P9-AQC-455

Black Hymnody

Black Hymnody:
A Hymnological History of
the African-American Church

Jon Michael Spencer

THE UNIVERSITY OF TENNESSEE PRESS / KNOXVILLE

Copyright © 1992 by The University of Tennessee Press / Knoxville.
All Rights Reserved. Manufactured in the United States of America.
First Edition.

The paper in this book meets the minimum requirements of the American National
Standard for Permanence of Paper for Printed Library Materials. ⊗ The binding
materials have been chosen for strength and durability.

Library of Congress Cataloging-in-Publication Data

Spencer, Jon Michael.
   Black hymnody : a hymnological history of the African-American
church / Jon Michael Spencer. — 1st ed.
     p. cm.
   Includes bibliographical references and index.
   ISBN 0-87049-745-6 (cloth: alk. paper)
    1. Afro-American churches—Hymns—History and criticism.
2. Afro-Americans—Religion.   3. Hymns, English—United States—History and
criticism. I. Title.
BV313.S64   1992
264'.2'08996073—dc20   91-31896
                                                CIP

To the late Wendell Whalum
for his pioneering work
in black church hymnody

Contents

Preface

This book documents the rich hymnological tradition of the black church in America through an analysis of the hymnbooks of ten denominations that represent every persuasion of the Afro-Christian faith: the Methodist, Baptist, Holiness, and Pentecostal denominations; as well as the Catholic, Episcopal, and United Methodist churches, whose black minority memberships produced supplemental hymnbooks reflecting their cultural ethnicity and distinct theological and social perspectives.

Because there is hardly any published research on the hymnody that constitutes black church hymnals, this documentation of the hymnological tradition of the black church is largely dependent on three sources of data: (1) the hymns and prefatory matter of the hymnbooks themselves, (2) the doctrinal disciplines and conference proceedings of the denominations, and (3) the histories and related biographies and autobiographies of denominational clergy and laity. The latter two secondary sources have been used primarily to provide information on the larger social and particular denominational milieus that have impacted the types of hymns compiled in the hymnbooks.

This hymnological history should be a helpful supplement to other histories of the black church, insofar as the hymns that black Christians sing are an essential aspect of their religious history and culture. A study of these hymns, as deposited in the collective memory and composite personality of denominational hymnbooks, is a primary means of tracing shifts and developments in a denomination's theological and doctrinal tenets and social perspectives. The intention of this book, then, is more than simply to record the types of hymns Afro-Christians have written, adapted, adopted, and sung during the course of the evolution of the black church in America; it is also to chronicle the history of the denominations themselves as viewed through the hymnological lens. What results may be a somewhat sketchy history, but it is one that reveals facts and nuances that would not be disclosed through histories that are not musicological. But probably this hymnological history is not as sketchy as one might presume; although I have tried not to duplicate regular, nonmusicological histories, I have attempted to contextualize all of the hymnological data in concrete historical timeframes, referencing important events and trends within the ten denominations covered. I hope it will be discovered that this is not only a novel way of reading black church history, insofar as it does so in the context of assessing the development of the rich tradition of black church hymnody, but also an enjoyable way of reading history.

The ten chapters of this book are divided into three parts covering (1) black Methodists and Baptists, (2) black Holiness and Pentecostals, and (3) black Episcopalians and Catholics. This arrangement is a means of facilitating the discussion of similarities and interrelated histories of the (1) black and white Methodist churches and their kindred Baptist churches, (2) the black Holiness and Pentecostal denominations, and (3) black Episcopalians and Catholics, who have been involved in identical struggles to indigenize their church liturgies.

Each of these three sections will provide valuable background information on the numerous hymnwriters of the black church and the historic figures who did the important work of compiling the hymnbooks. Some of the hymnists have been recognized in previous books on gospel music: Rev. Charles Albert Tindley of the black gospel hymn era; Thomas A. Dorsey, Lucie E. Campbell, Kenneth Morris, Roberta Martin, and Doris Akers of the golden age of gospel; and Andrae Crouch, Edwin Hawkins, and Elbernita Clark of the modern age of gospel. Well known among the historic arrangers of spirituals are H.T. Burleigh, R. Nathaniel Dett, and John Wesley Work, Jr. However, there are many more black hymnists, some of whom were also hymnbook compilers, whose names are generally unknown: nineteenth-century clergy such as Daniel A. Payne of the African Methodist Episcopal Church, Rev. Benjamin Franklin Wheeler and Rev. William Howard Day of the African Methodist Episcopal Zion Church; early twentieth-century musicians such as William Rosborough of the National Baptist Convention, USA; and hymnists of the later half of the twentieth century. These latter hym-

nists include Roland M. Carter of the African Methodist Episco-
pal Church; C. Eric Lincoln and the late J. Jefferson Cleveland of
the United Methodist Church; Juanita Griffey Hines, Elizabeth
Maddox Huntley, Margaret P. Douroux, and Rev. D.E. King of
the National Baptist Churches; Iris Stevenson and Elder Wallace
M. Cryor of the Church of God in Christ; David Hurd and
William B. Cooper of the Episcopal Church; and Clarence Joseph
Rivers, Leon C. Roberts, Grayson Warren Brown, and Edward
V. Bonnemere of the Roman Catholic Church. All of these hymnists, and others, are herein recognized. Their contributions to
the sacred black song tradition are documented as important
artifacts that reveal the Afro-Christian worldview at different
historical stages within their particular denominations.

My primary interest, then, is in the hymns (texts), not the
musical settings of hymns; for I am in pursuit of documenting
the doctrinal, theological, and social developments within the
black church. While for some musicologists the agenda is an-
thropological (ethnomusicology) and for others it is philosophical (the philosophy of music), my agenda is basically hymnological, which implies the centrality of the hymns (texts). The
fact is that in many of the early hymnbooks, music is not even
provided; only meters are given for the hymns. But even in the
cases where a tune is suggested or a setting is provided, an
examination of the music usually yields little (if anything) that
enhances the kind of data I seek. In the fields of hymnology and
theomusicology, the analysis of hymns is a legitimate undertaking, not to mention that, in view of the dearth of documentation
on black church hymnody, it is a needed undertaking. This is not
to say that I never discuss the musical settings of hymns. On
occasion, a musical setting is significant; and when that is the
case I process the sociohistorical information. However, characteristically, this book is more historical and hymnological than
strictly musicological.

Additionally, since I use hymnody to read the theological,
doctrinal, and social history of the black church, the hymnological lens through which I peer is not one that leads me to
determine whether particular hymns are of good or bad poetic
quality. For instance, while I do not attempt to determine the
poetic quality of the early nineteenth-century missionary
hymns, I do not hesitate to say that, given that they are tainted

with Social Darwinism, and given the changes in black social consciousness that occurred during the 1960s and 1970s, they are hymns out of touch with the new black mindset because they depict Africans as irreligious barbarians.

This new black mindset was fully in place by the late sixties. Thus, throughout this hymnological history, I use the Civil Rights movement (and the new social mindset that it brought to the masses of African Americans) as a point of measurement for the progressiveness or backwardness of hymnbooks and hymns published after this historical epoch. For instance, the debate as to whether James Weldon Johnson's "Lift Every Voice and Sing" should become the "Negro National Anthem" was going on as early as the late 1930s, but it was only after the 1960s that the popular hymn began appearing in denominational hymnals. Many members of the emerging black middle class during the first half of the twentieth century were against the notion of a separate national anthem because they believed it would undermine their thrust toward assimilation into the mainstream of society. But following the events of the sixties, the inclusion of this hymn in black denominational hymnbooks made an intentionally strong social statement, particularly when its inclusion was buttressed by the addition of black spirituals and other hymns by African Americans and the exclusion of the Social-Darwinist missionary hymns.

My criticism of the continued use of hymnals of the pre–Civil Rights era is usually direct, because these volumes subtly maintain outdated and problematic traditions that perpetuate black oppression. In order to focus criticisms that I have dispersed throughout the book, my postscript gives a brief critical assessment of the black church as seen through the hymnological lens, while suggesting needed future developments.

For suggesting that I write such a postscript and for his many other helpful comments toward the improvement of this book, I am grateful to William B. McClain, professor of homiletics and worship at Wesley Theological Seminary. Also requiring recognition is C. Eric Lincoln, professor of religion and culture at Duke University, whose mentorship has always provided me with clear direction and deep inspiration. I am grateful to sociology of religion professors Alton B. Pollard III of Wake Forest University, Mary R. Sawyer of Iowa State University, and

William C. Turner, Jr., of Duke University for their comments on various chapters in this book. Finally, I must express special thanks to Tana McDonald, acquisitions editor of the University of Tennessee Press, for her highly informed direction and pleasing personality, which facilitated this book's publication.

PART 1

BLACK METHODISTS AND BAPTISTS

CHAPTER 1

The African Methodist Episcopal Church

A number of us usually attended St. George's church in Fourth street; and when the colored people began to get numerous in attending the church, they moved us from the seats we usually sat on, and placed us around the wall, and on Sabbath morning we went to church and the sexton stood at the door, and told us to go in the gallery. He told us to go, and we would see where to sit. We expected to take the seats over the ones we formerly occupied below, not knowing any better. We took those seats. Meeting had begun, and they were nearly done singing, and just as we got to the seats, the elder said, "Let us pray." We had not been long on our knees before I heard considerable scuffling and low talking. I raised my head up and saw one of the trustees . . . having hold of the Rev. Absalom Jones, pulling him up off of his knees, and saying, "You must get up—you must not kneel here." Mr. Jones replied, "Wait until prayer is over . . . and I will get up and trouble you no more." With that he beckoned one of the trustees . . . to come to his assistance. . . . By this time prayer was over, and we all went out of the church in a body, and they were no more plagued with us in the church.

—*Richard Allen,*
founding bishop of the
African Methodist Episcopal Church[1]

Of the black Protestant denominations founded in North America, the African Methodist Episcopal (AME) Church has the longest and most informative hymnological history. Its genealogy of hymnbooks, the principal source of the following historical sketch, only recently culminated in the *AMEC Bicentennial Hymnal* (1984). This excellent compilation of a cross-section of Afro- and Euro-American hymnody was published for the 1987 commemoration of the two-hundredth anniversary of the church. (The founding date was calculated not from the first General Conference of 1816, but from the year 1787, when Richard Allen and his fellow black worshipers are said to have withdrawn from Philadelphia's Saint George's Methodist Episcopal Church in protest against racial discrimination.) An analysis of the 1984 hymnal, as the culmination and commemoration of a long and fruitful hymnic history, is best entered into following a historical survey of the full genealogy of AME hymnals. These hymnals were published in 1801, 1818, 1837, 1876, 1892, 1941, and 1954.

What seems somewhat inconsistent, from a hymnological purview, about the history of the AME church is that, while 1787 is the official founding date of the church, Richard Allen's hymnbook of 1801 is never even remotely figured into that history. All of the authorized denominational records consider the hymnbook of 1818 (published subsequent to the inaugural General Conference of 1816) the first denominational hymnbook of the church.

Titled *A Collection of Spiritual Songs and Hymns, Selected from Various Authors* (1801), Allen's compilation of fifty-four classic and "folk" hymns (printed in Philadelphia by John Ormrod) remained relatively unknown until Eileen Southern in the early 1970s documented her in-depth research on this pivotal hymnological work.[2] In identifying its historical importance, she said, "The novelty of the 1801 publication arises from the fact of the enterprising young minister's publishing his own hymnal instead of using the official Methodist hymnal."[3] Southern praised the 1801 hymnbook for several additional reasons: (1) it is the first published black denominational hymnal, (2) it is the very first published hymnbook to include the "wandering chorus"—unrelated choruses freely attached to one or more hymns, (3) it is the first hymnbook to include songs of the oral tradition (pieces which Allen probably picked up while preaching on the circuit), and (4) it is a document that reflects the musical taste of early-nineteenth-century black Protestants.[4] Regarding the latter point, just as John Wesley edited his brother Charles Wesley's hymns for inclusion in his hymnbooks, so did Richard Allen make minor textual modifications in his selected hymns in order to make them more appropriate or meaningful to his African Methodist parishioners.

Because a second edition of Allen's hymnbook was published later in 1801, Southern surmised that the first edition was well received and enjoyed substantial distribution.[5] Titled *A Collection of Hymns and Spiritual Songs, from Various Authors*, this second edition was printed privately in Philadelphia. Among its sixty-four hymns (ten more than its antecedent), several of the pieces incorporate moderate modifications in the texts of the original edition.[6] As was typical in hymnbooks of the eighteenth and early nineteenth centuries, hymn authors are not named. It is determinable, however, that many of the pieces were written by such hymnists as Charles Wesley, Isaac Watts, and John Newton. And at least one piece included was by Allen himself— "See! How the Nations Rage Together," the authorship of which can be inferred from the fact that it shares lines and stanzas (see italics) with one of the two original hymns in Allen's autobiography:

> See! how the nations rage together,
> Seeking of each other's blood;
> See how the scriptures are fulfilling!
> Sinners awake and turn to God.
>
> We see the fig-tree budding;
> You that in open ruin lie,
> Behold the leaves almost appearing,
> Awake! behold your end is nigh.
>
> *We read of wars, and great commotions,*
> To come *before* that *dreadful day;*
> *Sinners* quit *your sinful courses,*
> *And trifle not your time away.*
>
> Consider now the desolation,
> And the shortness of your time;
> Since there's none but a dark ocean,
> For all that don't repent in time,
>
> *Ye ministers that* wait on *preaching,*
> *Teachers and exhorters too,*
> Don't you see *your harvest wasting,*
> *Arise, there is no rest for you,*

O think upon that strict commandment,
God has on his teachers laid:
The sinner's blood that *dies unwarned,*
Shall fall upon the teacher's *head.*

Arise *dear brethren, let's be doing,*
See *the nations in distress;*
The Lord of hosts forbid their ruin,
Before their *day of grace is past.*

To see the land lie in confusion,
Looks dreadful in our mortal eye;
But O dear sinners, that is nothing,
To when the day of doom draws nigh.

To see the Lord in clouds descending,
Saints and angels guard him round;
The saints from earth will rise to meet
But sinners speechless at his frown.

To see the mountains a burning,
Mountains and hills must forward fly;
The moon in blood, the stars a falling,
And comets blazing thro' the sky.

O sinners! that's not all that's dreadful,
Before your Judge you must appear;
To answer for your past transactions,
How you ran your courses here.

The book of Conscience will be open'd
And your character read therein;
The sentence is, depart ye cursed,
And every saint will cry, Amen.

O Lord, forbid that this our nation,
That this should be their dreadful case;
O sinners turn and find salvation,
While now he offers you free grace.

'Tis now you have a gospel morning,
And yet the lamp holds out to burn;
'Tis now you have sufficient warning,
O sinners! sinners! will you turn?[7]

In 1816, at the inaugural General Conference of the AME Church, Allen was ordained a bishop by four ordained elders and Absalom Jones (a priest in the Protestant Episcopal Church). A year later, in 1817, he had John H. Cunningham of Philadelphia publish the church's inaugural discipline,[8] which was basically that of the Methodist Episcopal (ME) Church, with the

AME appellation and an original preface. The following year (1818), Allen published the first official hymnbook of the newly founded denomination, *The African Methodist Pocket Hymn Book*, also printed by Cunningham. Compiled by Daniel Coker, James Champion, and Richard Allen (the committee chairman), the 1818 hymnal was the first published document produced by the newly established AME Book Concern, the oldest black-owned publishing company in the country. The enterprising Allen, the company's founder, served as its business manager until 1826, while also serving as lifetime pastor of Bethel (the church he built in Philadelphia in 1793) and as the sole bishop of the church. While Allen was finally superseded as book manager by the astute young Rev. Joseph M. Corr, who served in the managerial capacity from 1826 to 1835, he remained the sole bishop of the church until Morris Brown was elected in 1828.

Containing 314 hymns, the 1818 hymnbook is divided into subject headings identical to those in the *The Methodist Pocket Hymn-Book* of 1807, the volume after which the AME hymnbook was closely modeled. Of the 314 hymns, Southern calculated that 244 were also in the ME hymnbook and that 18 hymns (which did not include Allen's own) were carried over from the 1801 volume.[9] In reference to the preface by Allen, Coker, and Champion, Southern said, "Richard Allen obviously was concerned about meeting the high standards of the Methodist hymnal in this new publication, although he had no intention of abandoning his independent stance."[10] The hymnal's preface reads:

> In April last, we presented you with the Discipline of our Church: It was requisite that we should exhibit to the Christian world, the rules of government and articles of faith, by which we intended to be influenced and governed. . . . Having become a distinct and separate body of people, there is no collection of hymns, we could, with propriety adopt. However, we have for some time, been collecting materials for the present work; and we trust, the result of our labour will receive the sanction of the congregations under our charge.
>
> In our researches, we have not passed over a selection of Hymns . . . but have endeavored to collect such as were applicable to the various states of Christian experience.
>
> A number of new hymns have been introduced into this work, in consequence of the estimation in which they were held. And we flatter ourselves, the present edition, will not suffer by a comparison with any collection of equal magnitude.

The closing statement that the hymnbook was "designed to supersede those heretofore used among us" may be indicative that Allen's 1801 hymnbook and perhaps the Methodist hymnbook of 1807 were among the predecessors of the 1818 hymnbook.

It was only after Allen's death in 1831 that the 1818 hymnbook was revised (in 1837) under the mandate of the General Conference of 1836. Titled *The African Methodist Episcopal Church Hymn Book*, this edition was published in Brooklyn, New York, by Rev. George Hogarth, a local African Methodist deacon in Brooklyn who moved the Book Concern there from Philadelphia. Having picked up the administration of the Book Concern, so ably managed by Rev. Corr until his death in 1835 at the early age of twenty-nine, Hogarth served as general book steward until 1848.

Although the subject categories of the 1837 hymnbook resemble those found in the extant ME hymnbook, like its antecedent of 1818 it was no mere duplication of its model. The preface, signed by the church bishops, Morris Brown and Edward Waters, indicates that the AME hymnbooks may have faced some competition from other existing collections, perhaps even the hymnbook of the ME Church: "We must, therefore, entreat you, if you have any respect for the authority of our Conference, or any regard for the prosperity of our church, of which you are members and friends, to purchase no books used in our church but what are assigned by the present bishops." Of course, this concern was one probably common to most denominations, so much so that the exhortation was actually taken almost verbatim from the ME hymnbook of 1836, which reads: "We must, therefore, earnestly entreat you, if you have any respect for the authority of the Conference, or of us, or any regard for the prosperity of the Church of which you are members and friends, to purchase no Hymnbooks but what are published by our own Agents, and signed with the names of your Bishops."

It was probably during the period in which the 1837 hymnbook was in use that choirs began to develop rapidly throughout the AME connection. The first African Methodist church choir is said to have been organized in 1830 in New York, according to one source, and in 1841 in Philadelphia (at Bethel), according to another.[11] AME historian Bishop R.R. Wright explained that choirs were first formed amid the congregation, wherein those with good voices and the desire to cultivate good singing sat together to sing, and that, later, pastors and parishioners consented to their having a designated place apart from the congregation.[12] Regarding the choir organized in 1841 at Bethel African Methodist Church in Philadelphia, Bishop Daniel A. Payne said there was fervent resistance to admitting choral singing into the church liturgy: "It gave great offense to the older members, especially those who had professed personal sanctification. Said they: 'You have brought the devil into the Church, and therefore we will go out.'"[13] Payne continued in his memoirs of 1888, "Similar excitements and irritations, resulting in withdrawals and small splits, followed the introduction of choral singing in the majority of our Churches. . . . But now it is the aim of every Church in the Connection to have a good choir."[14] Choral singing was quite acceptable to Payne, whose advanced learning and cultivated sophistication always seemed to place him on the side opposite the common people with respect to religious matters. He said, "The moral and religious effects of choral singing have been positive, especially when all or most of the choristers are earnest Christians and the congregation is involved in the singing."[15] By the time the next AME hymnal was published in 1876, it probably was, as Payne said, the goal of every church in the connection to have a good choir.

The 1876 volume, *The Hymn Book of the African Methodist Episcopal Church*, was compiled by the eminent clergyman and statesman Rev. Henry McNeal Turner. Twice elected (in 1868 and 1870) state senator in the Georgia legislature and later elected to the episcopacy of the AME Church in 1880, Turner was the first clergyman from the Lower South to achieve wide influence in the church. The fact that Turner's work was the first hymnbook published by the denomination following the Civil War is recognized by the church as having special significance: "In the organization of the Church after the war, many thousands were sold and much good was done. The old hymns gave way to the new, and the children of freedom sang a new song from their own Church Book."[16] Because of the historic setting in which this hymnbook was composed and the prominence of the man who compiled it, a rather detailed examination of its content is a valuable means of determining how the "new hymns" reflected the theological and social direction the church would take during and following Reconstruction.

The 1876 hymnbook was printed in Philadelphia by the Publication Department of the AME Church, during Turner's four-year term as business manager of the Book Concern (1876–1880). Compiling the large pocket-size volume containing 958 pages and 1,115 hymns was an onerous task for Turner. In his "Compiler's Remarks" he describes the job as one which should have been assigned to two hymnologists:

> In pursuance of a resolution adopted by the General Conference during its session in 1868, at Washington, D.C., doing me the honor of appointing me as compiler of the new edition of our hymn book, I now have the honor herewith to submit the manuscript of the same for your inspection. As you well know I have been about five years working on this manuscript; and yet it falls far short of what I would have been pleased to have given the church. But when you take into consideration the fact that I have had to execute the work amid the most busy and onerous years of my life, traveling most of the time day and night, planting and organizing new churches and missions, superintending most of the time the interest of our beloved connexion in the Empire State of the South, preaching thousands of sermons and delivering thousands of addresses, with no money appropriated to assist me in procuring clerical help—you will, I know, be more charitable with its defects and probable omissions, than you would have been had my facilities been otherwise. I have the satisfaction of knowing, however, that I did the best I could under my embarrassed circumstances.

In his actual presentation of the completed hymnbook manuscript before the bishops and members of the 1876 General Conference, Turner was both more candid about the complexity of the undertaking and less modest about his due acclaim. On the one hand, he complained that he had spent so much of his time and money on the project without any remuneration or thanks from the church that he was "glad to get rid of it." "I would not undertake the job again," he avowed, "for any consideration." On the other hand, Turner rightfully boasted (as had Allen in the preface to the 1818 hymnal), "I flatter myself that in it you will find a selection of the best hymns, and as appropriately arranged, as any book extant contains." Turner added, "I am a far better theologian than I possibly ever would have been, had it not been for my poetic examinations." Finally, his closing: "Hoping that the church will never assign me another duty so arduous and perplexing, I am most truly, H.M. Turner."[17]

Obviously, Turner's compilation was neither a thoughtless duplication of any extant hymnbook nor a mere revision of the former volume of 1837. In his "Compiler's Remarks" he explained that the collection was drawn from thirty-two of the best and most orthodox hymnbooks available. He also identified the volume as largely Wesleyan—"so much so," he said, "that it may be regarded as strictly a Wesleyan hymn book." In fact, of the 1,115 hymns comprising the volume, almost half (461) were Wesleyan—430 by Charles Wesley, 25 (including translations) by John Wesley, 5 by Samuel Wesley, Jr., and 1 by Samuel Wesley, Sr. Yet, in spite of this strong Wesleyan bent, for the fist time in the history of the denomination (save the 1801 collection), original hymns by African Methodists were incorporated. Many of the hymns submitted for publication by his fellow clergymen were, as Turner said, carelessly prepared and therefore rejected. Nonetheless, included were five pieces by Bishop Payne, two by the Reverend (later Bishop) Benjamin Tucker Tanner, one by the Reverend (late Bishop) James Anderson Handy, and one by Turner himself. While Turner was a gifted speech maker, he was no natural poet like Bishop Payne; however, his single hymn was a needed practical piece to be sung at church dedications.

The table of contents further attested to the originality of the 1876 hymnbook, for its subject headings comprised an integration of reordered and rephrased headings borrowed from the ME Church and ME Church, South, hymnbooks of the period and other categories either borrowed from other sources or formulated by Turner himself. The hymnbook's preface, signed by the bishops of the church (headed by Daniel Payne), lauded Turner's compilation as "excellent" and "more varied, comprehensive and useful than that, which we have been using for the last forty years."[18]

The historic location of this hymnbook as the first one published by the AME Church following the Civil War was reflected in the inclusion of the heading "Anniversary of Freedom," and in the fact that the two hymns placed therein appeared in no later hymnbook of the denomination. In fact, no comparable hymns appeared in any other black denominational hymnbooks in the history of the black church in North America. These pieces (both by W.H. Young) reflected the radical stance of a Turner who forbade his congregation to sing "Wash me and I shall be whiter than snow"—explaining to them that washing is meant to make one clean, not white[19]—and who in 1898 claimed that "God is a Negro."[20] The type of social conscientiousness evident in Turner's selection of these hymns (later embodied in the person of social gospeler Bishop Reverdy Ransom) was not again reflected in another AME hymnbook until after the Civil Rights movement. For this reason, both hymns are worth citing in full. Judging from the metrical irregularity of the first piece, titled "Freedom's Morn," it was probably intended to be sung to the tune of "My Country 'Tis of Thee":

> All hail! fair Freedom's morn,
> When Afric's sons were born,
> We bless this day.
> From slavery we are freed,
> No more our hearts will bleed—
> Lord, make us free indeed.
> To Thee we pray.
>
> Bless'd day of liberty,
> We raise our songs to thee,
> Day of the free;
> Our voices loud we raise,
> In Freedom's joyful lays,
> In songs of joy and praise,
> O God to thee.
>
> Long may this nation stand—
> Long may this glorious land
> Be fair and bright:
> May peace her arm extend
> O'er every foe and friend;
> May God the right defend
> With His great might.
>
> Lord, bless this Government,
> O'er all its broad extent,
> On land and sea.
> Oh! bless this glorious land—
> May Thy protecting hand
> Over the world expand,
> God of the free.

The second piece by Young was entitled "Freedom's Jubilee":

> Sons of Freedom, wake to glory!
> Let your anthems fill the sky;
> Children, men, and fathers hoary,

Raise your voices loud and high.
Join your voices altogether,
Sing the song of liberty,
Freedom reigns on land and water—
This is Freedom's jubilee!

Sons of Freedom, wake to glory!
Tune your hearts in grateful lays;
Freedom reigns—O, blessed story!
Sing a joyful song of praise.
Praise the Lord with hearts and voices—
He has gained the victory;
Every Freedman now rejoices,
On the land and on the sea.

Sons of Freedom, join the chorus!
Sing together with accord;
Brighter days are now before us—
Let us sing and praise the Lord;
Praise the Lord who reigns in heaven,
On the earth and on the sea;
Every shackle He has riven,
He has let the oppressed go free.

In contrast to these antislavery songs on the one hand and the orthodox Wesley hymns on the other, are the revival songs, which Turner, in his prefatory remarks, called "the old Zion songs." Nearly all of the fifty-nine pieces in this section were anonymous. Some contained the characteristic chorus, and others were responsorial (call and response) in form. Twelve of the revival songs were credited to Ira Sankey's gospel song collections that began appearing in print in 1875, while several others also were included in (and may have been carried over from) the AME hymnbooks of 1801 and 1837. In anticipation of a disapproving reaction to the inclusion of these "old Zion songs" by the conservative religionists of the church, Turner defended their inclusion in his prefatory remarks:

This may elicit the disapproval of some of our poetic neologists. But they must remember we have a wide spread custom of singing on revival occasions, especially, what is commonly called spiritual songs, most of which are devoid of both sense and reason; and some are absolutely false and vulgar. To remedy this evil, and to obviate the necessity of recurring to these wild melodies, even to accommodate the most illiterate, these time honored and precious old songs . . . have been as it were resurrected and regiven to the church. Besides, I am not ashamed to say that I love those good old soul-inspiring songs a thousand fold more than I do these later day operatio songs, most of the music of which is composed by persons who know nothing of God or religion, and some of whom are avowed atheists. And my experience in this respect, I am sure, is the experience of thousands of the ministry and laity.[21]

It is quite possible that Turner's vindication was directed at Bishop Payne, the pious, idealistic, autocratic religious conservative from Charleston, South Carolina. Payne, for instance, viewed the "praying and singing bands" of old-time southern black religion as little more than fetishism. Attending a "bush-meeting" (as he called it) on a visit to one of his clerics' circuit, Payne disdained the "heathenish" tumult of the congregants:[22]

After the sermon they formed a ring, and with coats off sung, clapped their hands and stamped their feet in a most ridiculous and heathenish way. I requested the pastor to go and stop their dancing. At this request they stopped their dancing and clapping of hands, but remained singing and rocking their bodies to and fro. This they did for about fifteen minutes. I then went, and taking their leader by the arm requested him to desist and to sit down and sing in a rational manner. I told him also that it was a heathenish way to worship and disgraceful to themselves, the race, and the Christian name. In that instance they broke up their ring; but would not sit down, and walked sullenly away.[23]

Turner may not have embraced the "ring" leader's theological claim that sinners will not get converted without a ring,[24] but, as his prefatory remarks showed, the native-born South Carolinian and longtime pastor of Savannah could understand and sympathize with the common people in a way that Payne could not. This may explain why the two men frequently came into conflict, and why Payne, as senior bishop, attempted to prevent Turner from being elected to the episcopacy in 1880.[25]

In spite of the dissimilarities between these two great churchmen, Turner included five pieces by Bishop Payne in the 1876 hymnbook. The best known of them appeared again in the 1892 and 1984 volumes, as well as in the 1954 AME Zion hymnal. Titled "Father, Above the Concave Sky," the hymn is representative of both the type of music Payne would have had the "fist and heal worshipers" sit down and sing in a rational manner, and the type of evangelical hymn being written by his fellow African Methodist churchmen during the nineteenth century. Of the seven verses in the 1876 hymnbook, the five which repeatedly appear in the later hymnbooks are as follows:

Father, above the concave sky,
Enthroned in light profound,
At Thy command the lightnings fly,
And thunders roar around.

O who can see the beaming sun,
The smiling moon at night,
The snowy clouds, the countless stars,
Enrobed with dazzling light,

And yet refuse to sing Thy praise
In sweetest notes of love?
Or echo to angelic lays,
Which fill the worlds above?

Whene'er I tread the blooming plains
And pluck the fragrant flower,
The luscious fruits, the yellow grains,
I see Thy matchless power.

What moves on earth, or wings the air,
Or swims the swelling sea,
Is but a ray of life to point
Immortal man to Thee.

The 1892 hymnbook, *Hymnal Adapted to the Doctrines and Usages of the African Methodist Episcopal Church,* was compiled under a mandate of the Episcopal Council at their January 1892 meeting in Macon, Georgia. The work was carried out by the Reverend (later Bishop) James Crawford Embry under the supervision of Bishops T.M.D. Ward and B.T. Tanner. According to the "Publisher's Preface" (probably written by Embry, who was manager of the Book Concern from 1884 to 1896), the intention of the Episcopal Council's mandate was to compile a *hymnbook* (without music) from which a *hymnal* (with music) subsequently could be formulated. This prospect necessitated a hymnbook with substantially fewer pieces than the 1876 volume had had, as well as one arranged metrically in order to facilitate the pairing of texts and tunes. The preface indicated that the hymns had been selected chiefly from the 1876 volume and the existing hymnbook of the ME Church, while a few pieces had been borrowed from such miscellaneous sources as the extant Baptist hymnbook and the psalmody of the United Presbyterian Church. Supplementing the prevailing Wesleyan hymns were original pieces by Bishops Payne, Turner, and Tanner, and by Rev. H.T. Johnson, Rev. J.R. Scott, and Rev. J.C. Embry.

That the work was completed expeditiously, in a brief ten months, is evidenced by the fact that the hymnbook was mandated in January 1892, while the prefatory matter is dated October 1892. Furthermore, in the prefatory "Note of Approval from the Bishops," Embry was commended for his "rapid, but arduous labor."[26] The bishops also confirmed that the work was essentially a revision of the 1876 hymnbook: "Most of these hymns are the same contained in our old book, in use the past seventeen years, and therefore not new or strange. The comparatively few collected from other sources, are largely Wesleyan in authorship and spirit." In terms of the original contributions to the volume, the bishops indicated that it was Bishop Ward who had suggested that a few of the original pieces in Turner's compilation be retained in the new hymnbook, alongside more recent newly added AME contributions. Completed late in 1892, the work was not officially approved until the General Conference of 1896.

As scheduled, the denomination's first hymnal (with music), *The African Methodist Episcopal Hymn and Tune Book,* was published several years later (1898) in Philadelphia by the AME Book Concern. The bishops' prefatory statement exclaimed: "We are more than pleased that we have lived to see the consummation so devoutly wished for and prayed for by our fathers—a Hymn and Tune Book of our own to use by our people." Also new was an extended essay titled "Methodist Hymnody," following the prefatory matter, in which brief introductory paragraphs lead into an extended excerpt from John Julian's *Dictionary of Hymnology.* Although the essay failed to mention black contributions to Methodist hymnody—spirituals, folk hymns, standard hymns, and the hymnbooks of 1801 through 1892— the leaders of the church felt that the essay would give their ministers a general overview of their hymnic history. Proud of their accomplishment, the bishops stated, "To be convinced of the excellency of the work, one only has to examine the arrangement of the subjects, and to note the versatility of authors, words and music, embracing as they do every phase of life, from the cradle to the grave, from the Jordan to the Throne."[27] Although Bishop Embry, chair of the hymnal committee, died in August 1897, prior to the completion of the work he had initiated, the extended version of the essay on "Methodist Hymnody," as it appears in the 1941 AME hymnal, says, "This volume will stand as a memorial to the work of the Rev. J.C. Embry, who worked on it until the last hours of his life. His last work, his last words, and last thoughts were in this Hymnal."

The "word hymnbook" compiled by Embry in 1892 had been intended to be the volume to which tunes would be added to comprise the long-awaited hymn and tune book. However, to the 1892 volume were added 149 new hymns, as well as 5 hymns by Bishop Tanner, 3 by Bishop Payne, and 1 each by Bishop L.J. Coppin and Rev. C.S. Smith (whose piece lyricized the contributions of twelve of the first nineteen bishops of the church). This addition of 149 new hymns required some modification in the use of the old printing plates. In the "Publisher's Word," Rev. T.W. Henderson, the business manager of the Book Concern, explained: "In order not to destroy the plates of the *word edition*, when we have found it necessary to add a hymn in *this*, not found in *that*, we have put the letter '*b*,' after the number, which will indicate that if the hymn is wanted in the *word edition*, it will be found after that number in the supplement, which is found at the rear of the book." In order to include the supplement (the added 149 hymns) in the word hymnbook of 1892, a "revised and enlarged edition" subsequently was printed. At least two of these editions appeared under Book Concern business managers Rev. J.I. Lowe in 1915 and Rev. (later Bishop) R.R. Wright, Jr., in 1917.

Two decades later, in an essay titled "Our Church Hymnody," published in the *AME Review* in 1919, came some criticism of the 1898 hymnal by Rev. Charles E. Stewart, one of the musically and theologically trained ministers of the church: "The hymnal of the African Methodist Episcopal Church is still the subject of needed revision. . . . Our hymnal is not comprehensive enough for the uses to which it should be put. Why cannot our hymnal contain the 'Star Spangled Banner' and the 'Battle Hymn of the Republic,' 'Onward Christian Soldiers,' Luther's famous 'A Mighty Fortress Is Our God,' and many others which could be used most effectively by Sunday School and Church."[28] The compromising dichotomy, with which all of the African Methodist hymnbook compilers, from the 1801 hymnbook forward, have had to wrestle, was evident even in Stewart's proposal. On the one hand, he suggested that the denominational hymnal should contain principally pieces that are able to stand the test of time, thereby eliminating "hymns and tunes of any light order"; while, on the other hand, echoing Turner's preface to the 1876 hymnbook, he suggested that selected revival hymns be added to the supplement in order to prevent so many hymns and hymnbooks with questionable texts and music from entering the church liturgy.[29] Stewart closed with this petition:

> While our hymnal at the time it was last revised, was a most worthy effort and a distinct credit to the church and race, it is not today in touch with the wonderful progress of the church and race since that time. We have grown very rapidly and with our growth the world of religion and music and people has also wonderfully changed, therefore our hymnal which was admittedly a new adventure for us and experimental, is in need of hands in touch with the spirit of the church and a musical knowledge sufficient to give us today another hymnal based upon the present one and sufficient to meet the needs of our present church efforts.[30]

Although Stewart's call for a new denominational hymnal went unheeded in the years to come, when an official mandate for a revision of the 1898 hymnal was issued at the General Conference of 1940, Stewart was among the clerical scholars placed on the hymnal revision committee. Perhaps his proposition should have been heeded earlier, for the bishops' statement prefacing the 1941 hymnal admitted that the dated hymnbook of 1898 had fallen into disuse and was frequently replaced by hymnbooks of other denominations, resulting in disparities in the liturgy used in the AME churches.

The committee that was appointed to revise the 1898 hymnal consisted of Bishops John A. Gregg (chairman), W.A. Fountain, Sr., and D. Ward Nichols; Rev. W.K. Hopes, Rev. Charles E. Stewart, Rev. W.H. Peck; and musical experts E.C. Deas, F.A. Clark, and Frederick Hall. Hall was a nationally known educator who, from the early twenties through the mid-seventies, directed the music departments at a number of black universities and colleges—Jackson State, Dillard, Alabama State, and Southern. E.C. Deas was a music publisher, composer of gospel hymns, and arranger of black spirituals, whose service to the hymnbook revision committee and contribution of hymns to the compilation followed a long and close affiliation with the AME Church. He had studied music at the denomination's Edward

Waters College; represented the AME Book Concern in Florida in 1911 and 1912, under R.R. Wright's management; and, at the time of his death in 1944, served as a member of the commission for the proposed combined hymnal of the AME and AME Zion churches.[31] F.A. Clark was known for his arrangements of Rev. Charles Albert Tindley's gospel hymns, several of which were included in the 1941 hymnal.

When the committee completed its revision of the 1898 hymnal late in 1940, the manuscript was given to Deas, who was to have plates made and sent to Hopes, the manager of the Book Concern. According to the prefatory "Publisher's Word," the plates were received by Hopes in February 1941, and instructions were given him to have the hymnal ready in ninety days. When the volume was nearly complete, Bishop Gregg, the committee chairman, had its publication suspended, pending a plan between the AME and the AME Zion churches to publish a "combined hymnal." As a result of this interruption, the hymnal evidently was not presented for official approval at the General Conference of 1944. When, in 1946, the "combined hymnbook" still remained incomplete, Bishop Gregg carried through the church's plan to publish the revised hymnal mandated by the General Conference of 1940. Apparently published in 1946 (or sometime between 1941 and 1946) by the Book Concern under Rev. W.K. Hopes, the hymnal was entitled *The Richard Allen AME Hymnal*. In a later printing of it, an added prefatory note by Bishop Gregg—dated 1 March 1950—explained that, because the progress of the combined hymnal had lagged, the bishops of the AME Church had decided that the "Allen AME Hymnal" would become the official hymnal of the church.

Perhaps the only substantial hymnological improvement in this hymnal over the 1898 volume (of which it is a revision) was that the essay on "Methodist Hymnody" in the latter was amended by an expanded historical survey of the AME hymnals of 1818, 1876, 1892, 1941, and 1954. Containing basically the prefatory matter of the above hymnbooks, this essay (which followed the end of the excerpt from Julian's *Dictionary of Hymnology*) was the first and most comprehensive documentation of the church's hymnic history to date. The only historical oversight was that the essay, which now commenced with the hymnic legacy of John and Charles Wesley and proceeded through the 1941 hymnal, neglected to mention Bishop Allen's two hymnbooks of 1801.

In 1953, a committee was appointed to review the "Allen Hymnal" of 1941, and the bishops voted to remove the Allen eponym from the title.[32] Simply titled *AMEC Hymnal*, the new work was completed in 1954 and published the same year, under the management of the Reverend (now Bishop) Henry A. Belin, Jr. The volume contained 645 pieces (184 more hymns than the 461 pieces in the previous volume), and it included four spirituals, whereas none of the previous volumes had contained any. Several of the original and racial pieces published in the 1941 hymnal were maintained in the 1954 volume, as was the amended essay on "Methodist Hymnody." Among these original pieces were the seven hymns written or arranged by Deas, the four Tindley songs arranged by F.A. Clark, the setting of a Bishop Tanner hymn by the Reverend (later Bishop) L.J. Coppin, and Coppin's "A Song I'll Sing to You," which poeticized the contributions of the first twenty-five bishops of the church.

This overview of the AME hymnbooks takes the present hymnological survey full circle, back to the current *AMEC Bicentennial Hymnal* of 1984. This most recent hymnal, resulting from a suggestion at the 1972 General Conference that a new hymnal be compiled for the bicentennial anniversary of the church (1787–1987), was published by the AME Publishing House in Nashville under Rev. Henry A. Belin, Jr. While this hymnal is substantially larger than its antecedent, the amended essay on "Methodist Hymnody" in the back of the 1941 and 1954 hymnals has been replaced by a brief two-page preface which highlights important facts about the earlier AME hymnbooks.

Even in the present age of ecumenism, it is understandable that this commemorative hymnal contains a number of denominational hymns. In fact, it contains more denominational hymns than any of the church's previous hymnals, and more than are found in any other black denominational hymnal in the history of the black church in North America. Among eight pieces under the subject heading "Founders Day" are "Our Church the Greatest on God's Earth" and "We Are Gathered to Pay Homage," both texts by E.M. Gordon; "A Song I'll Sing to You," by L.J. Coppin; "We Are the Children of the Church,"

Coppin's setting of a hymn by Bishop Tanner; "Bishop Richard Allen," text and music by H. Witboii; "Go Forward, Allen's Youth," text by William R. Wilkes; and "Allen's Youth Are Making Progress," text and music transcribed by Edith Ming from the Republic of South Africa.

The foreword to the bicentennial hymnal indicates that it is a volume that reflects many current theological concerns: "Major concern was given to questions of sexist language, ethnic identity, theological relevance, sectional usage, traditional consistencies, international inclusiveness, classification of material, valid entries, contemporary style, modern texts, and even personal favorites." Demonstrating the commission's concern for ethnic identity, the number of works (compositions or arrangements) by black writers has increased significantly over all of the previous hymnbooks. First of all, the Black National Anthem, "Lift Every Voice and Sing," is included in the church's hymnbooks for the first time in the history of the denomination. This addition is complemented by six hymns by C.A. Tindley, all but one of them arranged by F.A. Clark; four by Lucie Campbell; two each by Thomas Dorsey, Doris Akers, Kenneth Morris, and Andrae Crouch; and one by Charles Price Jones. As for AME clergy, there is one piece each by Bishops Payne and Tanner; AME laypersons are represented with eight arrangements by the late Wendell Whalum (longtime chairman of music at Morehouse College) and seven pieces (compositions or arrangements) by E.C. Deas. Hymns written or arranged by members of the Commission on Worship and Liturgy, which compiled the hymnal, include twenty-two transcriptions or arrangements by Edith Ming (wife of Bishop Donald G. Ming), three by Bishop Frederick H. Talbot, two by Vivienne L. Anderson, and one by Jimmie James, chairman of the music department at Jackson State University.

Further with regard to "ethnic identity," the number of spirituals has increased from the four located in the supplement to the 1954 hymnal to twenty-five dispersed according to subject throughout the body of the 1984 hymnal. Whereas no arrangers are listed for the four in the 1954 edition, the twenty-five in the 1984 volume are arranged by such well-known black composers as H.T. Burleigh, John Wesley Work, Jr., and Wendell Whalum. Also of significance is the deletion of the Social Darwinist missionary hymns found in the 1941 and 1954 editions—"From Greenland's Icy Mountains" and "Over the Ocean Waves, Far, Far Away"—which refer to Africans as "rude barbarians," "dark benighted pagans," and "heathens" who "bow down to wood and stone." In place of these derogatory pieces are modern missionary hymns such as "Give a Thought to Africa," a song transcribed by Edith Ming, as heard in the Republic of South Africa.

Compared with the 1954 hymnal, the 1984 volume also has an increase in hymns of a social nature—that is, hymns concerned more with social issues than with personal piety and evangelizing. This socialization of American hymnody and hymnals directly reflects the legacy of the era of Social Christianity (1830–1880) and especially the Social Gospel movement (1880–1930). The extent to which Social Gospel hymnody penetrated the hymnody of the AME Church can be gauged partially in a survey of hymns included in the hymnbooks compiled over the decades leading up to the 1960s. Excluding the hymnbooks of 1801, 1818, 1837, and 1876, which predate the Social Gospel, the following is a survey of the collective memory of the AME Church, as it appears in its hymnbooks of 1892, 1941, 1954, and 1984. Out of a total of 760 pieces, the 1892 hymnbook has 23 Social Gospel hymns. The 1941 hymnal shows an increase of 12 such hymns, so that, out of 461 pieces, 35 have substantive social strains. (It is in this 1941 hymnal that some of the great hymns of the Social Gospel movement first appear—William G. Ballantine's "God Save America," Katherine L. Bates's "O Beautiful for Spacious Skies," Washington Gladden's "O Master, Let Me Walk with Thee," William Merrill's "Rise Up, O Men of God," and Frank Mason North's "Where Cross the Crowded Ways of Life.") The 1954 hymnal has an increase of 7 social pieces, so that out of 673 hymns, 42 are social gospel ones. The 1984 hymnal—whose changes actually are more directly attributable to the Civil Rights movement—has an increase of 19 social hymns, so that out of a total of 670 hymns, 54 are social. In sum, in the span of half a century, the 54 social hymns in the 1984 hymnal are more than twice the number (23) found in the 1892 volume. This slow but steady increase in the number of pieces of a social nature is best understood in light of the steady decrease in the number of evangelical hymns (preeminently represented by the Wesleyan hymns). There were 461 Wesleyan hymns in the 1876

hymnbook, while the 1892, 1941, 1954, and 1984 volumes regis-
ter a steady decrease in the percentage of Wesleyan hymns (respectively, 210 hymns out of a total of 600 pieces, 47 out of 461
pieces, 58 out of 673, and 46 out of 670).

An example of a social hymn that appears in the 1984 hymnal
(its first appearance in an AME hymnal) is "In Christ There Is No
East or West" by John Oxenham (1852–1941). Far removed from
the pious poems of Bishop Payne, from the evangelical works of
Wesley, Watts, and Newton, and from the songs of AME clergy
who maintained that literary tradition, this hymn is emblematic
of a move toward social consciousness began with H.M. Turner's landmark hymnbook of 1876. Listed in the 1984 hymnal
under the heading "Kingdom of God on Earth—Patriotic," its
opening stanzas celebrate the hallmarks of the Social Gospel,
kingdomhood and fellowship.

> In Christ there is no east or west,
> In Him no south or north,
> But one great fellowship of love
> Throughout the whole wide earth.
>
> In Him shall true hearts everywhere
> Their high communion find;
> His service is the golden cord
> Close binding all mankind.

These two stanzas progress developmentally toward the third,
which draws a conclusion which the black oppressed long to
have affirmed—that not only is there no East or West and no
South or North, but also (in the sense of egalitarianism) no black
or white:

> Join hands, then, brothers of the faith,
> Whate'er your race may be;
> Who serves my Father as a son
> Is surely kin to me.

In addressing the idea of human homogeneity in the body of
Christ, the hymnist also suggests that there is an equality in
Christ, regardless of race:

> In Christ now meet both east and west,
> In Him meet south and north:
> All Christly souls are one in Him
> Throughout the whole wide earth.

Reflecting on the ethos intended by this great Social Gospel hymn, AME clergyman Rev. James Lynch—probably writing during his 1866–67 editorship of the AME *Christian Recorder*—made a comment that serves not only as an appropriate close to this brief examination of African Methodist hymnody, but also as a reminder of how, at the critical historical juncture of the Emancipation Proclamation, AME hymnody began to secure its independence from the Methodist Episcopal Church:

> Minute guns may be fired, cannons boom, and huzzas rend the air in consequence of what may be deemed a turn in national affairs against us. The telegraph may dolefully sound with the news of persecuted and murdered freedmen. The journals may teem with accounts of oppressive legislation against them, and volumes of testimony of outrage and injustice be chronicled by congressional committees, and yet we will know no man on account of his color, or the place of his residence and birth. We will know no *North*, no *South*, no *East*, no *West*, but the whole country—to *help*, to *feel* a kindred sympathy with every man that God has made.[33]

CHAPTER 2

The African Methodist Episcopal Zion Church

And now, it seems, the time is come when something
must be done for the prosperity of the ministry
amongst our coloured brethren; and how shall this be
accomplished? for we have not the least expectation that
African or coloured Preachers will be admitted to a seat
and vote in the Conferences of their white brethren, let
them be how much soever qualified for the work of the
ministry; nor do we desire to unite with our brother
Richard Allen's connexion, being dissatisfied with their
general manner of proceedings; . . . therefore, our
brethren in the city of New-York, after due consideration,
have been led to conclude that to form an itinerant
plan and establish a Conference for African Methodist
Preachers, under the patronage of the white Methodist
Bishops and Conference, would be a means of
accomplishing the desired end.

—*James Varick,*
founding bishop of the
African Methodist Episcopal Zion Church[1]

The current denominational hymnal of the African Methodist
Episcopal Zion (AMEZ) Church is *The AME Zion Hymnal,* published in 1957 by the AME Zion Publishing House in Charlotte,
North Carolina. At the time of its publication, the hymnal was
a commendable accomplishment. Insofar as it was published
prior to the social awakening of the Civil Rights movement,
however, it is currently a theologically dated compilation. Nonetheless, this assessment that it is a dated hymnal now over thirty
years old is qualified somewhat by the recognition that seventeen years went into its making, and that it is the first *original*

hymnal produced by the church. Therefore, in an effort to appreciate fully the historical significance of the 1957 hymnal, the primary concern here will be to outline in considerable detail the hymnic history of the Zion Church, from the first denominational hymnal to the current one. This will entail a survey of the AMEZ hymnbooks of 1839, 1858, 1872, 1892, 1909, and 1957.[2]

The inaugural AMEZ hymnbook apparently was published in New York in 1839 by Rev. Samuel M. Giles, Bishop Christopher Rush, and Rev. Joseph P. Thompson. Reference to this obscure volume was found in the preface to its 1858 successor, *Hymns for the Use of the African Methodist Episcopal Zion Church*, which supposedly was an enlarged edition of the 1839 hymnal:

> In consequence of the great difficulty our Societies labored under, as a denomination, in divine worship, for the want of an established Hymn Book, the following work was compiled with great care from the best of authors, under the direction of the New-York and Philadelphia Annual Conferences, during the administration of Right Reverends Christopher Rush and William Miller, which was published in 1839.
>
> Further improvements being essential, the Book Committee, by the authority of the last General Conference, has with great care improved it, by an additional number of hymns, etc. so that the work is superior to any of the previous editions.[3]

The General Conference of 1856 appointed Giles, Rush, and Thompson to constitute the general book committee whose responsibilities would include full supervision over the Book Concern.[4] Published two years later under their management, the 1858 hymnbook was adopted by the church at its General Conference of 1860.[5]

Akin to the early hymnbooks of the AME and CME Churches, which were modeled after the hymnbooks of the Methodist Episcopal Churches from which the denominations had defected, the 1839 AMEZ hymnal and its 1858 successor were abridged editions of the Methodist Episcopal (ME) Church hymnbook of 1831.[6] This derivativation is evident both in the subject headings (modeled after the 1831 hymnal) that order the 1858 hymnbook and the customary Methodist content. With Wesley hymns comprising the mass of the volume (nearly half of the 596 hymns), the remaining pieces were by such evangelicals as Watts, Steele, Hart, Fawcett, Cennick, Stennett, Heber, Cowper, Newton, Doddridge, Montgomery, and Beddome.

It is significant that the Zion Church elected to model its hymnbooks after the thoroughly evangelical hymnbooks of the ME Church, rather than after, for instance, the Wesleyan Methodists' *Miriam's Timbrel: Sacred Songs, Suited to Revival Occasions; and also for Anti-Slavery, Peace, Temperance, and Reform Meetings* (1853),[7] which synthesized the evangelical and the social. This is particularly telling considering the backgrounds of the compilers. Born a slave in North Carolina, Christopher Rush escaped to New York in 1798 and later became one of the inaugural pastors of the Zion Church, its second bishop, and an antislavery activist contemporary with Richard Allen, Nathaniel Paul, and Samuel Cornish. Joseph Thompson, who was also born a slave, in Virginia, and later became a bishop, played an active role in running the underground railroad. Samuel M. Giles, too, was an ardent abolitionist. In spite of their strong stance against slavery in the South and Jim Crow in the North, the hymnbook compiled by Giles, Rush, and Thompson clearly reflected their evangelical Methodist background while neglecting their quest for racial liberation and identity. In other words, while the nineteenth-century black conventions held in Philadelphia, Boston, New York, Rochester, and Columbus were concerned with such reform issues as temperance and abolitionism, the church's mission evidently was to be concerned mainly with the personal salvation of its members.

Although written by the superintendents rather than by the publishers (Giles, Rush, and Thompson), the preface to the 1858 AMEZ hymnal seems to reflect the provincialism of northern, second-generation freedmen in the Zion Church, a stance that was unaccepting of worship styles characteristic of the southern "invisible institution." As fugitive and manumitted Africans fled to the North and joined Zion churches, and as the Zion Church evangelized the South, the Zion leaders perhaps found it necessary to instruct converts who were unfamiliar with their Methodist form of worship. The preface to the 1858 hymnal reads: "In submitting this to you, we would recommend the laity to be more prudent, in their social prayer-meetings and similar exercises, by avoiding that irregularity in the singing which destroys the harmony that should exist in this part of Divine worship. We are commanded to *sing in the spirit and with the understanding:* by strictly observing this precept, we cannot but be blessed under its influence." This admonition against imprudence in worship and irregularity in singing strikingly recalls AME Bishop Daniel A. Payne's disparagement of "fist and heal religion." The only "irregularity" that possibly could have destroyed the harmony was heterophonic singing, where the hymn tune was freely embellished as in the singing of the "slave songs." Too, the superintendents' underscoring of the command to sing "with the understanding" suggests that the "irregularity in the singing" of those to whom the preface was intended was not only inharmonious but relatively incomprehensible. When coupled with the facts that the Zion Church was essentially a northern denomination and that its hymnals were modeled after those of the ME Church, the superintendents' predilections suggest a denomination still in its infancy, one that had not yet forged its own liturgical identity.

Typeset and printed in New York by D. Fanshaw, the 1858 hymnal was reprinted in 1869 by the *Zion's Standard and Weekly Review.* Founded in the mid-1860s by Rev. Singleton T. Jones, during his pastorate of Mother Zion Church in New York, the weekly journal functioned successfully under the editorship of Rev. Jones and William Howard Day until the General Conference of 1868 purchased it from Mother Zion in the year Jones was elevated to the episcopacy. Rev. J.N. Gloucester was elected the journal's new editor,[8] and a year later the journal reprinted the 1858 hymnal. The same printing plates were used, with no modifications other than the new publisher's name, the name of the journal now replacing that of Fanshaw.

This 1869 reprint of the 1858 hymnal was to be shortlived, for, in 1872, the church officially adopted and had published under the AMEZ insignia the ME Church hymnbook of 1849.[9] Titled *A Collection of Hymns for the Use of the African Methodist Episcopal Zion Church in America* (1872), this volume was printed in New York by the Methodist Book Concern. It began with a brief introductory "Bishops' Address" similar to the preface of the 1858 hymnal: "In consequence of the great difficulties our societies have labored under for the want of a suitable Collection of Hymns, the General Conference, at its session of 1872, adopted the following book, as used by the Methodist Episcopal Church."[10]

That the 1872 volume, like the earlier Zion hymnbooks, was modeled after a hymnbook of the ME Church was characteristic of the denomination, for it still considered the ME Church to be the "mother" of its organization. This very term had been used only a few years earlier when, at the General Conference of 1868, the Zion Church had devoted itself to the idea of organic union with the ME Church. Dispatched by the AMEZ General Conference of 1868 to address the ME Church Conference, Rev. Singleton T. Jones (elected bishop *in absentia*) appealed to the Methodist bishops with this message: "I am instructed by the General Conference of the African Methodist Episcopal Zion Church in America to say, that the M.E. Church is still regarded the mother of our organization, and that, as we were induced to leave her, simply because she made a distinction among her children which seriously affected our interests, we are ready to return, if we can be assured that no invidious distinction will be made in regard to us."[11] Although the Methodists scandalously declined to assure the equal rights of those who had defected from their ranks three-quarters of a century earlier, and thus no organic union was to be effected, the Zionites nevertheless continued to model their hymnbooks after those of the ME Church.

The 1892 hymnbook, *New Hymn and Tune Book: An Offering of Praise for the Use of the African M.E. Zion Church of America*,[12] was essentially an edited version of the 1872 Zion hymnal (which was a duplicate of the 1849 ME hymnal). Edited by Philip Phillips, publisher of hymn and gospel song books, hymnwriter, and evangelistic singer,[13] the 1892 volume was published by the AME Zion Book Concern. Like its three progenitors (the hymnals of 1839, 1858, and 1872), it too was typically Methodist. Regarding the large number of Wesleyan hymns—of the 1,216 hymns, about half (595) are Wesleyan—the "Committee's Address" examined itself: "What is the first requisite to congregational singing? Let the people provide themselves with hymn and tune books. . . . What kind of books should be procured? Such as contain the hymns of our denomination."[14] Although the 1892 volume was an edition of the ME hymnbook of 1849, it was, on the other hand, the very first Zion hymnal containing substantial original contributions. It supplements the 1872 Zion hymnal (the ME hymnal of 1849) with sixty-six new pieces. Of these sixty-six added hymns, thirty-seven (hymn nos. 1152–

1187)[15] included some of the popular gospel hymns of the day and five pieces by the editor himself, while twenty-nine (nos. 1188–1216) were a collection of hymns by Zion ministers.[16]

The hymnbook's closing section, containing the pieces by Zion ministers, had this explanatory heading: "The following Hymns were written by our own Ministers, and carefully compiled by Rev. B.F. Wheeler, A.M., B.D."[17] The title page of the hymnbook read similarly: "Several Original Hymns have been Written by our own Ministers and Carefully Compiled by Rev. B.F. Wheeler, A.M., B.D." Included among these twenty-nine selections were works by Rev. Benjamin F. Wheeler (the compiler), Rev. John Wesley Smith (later a bishop), Rev. George Wylie Clinton, Rev. Smith Claiborne, Rev. James T. Gaskill, Rev. Robert Russell Morris, Rev. William Howard Day, Rev. Richard Haywood Stitt, Rev. John H. White, Rev. H.P. Thomas, Rev. William T. Biddle, Rev. W.H. Marshall, Rev. H.W. Smith, Rev. John E. Price, Rev. J.A.D. Bloice, Rev. E. George Biddle, and Bishops Singleton T. Jones and John J. Moore. While most of the above clergymen were represented by only one hymn, included were six by Bishop Moore, four by Rev. Wheeler, three by Bishop Jones, and two by Rev. Bloice. Perhaps this compilation of hymns by Zion ministers was what the prefatory "Committee's Address" meant by its statement that "all the different evangelical Churches have their own hymns set to tunes, and published by their respective societies"—i.e., now the Zion Church had its own hymns as well.

The hymns by the Zion ministers were Methodist in theology, classic and evangelistic in language, and centered around such topics as faith, endurance, crucifixion, resurrection, sanctification, and salvation. In short, they poeticized the temporality of this life and the eternal verities of the afterlife. The Methodist influence was evidenced in the Zionite poets' use of phrases first lyricized by the traditional hymnists whose pieces long had dominated the pages of Zion hymnbooks. A few examples are Rev. Claiborne's reference to the Lord's name as "awful" (after Philip Doddridge), Rev. Bloice's and Bishop Jones' respective use of the familiar phrases "Holy Spirit, Heavenly Dove" and "amazing bliss" (both after Watts), and Bishop John J. Moore's reference to heaven as the realms of "endless day" (after Thomas Kelly).[18] Furthermore, like the hymns of the traditional evangelical writers, the works by the Zion ministers were concerned with personal sanctification rather than social reformation. This was evinced in such pieces as Rev. Stitts' "A Soldier I Would Be" and Bishop Moore's "The Christian Warrior, Brave and Stout," both of which employed military imagery to depict, during the hostile years of Reconstruction and Jim Crow, their personal "warfare" against sin rather than against social injustice.

Whether the Zion hymnist was from the North or the South, born enslaved or free, nearly all of the hymns had a strong heavenward bent in their tendency to portray heaven as the eternal alternative to the world of perpetual sorrow. Bishop Jones (known among Zionites as an adept organist)[19] depicted life as a "vale of tears" through which "life's pilgrims roam," while of heaven he waxes exultant:

> No scenes of parting there,
> No pain, no grief, no fear,
> No murmuring sigh, no sad complaint
> Like those that grieve us here.

Not all of the Zion hymns in the 1892 hymnal are characteristically Methodist, for another piece by Bishop Jones assumes the call-and-response form of the spirituals. Here heaven is lyricized as "long-loved Zion":

> We shall reach the blissful shore,
>   Home in long-loved Zion,
> Where sighing hearts shall sigh no more,
>   Home in long-loved Zion.
>
> Oh! sinner! sinner! why delay!
>   Far from long-loved Zion;
> Come seek the Savior while you may—
>   Come to long-loved Zion.[20]

In a piece titled "The City of My Dreams," Rev. J.W. Smith also portrays life as "sad and dreary," but his jubilance comes from the assurance that the angels are waiting to "bear [him] o'er the tide/Across the dark, deep waters/Where Jesus Christ resides." As he dreams of the city of his longings, Rev. Smith envisions a glorious procession:

> I see the long procession
> Of friends both young and old;
> Of those whose locks are hoary

> And those with locks of gold;
> And some are smiling infants,
> And all have snow-white wings,
> Around each brow the halo
> Which rest with Jesus brings.

Although Smith concludes this hymn with the biblical image of the river so prominent in spirituals, references to the "Golden City" beyond the river now are interpreted as ethereal rather than empirical:

> I know beyond the river—
> Beyond the turbid stream—
> There lies the Golden City,
> The city of my dreams.[21]

One of the hymns, "Trust in the Lord," by Rev. J.A.D. Bloice, is typically Methodist in its treatment of God as incomprehensible, untraceable, unreachable, and yet, paradoxically, omnipresent and personal. It is unique, however, in its atypical meter:

> I cannot understand Thee,
> Thou God of Light;
> In dark clouds Thou movest
> Dark as night.
> I cannot see Thee,
> Yet in Thee I trust,
> To guide, protect and lead me
> Home at last.
>
> I cannot even trace Thee,
> Thou God of Life;
> In trackless path Thou walkest
> Unseen Life.
> I cannot see Thee,
> Yet to Thee I come,
> To save, direct and bring me
> Safe to home.
>
> I cannot hope to reach Thee,
> Thou God of Heaven;
> In highest heights Thou dwellest
> High as heaven.
> I cannot hold Thee,
> Yet to Thee I look,
> So bend Thine ear and hear me
> In Thy Book.

I cannot lose Thee,
Thou God of Grace;
In mercy mild Thou waitest,
Mild as grace.
I cannot miss Thee;
Thou art to me,
In Life, in Death, forever
My best Friend.

William Howard Day's hymn, "The Nation's Woe," is the only piece among Rev. Wheeler's compilation in the 1892 hymnal that falls under the rubric of social reform. An active abolitionist, Day's hymn resembles the solemn pacifist verse of the great reform hymnists, who prayerfully petitioned God to redress the nation's transgression. Composed in the communal (first person plural) language of antislavery hymnody rather than in the personal (first person singular) language of evangelical hymnody, Day's hymn reads:

O God, our plea to Thee we lift—
Our ever-present Helper Thou;
We cling to Thee when all things drift—
To Thy blest will we humbly bow.

Asleep or wake, we helpless are,
The frail rememberers of Thy power;
In this dark hour we need Thy care—
We need Thee in our happiest hour.

Appear for us Thou Father, God—
Lift from us now Thy chastening hand;
Scatter the darkness with Thy rod,
And smile upon our sorrowing land.

As we sit listening for Thy voice
God of the nations speak Thy love;
Make all our sickened hearts rejoice,
In view of mercy from above.

And when, as now, with plaint sincere,
The sore heart of the nation bleeds,
Let Mercy touch us; may we hear—
"I am thy help for all thy needs."

Fifteen years following his compilation of the Zion hymns for the 1892 hymnal, Rev. Wheeler edited and had privately published a work titled *Cullings from Zion's Poets* (1907). One of the pieces in that anthology—which was not to appear in any of the

Zion hymnals—had been written for the centennial celebration of the church by Rev. William Howard Day (1825–1901). That Day, a native of New York City and the first black graduate of Oberlin College (1847), was an abolitionist who had been raised and educated in centers of antislavery activity was evident in the words of this hymn. At the 1896 centennial celebration that opened on 12 October in New York City, the birthplace of the Zion Church, Day's "Hail to the Church that Varick Started" was led by Bishop Isom Caleb Clinton:[22]

> Oh God, our Father, come we now,
> And in Thy presence humbly bow
> In thanks that for one hundred years,
> Thy church has stood through blood and tears.
>
> We bless Thee for Thy early care
> To help Thy people do and dare,
> When foes without blasphemed Thy name,
> And friends within were clad with shame.
>
> To recognize Thine image here,
> Because 'twas cut in ebon clear,
> We thank Thee for our color now,
> We bless Thee that we did not bow
>
> To the behest of slavery,
> Nor spurn the price of Liberty—
> And thank Thee for the friends who stood,
> In early days and sought our good.[23]

AME Bishop Henry McNeil Turner had claimed that "God is a Negro," and Day seems to affirm this idea in his third stanza, where he asserts that God's image is "ebon." His rejection of slavery and affirmation of his race and of liberty in the third and fourth stanzas are potent theological statements that would be integrated into Zion's evolving theology of liberation.

The 1909 hymnbook, *New Hymn and Tune Book for the Use of the African ME Zion Church*, was the first hymnbook printed by the AMEZ Publishing House of Charlotte, North Carolina.[24] Insofar as the 1909 hymnal was a duplicate of the ME hymnal of 1882[25] (albeit with the AMEZ's original prefatory matter and "Formula of Service"), the printing plates likely were loaned to the Zion publisher by the Publishing House of the ME Church. The hymnal was decided upon by a resolution adopted at the church's Connectional Council meeting in New York City in August

1909.[26] The "Bishops' Address" prefacing the hymnal had little to say about the selection, other than that the church leaders believed it would serve the church's needs:

> For some time we have realized the need of a Hymn Book containing more of the modern hymns than the one we have been using, therefore, in answer to the great need, we have taken steps to supply the Church with a Hymnal which we believe will meet the demand.
> We unanimously approve the report of the Committee appointed by the Connectional Council and do most cordially commend their selection.[27]

The prefatory "Committee's Report" gave a few more details about Zion's selection and adoption of the 1882 ME hymnal. It said, "After carefully examining and comparing the various Hymn Books in use by the Methodist bodies, it is our opinion that the Special Edition of the Methodist Episcopal Hymn and Tune Book comes more nearly suiting our needs than any other."[28] When the Zion Church renewed the copyright to the 1909 hymnal in 1937, it was evidently with the intention that it would continue to serve the church until action was taken to revise it. Such action was initiated in 1941. But unforseen circumstances insured that the recopyrighted volume—already fifty-five years old, since it was based on the 1882 ME hymnal— would be used for another twenty years.

While the 1909 hymnal was a duplication of the 1882 ME Church hymnal, that same year an original collection of hymns appeared which involved two of the Zion bishops. Titled *Soul Echoes: A Collection of Songs for Religious Meetings*,[29] the small pamphlet was published cooperatively by Bishops J.S. Caldwell and G.L. Blackwell of the AMEZ Church, Bishop L.J. Coppin of the AME Church, and Rev. Charles Albert Tindley of the ME Church. While all efforts by the black Methodist denominations over the next half-century to compile a common hymnbook failed utterly, here was a small but successful effort by an ecumenical group of black Methodist leaders to work cooperatively. The interdenominational nature of the work was obviously intentional; otherwise it would have been impractical for four clergymen to compile a small pamphlet of a mere fifty hymns, half of which were composed by Tindley, who was quite experienced at publishing his own songs. Yet the front matter neither identified the denominational affiliation of the compilers nor commented on the cooperative nature of the work. In fact, the opening remarks were not only brief, but rather figurative:

> A long felt desire for songs with words of Hope, Cheer, Love and Pity; for melodies that can sink to the depths of sorrow, and rise to the heights of joy, has had most to do with the publication of this book.
>
> It is the prayer of the publishers that these messages in rhyme shall float from soul to soul until the hills and valleys shall awake into joyful singing.

Published in Philadelphia, where Tindley was pastor of a Methodist Episcopal church, and made available for purchase through the AMEZ Publishing House in Charlotte, North Carolina, the first edition of *Soul Echoes* sold out within thirty days. This success necessitated the immediate publication of a second edition, which came out the same year. The inside cover of the enlarged edition explained: "The fact that the first issue of 'Soul Echoes' was sold within thirty days, is sufficient testimony of the popularity of the book. This revised edition contains several new and beautiful selections, never before sung or published, and is calculated to be even more popular than the First Book."[30] Insofar as all of the denominational hymnals of the Zion Church either adopted or adapted the ME hymnbooks—containing few revival songs, virtually no spirituals, and large numbers of Wesleyan hymns—it was understandable that the gospel hymns of Tindley would be readily and warmly received. Written in the vernacular characteristic of the spirituals, Tindley's hymns captured the mood of disconsolation among the black urban population. They expressed their own ethnic brand of hope, cheer, love, and pity, quite distinct from the classic Methodist hymns.

The second or revised edition of *Soul Echoes* contained fifty-one hymns, most of which were set to music. Almost half of the pieces (twenty-five of the fifty-one) were by Tindley, whose gospel hymns had been set to music by himself or arranged by F.A. Clark or William D. Smith. Among the remaining pieces were "Hymn for Baptism," by AME bishop Daniel A. Payne, a piece by R. William Fickland set by AME Bishop L.J. Coppin, and a scattering of old favorites by the evangelical contemporaries of Wesley and Watts. The 1964 volume produced by Bishop William J. Walls was a facsimile reprint of the second issue, with five pieces added at the back. One of those five pieces, titled

"Freedom," was a hymn by Bishop Walls, with music by K. Eloise Simpson.

Although *Soul Echoes* was never adopted by the Zion, Bethel (AME), or Methodist churches as a hymnal supplement, it was a small harbinger of larger efforts at ecumenical cooperation that Zion, Bethel, and the Colored Methodists were to make in subsequent years. At the Tri-Council meetings of the bishops of these three denominations, held during the first three decades of the twentieth century, the principal item on the agenda was the possibility of union. As the churches pressed toward this goal, much was made of the idea that they publish a "common hymnbook." The Colored Methodists, however, withdrew from the proposed plan for organizational union during the early twenties, and talk of union continued between the Zion and Bethel churches. It was as part of this dialogue that, in 1940, the two African Methodist churches planned to publish a joint hymnbook.[31] Hence, according to Zion historian D.H. Bradley, the endeavor to produce what eventually would result in the 1957 Zion hymnal actually stemmed back to the Tri-Council's effort to compile a "common hymnbook": "The first effort at the production of a distinctly African Methodist hymnal began in the middle decades of the Twentieth Century—1930–1960. Progress was at first made with the idea of the three Black Methodist denominations working to produce a common book. Later, the A.M.E. and the A.M.E. Zion Church appeared very close to the obtaining of such a work, much of the work having been collected and put together."[32]

When Bethel's Bishop John A. Gregg visited Zion's General Conference of 1944, it was reported by the hymnal commission that a manuscript was in progress. According to the Zionites, it was not long afterward that some unknown difficulty arose with the Bethelites connected with the commission, with the result that the project was deferred until the problem could be resolved.[33] What occurred during the interim greatly disturbed the Zion Church, and members later would write about it in the preface to the 1957 Zion hymnal: "Our sister church published a hymnal of their own leaving the joint manuscript unused and announced, unjustifiably, that the African Methodist Episcopal Zion church had failed to meet conditions for the joint hymnal." Bradley interpreted the reaction of his church as being one of disappointment. "Keen disappointment," he emphasized, "was expressed when it became known that the A.M.E. Church was already proceeding towards the production of such a work without following through on the basic cooperation with Zion." A decade after the publication of the 1957 Zion hymnal, Bradley stated that reasons for Bethel's decision to publish its own hymnbook remained unknown.[34]

The hymnal allegedly produced by Bethel was *The Richard Allen AME Hymnal*, published in 1946. According to its prefatory "Publisher's Word" (written by W.K. Hopes, manager of the Book Concern), the AME General Conference of 1940 called for a revised hymnal, which was expeditiously completed and ready for publication in 1941. "When the book was nearly completed," wrote Hopes, "we received orders from the Chairman [Bishop Gregg] to withhold completion of the book pending a plan to have a joint hymnal by the A.M.E. Church and the A.M.E. Zion Church." Hopes concluded, rather demurely, "The book is still in the making." Thus, it was a full two years following Bishop Gregg's visit to the 1944 AMEZ General Conference that Bethel went through with its initial plan to publish the *Allen AME Hymnal*. In an addendum to the preface of a later printing of this hymnal, dated 1 March 1950, Bishop Gregg made this telling remark: "As the progress of the combined Hymnal between the A.M.E. and the A.M.E. Zion Churches has lagged, the Bishops of the A.M.E. Church in Council at Jacksonville, Florida, February 15–17, 1950, ordered that the 'Allen A.M.E. Hymnal' shall now become the official A.M.E. Hymnal of the Connection. We are therefore proceeding with the publication of the same and giving it to the church at this time." If Bethel in fact accused Zion of failing to meet conditions for the joint hymnal, it could have been, as Hopes and Gregg intimated, because Zion had lagged far behind schedule. Bethel seemingly had been patient for a sufficient period of time, for the adoption of the *Allen AME Hymnal* as the official hymnal of the church came ten long years after plans were made to produce the joint hymnal and to revise their own 1892 hymnal (then over fifty years old).

To the Zion Church, it was gravely unfortunate that the joint hymnal never materialized. Such a step toward consolidation could have resulted in more fruitful Christian fellowship and greater political and economic efficiency for the black church in

North America.[35] Too, Zion always had envisioned the black Methodists leading all the Methodist denominations of the world into organic union, thereby setting the example for other religious denominations.[36] The notion that a joint hymnal could constitute the inaugural step toward such union was not at all unreasonable. After all, *The Methodist Hymnal* of 1905, published jointly by the northern and southern branches of Methodism, had been preparatory for *The Methodist Hymnal* of 1935, which was published cooperatively by the ME Church, ME Church, South, and the Methodist Protestant (MP) Church. Following his discussion of these cooperative Methodist hymnbooks of 1905 and 1935, hymnologist Robert McCutchan asked in 1937: "Is it too much to expect that the next generation of Methodists may publish a hymnal in which all other branches of the Church may join?"[37] It was but two years later that the latter three Methodist denominations merged. It seems positively feasible, then, that a common hymnbook between Zion and Bethel later could have included the Colored Methodists, and that the resulting fruits of fellowship and economic benefit could have convinced them of the value of organic union.

Now, with Bethel having published a new hymnal and Zion having been left with its outdated hymnal of 1909 (the ME hymnal of 1882), Zion's General Conference of 1952 reconstructed its hymnal commission and authorized it to compile a hymnbook for the church. The resolution at the conference was given by Rev. J.E. McCall:

> *Whereas,* the A.M.E. Zion Church, like other churches has use of Hymnals in its service for the choir and congregation;
> *Whereas,* it has been quite some time since we have had any hymnals printed;
> *Whereas,* the services of our churches will be greatly enhanced by the use of our own hymnals, Be it
> *Resolved:* that a committee be appointed to work with the manager of the Publication House in printing new hymnals for the A.M.E. Zion Church.[38]

Four years later, at the 1956 General Conference, the hymnal was on the verge of completion (while Bethel had in fact published another hymnal two years earlier).[39] Bishop Stephen Gill Spottswood, one of the most active members of Zion's hymnal commission, reported that "since the order of the 1952 General

Conference, we have not lost any time in planning to have a hymnal for our church, and if we are able to get the money, we will have the hymnal in the near future."[40]

In his denominational history of the Zion Church, Bishop Walls, who was chairman of the hymnal commission, intimated that the 1957 hymnbook was at least partially based on the material compiled by the original joint commission: "The joint hymnal manuscript, which was in the hands of the Zion group, was practically ready for press. The African Methodist Episcopal Zion Church excluded the African Methodist Episcopal Church's specific connectional contribution and retained the major work which the Zion Commission had prepared and submitted it to the General Conference . . . in 1952." After Rev. McCall's resolution, concluded Walls, "The commission labored tirelessly to complete the manuscript with additional features."[41] That the Zion Church used the manuscript compiled by the joint commission, without Bethel's "specific connectional contribution," conceivably explains the intentional or unintentional inclusion of two hymns by Bethel's Bishops Daniel A. Payne and J.C. Embry.

Finally published in 1957, a full seventeen years following the initial proposal to compile a joint hymnal, it is understandable that the description given the new hymnal at the ensuing General Conference of 1960 proudly highlighted its comprehensiveness: "The New A.M.E. Zion Hymnal . . . contains a large selective number of hymns including many by Charles Wesley, John Wesley, Isaac Watts, Ancient Hymns and Canticles, Modern Authors, Spirituals, Zion Methodist Authors, Hymns for children, and for youth. In addition, there is part of the ritual, responses and sentences, Responsive Readings and eight Indices."[42] The prefatory "Bishops' Address" appears equally proud and relieved at having finally satisfied the church's dire need for a modern hymnbook: "For some time we have realized the need of a Hymn book containing more of the modern hymns than the ones we have been using. Therefore, in answer to the great need, we have taken steps to supply the church with a Hymnal which we believe will meet that need."

The address proceeded to list eight points that reflected some of the ecclesiastical and theological concerns of the day. One of the points was a cautionary reaction to the recent development of the gospel choir. "The minister must take and express deep and constant interest in congregational singing," it said. "We must redeem it from the failure into which it has drifted by the choir and chorus emphasis." In closing, the bishops not only boasted further concerning the merits of the new hymnbook but also revealed much about their theology of hymn singing and their view of it as a preeminent means of ministry:

> We have the hope that this work, which includes original hymns from people in our own communion and more of the original Wesleyan Hymns than any other book now extant in America, will stimulate all the people to sing in all the services and may contribute to a revival of spirituality in worship through the power of sacred song upon the heart. Thus it will aid many to turn to salvation who may be more moved by the suasion of the Gospel in appropriate song than by many other visible agencies; because it is the people repreaching the sermon which Protestantism submits as the most powerful Gospel and soul saving influence, when moved by the Holy Spirit.[43]

The "Commission's Statement" reiterated the claim made in the "Bishops' Address" that the Zion hymnbook contained the largest number of Wesleyan hymns to be found in any hymnbook in the nation. It also claimed to have restored some of the "appropriate" evangelical hymns that modern hymnbook compilers had excluded. Lastly, the statement said, "The commission has sought to make this book universal as a doctrinal and evangelistic instrument of song for the Christian church with emphasis on the Methodist approach to the way of salvation."

It is likely that Zion's claims were true, for, while they were filling their hymnbook with one hundred Wesleyan hymns[44] and restoring the evangelical pieces that modern hymnbook compilers had been omitting over the last half-century of social reform, other denominational hymnals, such as the recent AME hymnal of 1954, were still responding to the aftermath of the Social Gospel movement. On the other hand, while the 1957 hymnal is clearly Methodist and evangelical, there is some evidence that the church was affected by the Social Gospel. The influence is clear in the table of contents; under the heading "The Kingdom of God," forty-two hymns are categorized under these four subheadings: Service, Brotherhood, Missions, and National and International Life.

There are two aspects that help make this 1957 hymnbook the first completely original hymnological work produced in the history of the Zion Church. First, black spirituals are included in a Zion hymnbook for the first time. The nine spirituals in the volume may have been included at the insistence of Bishop W.J. Walls, chairman of the hymnal commission. "It is the responsibility of the black race of every age," wrote Walls elsewhere, "to keep inviolate and preserve this precious gift squeezed out of the toils and tears of our ancestral afflictions."[45] Second, the hymnal includes almost all of the twenty-nine hymns by the Zion ministers initially published in the 1892 hymnbook.[46] While in the 1892 volume the hymns of the Zion ministers appeared without tunes (as do all the hymns in that volume), in the 1957 "hymn and tune book" they are paired with traditional tunes by such classic composers as Beethoven, Haydn, Weber, William Bradbury, and Lowell Mason.

In addition to these historic hymns by Zion ministers, there are several original pieces by contemporary Zion clergy. Among the bishops who signed the prefatory "Bishop's Address" and served on the hymnal commission are several who have one or two of their original hymns in the volume: Bishops William J. Walls, Cameron C. Allyne, James C. Taylor, and Stephen G. Spottswood. Also included is a piece by Bettye Lee Roberts Allyne, Bishop Allyne's wife. Titled "Work of Our Founders We Extol" and set by William Knapp, the hymn has a footnote indicating that it was written for the Sesquicentennial Celebration of the Zion Church. A characteristic verse (the fourth) reads:

> For liberty they struck the blow,
> Like them we toil—half million strong;
> Building our Zion we onward go,
> To God and them our praise belong,
> Work of our founders, noble work,
> We'll labor on and never shirk.

Another piece written for the 1946 celebration of the first 150 years of the Zion Church is "Hope of Ages Thou, Our God," by Bishop James C. Taylor. Its footnote reads, "Written for the Sesquicentennial celebration of the African Methodist Episcopal Zion Church, September 8–22, 1946. Dedicated to the Founders of the A.M.E. Zion Church, and to the late Bishop James Walter Brown, builder of the present Mother A.M.E. Zion Church edifice." Bishop Taylor's hymn was set by Andrades Lindsay Brown, the wife of Bishop James W. Brown, whose name is among those to whom the book is dedicated. The tune is appropriately named "Bishop Brown." A characteristic verse (the second) reads:

> God, whose truth alone shall free us,
> Loose our minds from fetters strong,
> That we, knowing Thy pure purpose,
> Make our deeds square with our song.
> Touch our minds, shake off our shackles.
> Hope of Ages Thou, our God.

These many hymns by Zion writers are what gives the 1957 AMEZ hymnal its original and uniquely denominational flavor. However, while it was a commendable accomplishment at the time of its publication, the 1957 hymnal is socially and theologically outmoded. Its pre–Civil Rights character makes it necessary that this work be supplanted by a volume reflecting the church's post-Civil Rights awareness—the kind of awareness that would allow its members to assert more forthrightly, with William Howard Day, that God is "ebon." Zion's hymnody soon must catch up with Zion's vision of the twenty-first century.

Chapter 3

The Christian Methodist Episcopal Church

The Colored Methodist Episcopal Church in America has had a remarkable career. As a branch or product of the Methodist Episcopal Church, South, it has been opposed by strong hands and accomplished leaders among the colored people, from its birthday to the present; though, happily for us, these oppositions are now subsiding and the young organization is taking on a firm and expanding aspect that is most interesting and extraordinary. To sustain and propagate such an institution amid so many opposing forces as those that have presented themselves for the last twenty years, seemed, at first, to be a forlorn and hopeless undertaking. Green from the fields of slavery, raw in the experiences of church tactics, in membership and ministry, without houses of worship or literature, with many of its organizing feats being performed out of doors and under trees, it overcame difficulties that make it more than an experiment. Being in the dews of its youth, it has not yet attained its destined dignity and power for good among the colored race. But it is advancing in every department.

—*Lucius H. Holsey,*
third elected bishop of the Colored Methodist Episcopal Church[1]

The most recent hymnological endeavor of the Christian Methodist Episcopal (CME) Church is *The Hymnal of the Christian Methodist Episcopal Church*, which was published in 1987 by the CME Publishing House, in Memphis, Tennessee. Its preface is probably the only printed document that chronicles the musical history of the denomination. Commencing with reference to John Wesley's *A Collection of Psalms and Hymns* (1737) and the hymns of Charles Wesley, the narrative proceeds to cover the creation of the black spirituals, the lining-out style of "Dr. Watts" hymn-singing, and the singing of "improvised hymns."[2] During the course of the present chapter, we shall draw on the preface's discussion of the CME hymnbook of 1891, its songbook of 1904, its 1950 adoption of the Methodist hymnbook of 1939, and its present hymnbook of 1987.

The new CME hymnal is a blue hardbound volume with gold lettering. On its spine, and on the back of the title page above the copyright data,[3] is displayed the official logo of the church—a globe encircling the Christian cross diagonally spanning its length, with a weather vane to the left of its lengthwise beam, an urban skyline to its right, and the unabbreviated church name and founding date stretching along the globe's upper curve. Adopted in 1970, the year of the denomination's centennial commemoration, the emblem is "indicative of the desire to 'serve the present age'."[4]

Ensuing is the preface, whose five pages conclude with the Hymn of Christian Methodism—Bishop Lucius H. Holsey's "O Rapturous Scenes." Apparently written by Bishop Holsey during Reconstruction, the hymn was set by his church contemporary, Rev. F.M. Hamilton, probably during the years leading up to its initial publication in 1904. The foreword to the hymn says: "During his years as a slave and the turbulent days of Reconstruction as the fledgling Colored Methodist Episcopal Church was facing fierce opposition, Holsey wrote the words of a hymn that captured the mood of sorrow and despair, faith and hope that was so much a part of the life of Black Christians." In his history of the CME Church, Bishop Othal Lakey further suggested that, "Though it is not known exactly when Holsey wrote the words of this hymn, they appear to have had their origin in the days of slavery, but reflect some of the persecution Holsey experienced trying to establish his beloved CME Church in the post-bellum days." Bishop Lakey concludes, "Holsey's hymn expresses the deep faith and hope shared by so many Black Christians."[5]

At the funeral of this Georgia-born freedman (1842–1920) and third elected bishop (1873) of the CME Church, Holsey's own "O Rapturous Scenes" was led by Bishop C.H. Phillips:[6]

O rapturous scenes that wait the day,
When Thou shall call me home,
When I shall here no longer stay,
No longer weep and moan.

Long has my heart look'd up to Thee,
My Master and my King,
No other hand can make me free,
And to thy bosom bring.

What wondrous grace is this that brings,
My waiting soul to Thee,
That makes me scorn all earthly things,
That I may holy be?

Say gracious Lord, where am I now?
Am I Thy servant still?
Shall flesh and blood my soul o'erthrow?
And set at naught Thy will?

Nay, but my soul shall rise and fly,
To that bright world above;
The heav'nly Canaan in the sky,
The city of Thy love.

Hallelujah! the race is run!
Eternal life is gained,
My happiness has just begun,
The crown of life obtained!

In an editorial review in the CME periodical, the *Christian Index*, Rev. Lawrence L. Reddick III commented on the method employed to produce the 1987 hymnal: "What has resulted in the production of a new CME hymnal was the choice by the commission to hire a publishing firm which specialized in hymnal printing to print for the Christian Methodist Episcopal Church a hymnal for which that firm already has publishing rights. This has also resulted in a hymnal which will look, in many respects, like another denominational hymnal with which many CME's are familiar."[7] The hymnal to which Rev. Reddick was referring is *The New National Baptist Hymnal* (1977). However, the CME hymnal does not "resemble" it; aside from having its own front- and backmatter,[8] the CME hymnal is an exact duplication of it. The only cosmetic modification in the body of the volume is that the two opening hymns are interchanged. While the Baptist hymnal opens with Heber's "Holy, Holy, Holy," followed by Perronet's "All Hail the Power," the CME hymnal does just the reverse. This explains the ability of the Christian Methodists to resolve in 1986 to compile a hymnal and then to publish it a short time later in 1987. It also explains why Rev. T.B. Boyd III, publisher of the National Baptist Publishing Board, is acknowledged as the associate publication supervisor to Rev. L.L. Napier, the publisher of the CME Publishing House.

Having himself served on the Hymnal Commission of 1978, which relinquished the project in 1982 when its chairperson, Bishop James L. Cummings, died, Rev. Reddick commented further, out of his own experience: "Though it would have been possible to spend the additional time and money to gather the church's musicians together, choose hymns, decide thematic structures for a hymnal, enter into negotiations for reproduction privileges and agree upon royalties with copyright owners, it could have proven a mammoth undertaking in money and time for this to succeed."[9]

As Rev. Reddick knew well, the ideal procedure for compiling an original hymnal was a task of proven enormity. Nevertheless, because hymnody is such a salient aspect of the church liturgy and for the church laity is a principal source of religious language, theology, doctrine, and denominational history, the church must maintain its crucial role as conservator of historical and cultural values. *The Hymnal of the Christian Methodist Episcopal Church* ideally should be a reflection of the elements that make the denomination what it is, doctrinally, theologically, historically, and culturally. The cultural aspect is fundamentally monolithic, in that all black worshipers—Methodist, Baptist, Holiness, Pentecostal, Episcopal, and Roman Catholic—generally sing the same hymns. Since the CMEs and the National Baptists are both black Protestant denominations, their minor theological and doctrinal distinctions have no real effect on the hymns they choose to sing. But historically, even in the present era of ecumenism, the CME Church has as great an obligation to preserve the hymns of its hymnists as larger Methodism has to perpetuate the hymnic legacy of Charles Wesley.

Had we already surveyed the hymnic history of the CME Church, then the unforeseen event would have been not that the church adapted the hymnal of another denomination, but that it adapted a Baptist hymnal. For the inaugural hymnal of the CME Church, the *Hymn Book of the Colored M.E. Church in America*

(1891), was more or less the hymnbook of the Methodist Episcopal Church, South (the church from which the black membership separated amiably in 1870 to form its own denomination), with the CME appellation appended. Among the concerns of the inaugural General Conference of 1870, held in Jackson, Tennessee, were a discipline, a periodical, Sunday school literature, catechisms, and a hymnbook. It was decided by the leaders of the nascent church that, until the connection could establish its own publishing facility, it would use the Sunday school literature and catechisms of the Methodist Episcopal Church, South, and have the latter's publishing house print their church's discipline and hymnbook.[10] At the time the 1891 hymnbook was published, the CME Book Concern was simply an office in Jackson, under the direction of a "book agent," where printed materials were ordered from the mother church, stored, and then sold and distributed throughout the CME connection:[11]

> At the Organizing General Conference of 1870 which made the Colored Methodist Episcopal Church in America a separate and independent church, the Hymnbook of the Methodist Episcopal Church, South, was approved as the official hymnbook of the CME Church, pending the establishment of a Book Concern and the printing of a CME Hymnbook. The General Conference of 1886 authorized Bishop Lucius H. Holsey to publish a hymnbook for the Church. Accordingly, it was in 1890 that the first hymnbook in the name of the CME Church was published.[12]

The publication date given on the title page was actually 1891, and the volume apparently was endorsed as the official hymnbook of the church by the General Conference of 1894.[13]

This 1891 hymnbook was clearly an adaptation of the 1889 *Hymn Book of the Methodist Episcopal Church, South.*[14] The table of contents of the CME volume was essentially identical to that in the model 1889 hymnal.[15] Of the 1889 volume, the preface of the 1987 hymnal says, "This hymnbook was based primarily on the hymnbook of the M.E. Church, South, with a preface by the bishops of the Church and the ritual of the CME Church added." In fact, there apparently was no ritual added,[16] and substantial modifications were made. In preparing the 1891 hymnal, Bishop Holsey deleted from the model hymnbook of 1889 334 of the 929 hymns (as well as two indices and the doctrinal back matter)[17] and added 46 hymns from other hymnbooks, to achieve a total of 641 hymns. Six of the 46 added pieces might have been transcribed from the earlier 1884 hymnal of the mother church, while 25 of them undoubtedly were borrowed from Ira Sankey's six-volume collection of gospel hymns that commenced publication in 1875.[18] Reducing the size of the model hymnbook was at least partly a financial decision by the CME Church. "We have long felt the need of a cheap Hymn Book among us," said the 1891 preface, "not cheap as to doctrinal and poetic merit—but cheap as for the price paid by those for whose use the book has its existence." Because Bishop Holsey compiled the CME hymnal, as Bishop Phillips said, "with great care and skill," it came to be known as "the Holsey Hymn Book."[19]

The hymnal's preface opened with the salutation, "Dear Brethren," and closed with the valediction, "Affectionately your chief pastors, W.H. Miles, J.A. Beebe, L.H. Holsey, Isaac Lane. January 16, 1891." Insofar as it was Holsey who wrote every message from the bishops between 1873 and 1914,[20] and insofar as the hymnbook was "the Holsey Hymn Book," it was most probably Holsey who wrote the preface which articulately expressed the need for it:

> We hope to see this Hymn Book in all the churches, congregations, Sunday-schools, and families. Let the pastorate remember that their duty is not done until this collection of hymns is placed in every church, congregation, Sunday-school, and family composing our expanding Connection. Our people should be taught congregational singing. Nothing can be substituted in its place. Our people are famous in the art of congregational singing, which should always be encouraged, but for the last few years there is a noted falling off in this respect. Many of our congregations have permitted themselves to drift into a stiff and dead formalism in their singing that is damaging to piety and detrimental to the growth in grace so necessary to a hearty and whole-soul Christianity. Whether we have organs or not, let every pastor teach his people the art and beauty of congregational singing.

Particularly replete with Wesleyan and Wattsian hymns, which together comprised nearly half the volume, the pieces were, as the preface said, "sound in their doctrinal teachings," "Wesleyan and Methodistic." The writer declared, "They breathe the spirit of elevated piety and true devotion."

In 1904, Rev. F.M. Hamilton, with the editorial assistance of Bishop Holsey, compiled a songbook for the church entitled *Songs of Love and Mercy.*[21] It was in this volume that Bishop

Holsey's "O Rapturous Scenes" first appeared. Printed by the CME Publishing House in Jackson, Tennessee, it was produced under the supervision of Rev. Henry Bullock, book agent from 1902 to 1912. Rev. Bullock wrote in the preface:

> In their Quadrennial address to the General Conference held in Nashville, Tennessee, May, 1902, the Bishops recommended that the Conference arrange to have a Young People's Hymnal devised and published, to meet the needs of our Sunday School, Epworth Leagues and other meetings of the public services.
>
> We are indebted to Rev. F.M. Hamilton for the preparation of this book. He has furnished many new songs which are given to the public for the first time. These songs were carefully examined by Bishop L.H. Holsey. . . .
>
> This song book is one among the very few produced by Negro authors, and should have a wide circulation among the music loving people of the race.
>
> We would call the attention of pastors, superintendents and others engaged in religious work, to the importance of good music in the various meetings.
>
> The songs contained here in are suitable for all religious gatherings; and we send them forth with the hope that they may find favor with the public; and that they may be the means of awakening religious enthusiasm among all Christian workers, and cause many who are yet unsaved to seek, and find Him who really *loves* and will have *mercy.*

Love and Mercy, as it was called,[22] contained 198 hymns, a substantial number of which were composed or set to music by members of the CME Church. Rev. Hamilton, the most prolific among CME writers, wrote either the text or music to 54 pieces. He wrote both text and music for 38 hymns, the text alone to 4 additional hymns, and the music to 12 pieces (5 hymns, 5 arrangements, and 2 anthems).[23] In addition to Bishop Holsey's "O Rapturous Scenes" (set by Hamilton) was 1 hymn by Rev. A.J. Cobb, the editor of the *Christian Index* from 1910 to 1914 (set by Charles A. Dryscoll), and one by Hattie Hamilton (set by her husband, Rev. F.M. Hamilton).[24] The remaining were classics by hymnists such as Wesley (13 pieces) and Watts (15 pieces), plus 2 spirituals (listed as "anonymous").[25]

While Bishop Holsey deserves to be called the father of CME hymnody, having compiled the church's inaugural hymnal and played a part in the making of *Love and Mercy*, Rev. F.M. Hamilton merits the title "the sweet singer of Colored Methodism." A native of Macon, Georgia, who during his career pastored in Alabama, Arkansas, Georgia, and Virginia, Rev. Hamilton (who died in 1912) was for about three decades one of the recognized leaders of the church.[26] He served as secretary to the General Conference from 1886 to 1910, editor of *The Christian Index* from 1886 to 1892, and book agent of the Publishing House from 1886 to 1890.[27] As author of numerous pamphlets and monographs on CME Church history and polity,[28] Hamilton was also "the most prolific writer in the early history of the church."[29]

Had the 1986 hymnal commission closely examined Rev. Hamilton's hymns in *Love and Mercy,* they undoubtedly would have found them to be historical gems well worth depositing in the "history book" of their hymnal. His hymns are just as well suited, theologically and culturally, to contemporary black worship as are the hymns of Charles Price Jones and Charles Albert Tindley. They typically petition God's "laborers" to "work" in the "vineyard" and in the "harvest fields" performing "deeds of loving kindness." The Lord's "willing workers" must carry out "the work of faith and love," Hamilton lyricized, in order to one day see "the endless day," that "land of endless glory." "Helping the helpless, helping the poor, Seeking for the lost and erring ones"—these are the things the Master calls them to do.

> Our work on earth will not be done,
> 'Till we in Jesus' name
> Fight the good fight of faith, and then
> The glorious crown obtain.

As well, said Hamilton, there are the poor in spirit whose souls thirst and hunger for the living water: "Go break to them the bread of life, To living waters lead them too."[30]

According to Hamilton's imagery, to work in the vineyard is to be at "war," and to be a faithful member of the "band of true believers" is to be a soldier in a "mighty army":

> They have pass'd thro' many conflicts,
> Many trials hard and sore,
> Still they're marching on to Zion,
> Where they'll study war no more.
>
> When the warfare here is ended,
> And the armor all laid down,
> They shall enter joys eternal
> And receive a starry crown.

The "band of true believers" is, of course, the church, which by "marching onward in the service of the Lord" is concurrently "marching to the land above." Those in the procession must "take the world for Christ," lyricized Hamilton, "no matter what the cost." It is a moral responsibility:

> Whatsoever things are pure,
> Things that will fore'er endure,
> And on things that are honest,
> Surely these are always best.

> Whatsoever things are just,
> Things in which all men can trust,
> And on things divinely true,
> Think on these in all you do.[31]

Occasionally in Hamilton's hymns the "land beyond the swelling tide"—that ethereal expanse embracing no sickness, death, or troubles—stands over and against the dark world of low-hanging clouds. In the mood of C.P. Jones and C.A. Tindley, he wrote:

> Tho' the way may seem dark and the clouds hang low,
> And the mutt'ring thunders lift their sullen roar,
> With our trust in our God we will walk straight on,
> Follow on until we reach the other shore.

> Tho' our friends may forsake and foes unite
> And the hosts of hell combine against us here
> Still we'll keep in the path and will follow on,
> Keeping sight of Him who casteth out fear.

Although Hamilton occasionally characterized the world as "not so friendly" and human relationships as sometimes deceiving, he never really depicted the "realm of endless day" as the absolute alternative to the world God so loved. At least once he referred to the earthly domain as a "world of woes," but more typically he denoted life "a contest" and its way as "narrow." Hence, "the golden shore" may not be portrayed in his hymns as the *absolute alternative*, as it is in the hymns of Jones and Tindley, but it is undoubtedly life's ultimate goal. For those who have fought the good fight of faith, it is the place where finally they will be reunited with friends and loved ones in communion, Hamilton said, with the angels, apostles, and martyrs:

> March on, press on, struggle day by day,
> Strive on, fight on, never leave the fray,

> For in the conflict we will overcome,
> And will be rewarded when the work is done.

Finally, as though tuning up his preaching for a climactic cadenza, Hamilton waxed poetic in his portrait of the "other shore" as infinitely "golden":

> There's a happy day soon coming, and the time will not be long,
> When we all shall join together in one grand glorious song,
> Singing with the holy angels in the bright forevermore,
> In that blessed land of promise, Over on the other shore.
>
> Thro' the pearly gates we'll enter, walk the streets of shining
>   gold,
> And behold the walls of Jasper as th' apostle once foretold,
> And we'll tell the wondrous story as we've never told before,
> As we walk and talk together, Over on the other shore.
>
> "There the wicked cease to trouble and the weary are at rest,"
> In that happy land of promise where we'll evermore be blest,
> There we'll meet with all our loved ones, who have journey'd
>   on before.
> It will be a joyous greeting, Over on the other shore.[32]

In sum, F.M. Hamilton's hymns are just as poetic, and borrow just as substantively from the vernacular of black culture, as the hymns of Charles Albert Tindley. Like Charles Price Jones, he apparently was a far more prolific musician and composer than Tindley. Also, while Tindley was a minister in the long-established Methodist Church, Hamilton, as his hymns seem to reflect, lived amid the severe struggles of an infant southern black church, fighting to establish itself in the wake of Reconstruction, in the face of African Methodist Episcopal (AME) and African Methodist Episcopal Zion (AMEZ) opposition, and in the shadow of parental skepticism on the part of the Methodist Episcopal Church, South. Yet throughout Hamilton's hymns, "the path the Master trod" remained the paradigm for Christian behavior and labor.[33]

Following *Songs of Love and Mercy* (1904), there would be no hymnological milestone in the CME Church for another half-century. During the interim, however, there was much talk of a "common hymnbook," to be published jointly by the three black Methodist denominations. In the bishops' message to the 1906 General Conference, Bishop Holsey claimed that a "common hymnbook," similar to the one used jointly by the Methodist

Episcopal Church and the Methodist Episcopal Church, South, was greatly needed.[34] As we have seen, the Tri-Council of bishops of the AME, AMEZ, and CME churches, which met in 1908, 1911, and 1918 to promote unity, cooperation, and joint religious effort, engaged in serious deliberation regarding this matter.[35] At the first meeting, held 12–17 February 1908, in Washington, D.C., committees were formed to cover a number of church concerns, one being the Hymnal and Catechism Committee.[36] A "common hymnbook," however, was never to materialize. In a 1920 address opposing the merger of the three denominations, Bishop Phillips noted that the bishops who had gathered at the Tri-Councils had resolved to produce a number of things in common, one being a "common hymnbook," but that their resolutions had "cooled down" after they parted and they never had carried out their promises.[37] Even as recently as 1921, the petition for a "common hymnbook" had been repeated. That year, in the 13 January issue of the *Christian Recorder* (the AME newspaper), an editorial accurately prophesied that, for the next twenty-five years, any hope of organic unity among the black Methodist bodies would be a mere wish. Nevertheless, wrote the editor, insofar as federation among the separate churches is feasible, then having in common such things as a hymnbook could reasonably be expected to lead to union under a future generation.[38]

In light of the aging CME hymnal of 1891 and the obvious limitations of *Songs of Love and Mercy*, for the CMEs a "common hymnbook" evolving out of a federation of the black Methodists would have meant a much-needed "new song" to sing. Because this cooperative venture was not to materialize by 1925, however, the church had to wait yet another quarter-century before formally authorizing the use of a "new" hymnal. What they settled upon then was even more dependent upon an existent hymnbook than what they had used in 1891— they *adopted*, without modification, the 1939 hymnal of the Methodist Church:

> Since the hymnology of American Methodism was so integral to the history of the CME Church and there were no differences in the printed rituals, the General Conference of 1950 decided that the 1939 hymnal of The Methodist Church, which for years had been used in many CME Churches, would be the official hymnal of the CME Church. This

hymnal, along with *The Gospel Pearl*, a collection of those songs which by 1930 had become so popular in Black churches, and a new type of songs, called "Gospel Songs" . . . have constituted the music in CME Churches over the past 40 or 50 years.[39]

In December 1968, *Songs of Love and Mercy* was reprinted for the 1970 centennial commemoration of the founding of the church. This historical milestone (perhaps coupled with the soul-converting social alchemy of the late 1960s) apparently prompted renewed sentiment for the compiling of a new denominational hymnal: "As the CME Church entered its second century following its Centennial in 1970, the need of a hymnal for the denomination was becoming paramount. A Commission on Hymnal for the CME Church was approved by the General Conference of 1978 with a mandate to begin preparation of a hymnal for the church. The College of Bishops appointed Bishop James L. Cummings as the Chairperson. The Commission agreed on the number and nature of hymns that the new hymnal would contain."[40] Because the death of Bishop Cummings was to leave the task unfinished, the only volume to emanate immediately from the centennial commemoration was the facsimile of *Songs of Love and Mercy*. Following that reprint, it was another two decades before the publication of *The Hymnal of the Christian Methodist Episcopal Church* (1987).

In retrospect, it is evident that the CME's 1987 adoption of an extant denominational hymnal was in keeping with its tradition. It is also more apparent that the decision to adopt the hymnal compiled by the National Baptists has resulted in a product which is less Methodist than it is Baptist (not to mention that it is even less CME than it is Methodist). First of all, the CMEs have forsaken the Methodist precedent of having a substantial representation of Wesleyan hymns. Their 1891 *Hymn Book of the Colored M.E. Church in America* included (out of a total of 641 pieces) 188 Wesleyan hymns—171 by Charles Wesley, 13 by John Wesley (10 being translations), 3 by Samuel Wesley, Jr., and 1 by Samuel Wesley, Sr. Its preface even boasted of the hymns being fundamentally "Wesleyan and Methodistic." It said further that "Methodists of all countries have been noted for their songs. 'The Wesleyan Hymns' are thrilling the hearts of the nations, and in verse and meter the Wesleys still talk to the heathen and preach the doctrine of the cross to the world." *The Methodist*

Hymnal of 1939, which the CMEs adopted in 1950, contained (out of a total of 644 pieces) 56 hymns by Charles Wesley and 1 by Samuel Wesley. Its preface also made a point of saying that "Methodism was born in song and has made a vitalizing contribution to evangelical hymnody." While even *Songs of Love and Mercy* (1904) contained (out of 198 pieces) 13 hymns by Charles Wesley, *The Hymnal of the Christian Methodist Episcopal Church* (1987) contains a mere 8 by the "sweet singer of Methodism." Absent from among those 8 is the "old conference hymn" of the CME Church, "And Are We Yet Alive"[41] (a favorite of the AMEs and AMEZs as well, and included in their hymnbooks).

The hymns of Isaac Watts, too, are Methodist. John Wesley marked them thus even before the people were called Methodists. Approximately half of the seventy pieces in his *A Collection of Psalms and Hymns* (1737)—the first hymnbook published in North America—were by Watts.[42] Even after Charles Wesley began writing hymns, following his conversion experience a year later, John Wesley continued to include a large number of Watts' hymns in his collections. But here again the CMEs have forsaken their deep-rooted Wattsian-Methodist tradition. Their hymnal of 1891 contained 93 Watts hymns, *Love and Mercy* contained 54, and the Methodist hymnal of 1939 (adopted in 1950) contained 18, while their "new" hymnal contains a mere 10.

The Baptist nature of the "new" Christian Methodist hymnal is further evident when compared to the current *African Methodist Episcopal Zion Hymnal* (1957) and *AMEC Bicentennial Hymnal* (1984). These two hymnals are ideal for such a comparison, in that one represents a pre-1960s and the other a post-1960s posture toward the time-honored Wesleyan and Wattsian hymns. The AMEZ hymnal contains 38 Wattsian and 100 Wesleyan hymns (90 by Charles Wesley, 7 by John Wesley, and 3 by Samuel Wesley). The AME hymnal contains 39 Wattsian and 58 Wesleyan hymns (52 by Charles Wesley, 3 by Samuel Wesley, and 1 each by John Wesley, Samuel Wesley, Sr., and Samuel Wesley, Jr.). Correspondingly, the "Baptist" CME hymnal has 7 hymns or arrangements each by Thomas Dorsey, Roberta Martin, Kenneth Morris, Lucie E. Campbell, and Doris Akers—gospel artists either raised in, associated with, or adopted by the Baptists. Conversely, the AME hymnal contains a mere 10 works by these writers (4 by Campbell and 2 each by Dorsey, Morris, and Akers), and the AMEZ hymnal not a one.

Hence, the statement made in the preface to the "new" hymnal—that it "represents the singing tradition of the Christian Methodist Episcopal Church"—is disreputable, as is the assertion that *"The Hymnal of the Christian Methodist Episcopal Church* brings together those hymns and spiritual songs members of the Christian Methodist Episcopal Church have found meaningful to their souls as they have sought to worship their God."[43] The preface also says, "The Scriptures tell us, 'Sing unto the Lord a new song.' This hymnal is presented to the members of the Christian Methodist Episcopal Church in hope that they will not only sing unto the Lord that 'new' song, but will, in the words of Alfred B. Haas, 'keep up the song forever!' " Actually, this hymnal permits neither. Because it was compiled prior to (and published in) 1977, making it by 1987 already ten years old, it contains no "new song." Because it does not embrace the hymns of the greatest hymnist in the history of Colored Methodism, it fails to "keep up the song forever."

To rehearse two-and-a-half centuries of Methodist history as a preface to an essentially "Baptist" hymnal belies the denominational heritage in which the CMEs have always taken great pride. In fact, it is a categorical denial of the CME's claim to what Bishop Lakey called "legitimacy of self-affirmation":

> The CME's constantly emphasized and took great pride in the fact that their first two bishops were ordained by the bishops of the Methodist Episcopal Church, South, upon the specific authorization of the General Conference of that church. Hence, the Colored Methodists claimed ministerial orders going all the way back to John Wesley, that were as valid as those of the Methodist Episcopal Church and the Methodist Episcopal Church, South. Such, in their opinion, was not the case in the ministerial orders of the independent Black Methodist bodies.
>
> Though their founders had been members of the Methodist Episcopal Church and had sought and petitioned the "Mother" Church for their acceptance, they were, nonetheless, never an official part of the Methodist Episcopal Church. So while the self-establishment of these Black Methodist churches was a most necessary consequence of the racial practices of the Methodist Episcopal Church, any claim based upon it— by way of what we might call the legitimacy of self-affirmation—was lost in the heated confusions, claims, and counter-claims of that hectic postbellum period.[44]

In this respect there is something both distinctive and not distinctive about this 1987 CME hymnal. It is not distinctive denominationally because it is actually the hymnal of the National Baptist Convention, Inc. It is distinctive historically because it is the only current hymnal of the black denominations that neglects earnestly to reflect its denominational heritage.

In his review of *The Hymnal of the Christian Methodist Episcopal Church*, Rev. Reddick suggests a possible means of updating the hymnal. He says: "For the present time, what has been excluded seems far outweighed by what has been included. But—what is left out may be important, and there must be some channel for those who would want to suggest improvements for the next printing of the hymnal. We should not let this hymnal become a stagnant instrument that slowly dies from irrelevancy, but we must update and adjust it as time goes on."[45] As shown by our brief textual analysis of Rev. Hamilton's hymns and our overview of the traditionally strong Wesleyan and Wattsian representation in the former hymnals of the church, what has been left out is indeed very important. As Rev. Reddick has said, the Christian Methodist Episcopal Church should not allow this hymnal to become "a stagnant instrument that slowly dies from irrelevancy."

CHAPTER 4

The United Methodist Church

> We, a group of black Methodists in America, are deeply
> disturbed about the crisis of racism in America. We are
> equally concerned about the failure of a number of
> black people, including black Methodists to respond
> appropriately to the roots and forces of racism and the
> current Black Revolution. . . .
>
> We are new men—the old man, "nigger," is dead. The
> "boy" is now a man!
>
> We now stand as proud black men prepared to embrace
> our blackness and committed to address ourselves
> unequivocally and forcefully to racism wherever we find
> it, in and outside the church.
>
> —*Black Methodists for Church Renewal Caucus*[1]

Within United Methodism there exists a Black Methodist Church which was institutionalized in 1939, when the delegates of the merging Methodist Episcopal (ME) Church, ME Church, South, and Methodist Protestant (MP) Church voted to segregate the new church's black membership.[2] Of the six administrative jurisdictions established by the Methodist Church, five were geographically based, with the remaining one being racially based to include virtually the entire black constituency of the church. According to the 1939 book of Methodist discipline, the five geographical sections were the Northeastern, Southeastern, Central, North Central, and Western Jurisdictions. The Central Jurisdiction included "The Negro Annual Conferences, the Negro Mission Conferences and Missions in the United States of America."[3] This arrangement was the ME Church's concession to the ME Church, South, which had unburdened itself of its black membership in 1870 by approving and facilitating the founding of the Colored Methodist Episcopal (CME) Church, and which wanted nothing to do with the hundreds of thousands of blacks in the northern church. As Harry V. Richardson explained, segregation was a matter of historical fact in the Methodist Episcopal Church, but the jurisdictional system it agreed upon made segregation legal according to the constitution of the church.[4]

In theory, the Methodist Church discouraged discrimination based on race and color. In fact, the same book of discipline (1939) that legalized segregation claimed in its social creed, "We stand for the rights of racial groups, and insist that [our] social, economic, and spiritual principles apply to all races alike."[5] In 1968, when the United Methodist (UM) Church came into existence upon the merger of the Methodist Church and the Evangelical United Brethren, the Central Jurisdiction (and legalized segregation) was abolished, and integration was supported by familiar theoretical statements rejecting racial discrimination. However, it was four years later, perhaps in response to the recent advent of liberation theology in North America and the work of the black caucus (Black Methodists for Church Renewal), before a more satisfactory statement against racial exclusion appeared in the church's 1972 book of discipline. "We rejoice in the gifts which particular ethnic histories and cultures bring to our total life," it said. "We commend and encourage the self-awareness of all ethnic minorities and oppressed peoples."[6] On the other hand, the denominational hymnal—the most public and popular document of the church—flagrantly failed to reflect this claim. Published in 1964, this hymnal, containing a mere six hymns representative of the largest ethnic community in United Methodism, continued to serve the church on into 1989. The committee that compiled the 1964 hymnal stated in its preface that the intent of the volume was to serve the present and future generation of United Methodists by compiling a hymnal "of sufficient diversity to allow for the variety of religious experiences." It is quite obvious that, with a mere six hymns representative of the black religious experience, this statement of theory was far from being put into practice.

In a sociological study of black pastors and churches in United Methodism, carried out during the decade ending in 1974, Grant Shockley, Earl Brewer, and Marie Townsend concluded that racial conditions had not improved substantially for black Meth-

odists since the 1968 merger and the abolition of the Central
Jurisdiction: "United Methodism in America has committed itself to the achievement of racial inclusiveness in its life, work,
fellowship, and mission. Over the ten-year period covered in
this study (1964–1974), there is less convincing evidence than
there should be that the church is not just as far from genuine
inclusiveness as it was before the merger process began."[7] The
authors stated further that there was a duplicity inherent in
theorizing about inclusiveness, on the one hand, and failing to
implement its realization, on the other.[8] By the early 1980s—half
a century since the formation of the Central Jurisdiction, two
decades since its abolition, and one decade since the publication
of the foregoing report—the majority race within the denominations that merged in 1939 to form the Methodist Church and
again in 1968 to form the United Methodist Church has long
been fully in general agreement regarding social issues; on the
other hand, there still remains within United Methodism a Black
Methodist Church. In fact, racial exclusivity, blatantly obvious
in the Methodist hymnal used for a quarter-century (1963–89),
was the single factor that led to the production of several hymnal supplements by the denomination's Board of Discipleship.
These projects began as early as 1973 and were published between 1981 and 1983.

According to the 1972 book of Methodist discipline, the Section on Worship of the Board of Discipleship existed for such
functions as to cultivate the best possible worship experiences in
the church through the use of music and the arts, to develop
resources for worship in the churches, and to advise the church
in the preparation and publication of liturgical materials.[9] Accordingly, that board, in 1973 in Atlanta, sponsored a workshop
on the black church, out of which came a proposal that the UM
Church publish a hymnbook supplement reflective of the musical heritage of black Christians. In the preface to the volume that
was to result from the recommendation, *Songs of Zion*, William
B. McClain (professor of homiletics and worship at Wesley Theological Seminary and chairman of the church's National Ad-
visory Task Force on the Hymnbook Project) recalled the inception of the project:

> Growing out of the Consultation on the Black Church in Atlanta,
> Georgia, in 1973, sponsored by the Board of Discipleship, was a specific

recommendation that the Section on Worship develop a songbook from the Black religious tradition to be made available to United Methodist churches. This urgent recommendation was made by a workshop on worship I conducted after we carefully surveyed the present *Book of Hymns* only to find it contains only one hymn by a Black composer and a mere five Negro spirituals, listed simply as "American Folk Hymns." This songbook, entitled *Songs of Zion*, is the realization of the dream of those persons who gathered in Atlanta eight years ago.

Songs of Zion was the second of three hymnal supplements produced by the Board of Discipleship's Section on Worship. These Supplemental Worship Resources (nos. 11, 12, and 13) were, respectively, *Supplement to the Book of Hymns* (1982), *Songs of Zion* (1981), and *Hymns for the Four Winds: A Collection of Asian American Hymns* (1983).[10] *Songs of Zion* not only was published prior to the *Supplement to the Book of Hymns*, it also appears to have been the source from which the latter took much of its black hymnody. While *Songs of Zion* and *Hymns for the Four Winds* were compiled for the African-American and Asian-American memberships of the UM Church, respectively, the *Supplement to the Book of Hymns* was the effort of the church to remedy the lack of ethnic hymnody in its 1964 hymnal by including hymns representative of all four of its major ethnic groups—African Americans, Asian Americans, Hispanics, and Native Americans.

The preface to the *Supplement to the Book of Hymns* identifies the volume as "a collection of alternative congregational song selected from that which has been used in the United Methodist Church and the wider Christian community since the canon of *The Book of Hymns* was closed in 1963." The small collection contains 128 pieces, whose numbering (854–981) picks up where the numbering in the 1964 hymnal ended. Supplementing the five spirituals and one Tindley hymn in the 1964 hymnal are an additional six black spirituals, two African hymns, and a single hymn each by C.A. Tindley, C. Eric Lincoln, and Margaret J. Douroux. Three of the six spirituals were co-arranged by J. Jefferson Cleveland and Verolga Nix, the editors of *Songs of Zion*. The inclusion of this black hymnody in the supplement was largely attributable to the input of William B. McClain, then a member of the Board of Discipleship's Section on Worship, and the late J. Jefferson Cleveland, the leader of the African-American consultant group to the supplement project.

The *Supplement to the Book of Hymns* was a positive gesture by the UM Church to remedy the racial exclusivity of its 1964 hymnal. Prior to the 1989 edition of *The Book of Hymns*, a vast improvement over the 1964 volume,[11] *Songs of Zion* was the only hymnbook produced by the Methodist Church that adequately and equitably represented the rich and expansive hymnic history of its largest ethnic constituency. The supplement produced by the ME Church, South, in 1851, *Songs of Zion: A Supplement to the Hymn-book of the Methodist Episcopal Church, South* (revised and enlarged in 1874), clearly was not published with the church's black membership in mind. Rather, according to its preface, it was compiled as a supplement to the connectional hymnbook in part to "contravene, to some extent, the circulation of those collections which seem to have been compiled on the principle that neither poetry nor common sense is an essential element in a spiritual song." Although the hymnbook was produced for the white membership of the ME Church, South, it does contain numerous campmeeting songs which might have made it equally attractive to black Methodists.

The *Songs of Zion* of 1981 doubtless was intended primarily, though not exclusively, for black worshipers. The compilation of 249 pieces, edited by two black United Methodist musicians, J. Jefferson Cleveland and Verolga Nix, includes black and white hymnody typically sung in the black church. In the preface to the collection, McClain insists that *Songs of Zion* was intended for the Christian church at large, rather than merely for the United Methodist Church or its black membership. "This songbook offers the whole church a volume of songs that can enrich the worship of the whole church," he says. "It is music that will broaden the musical genres in worship in any Christian church." In this respect, it was probably significant that neither the title nor the cover identified the volume as produced by or for the UM Church. Indeed, other than the fact that the cover was printed in the colors symbolizing African-American liberation—red, black, and green—there was no immediate indication that *Songs of Zion* was produced particularly for the black church. Just as the *Songs of Zion* of 1851/1874 probably enjoyed some circulation among early black Methodists, so has the *Songs of Zion* of 1981 enjoyed some circulation and continued use among white

Methodists, who have found in it favorite old hymns excluded from their 1964 and 1989 hymnals.[12]

Unlike the *Songs of Zion* of 1851/1874, the *Songs of Zion* of 1981 is ordered according to musical genre rather than theological category. Its five sections—"Hymns," "Negro Spirituals," "Black Gospel," "Songs for Special Occasions," and "Service Music"—actually render it more appropriate to be called a *hymnbook* or *songbook* than a *hymnal*. Further distinguishing it from a standard hymnal are the historical essays prefacing its first three sections: "A Historical Account of the Hymn in the Black Worship Experience," "A Historical Account of the Negro Spiritual," and "A Historical Account of the Black Gospel Song." The volume also is distinct in that several of its songs were in print for the first time, having been transcribed into musical notation by Cleveland as he remembered them sung during his upbringing in the church. Some hymns had been long out of print, for example, Tindley's "I'll Overcome Someday," which appeared in no other denominational hymnbook prior to this one.

As a supplement, *Songs of Zion* was basically an assemblage of hymnody excluded from *The Book of Hymns* of 1964. The few pieces that were duplicated in it had been arranged, principally by Cleveland and Nix, in the style in which black worshipers traditionally have sung them. An example was their arrangement of Tindley's "Stand By Me" (the only hymn by a black writer in the 1964 *Book of Hymns*). Another was "In Christ There Is No East or West," which, in *Songs of Zion*, was arranged by the renowned black composer H.T. Burleigh. *Songs of Zion*, then, was neither a standard hymnal (or hymnal supplement) nor an average hymnbook or songbook. It was a distinctive hymnic and historical document that re-presented to the black church many of its hymns long neglected or forgotten.

The first section of the songbook—"Hymns"—contains seventy-one pieces by such contemporary black hymnists as Margaret Douroux, Richard Allen Henderson, James Hendrix, J. Edward Hoy, Morris C. Queen, and William Farley Smith. Also among the contemporary pieces is Verolga Nix's setting of a hymn by Valerie Clayton (a soloist for Tindley Temple UM Church in Philadelphia). Among the more historic pieces included are a hymn setting by the late E.C. Deas and the Black

National Anthem (J. Rosamond Johnson's setting of his brother James Weldon Johnson's "Lift Every Voice and Sing"). As might have been expected in a volume produced by black United Methodists, the largest number of hymns by a single composer is the twelve by Rev. Charles Albert Tindley, the great hymn writer of the Methodist Church. In his introductory essay to this section, Cleveland writes: "The Rev. Dr. Charles Albert Tindley was an outstanding and world-renowned minister, and Tindley Temple United Methodist Church stands today as a tangible memorial to his memory. He ministered not only through the spoken word; he ministered through the song and was an astute and prolific composer, and his numerous hymns remain as self-memorials to his ministry through music."

Although Cleveland, in accordance with the characteristic assertion of most Methodists, considered Tindley to be the most prolific black hymnwriter in the history of the black church, actually the most prolific unquestionably is Bishop Charles Price Jones, the founder of the Church of Christ (Holiness), USA. While Tindley composed approximately forty gospel hymns and has been credited as the first African American to publish (in 1901) an original song collection, a study of the hymns and anthems of Jones, who composed over one thousand pieces, reveals that he was undoubtedly the more prolific composer, as well as the first to publish an original collection of hymns, *Jesus Only*, which saw print in 1899. The year Tindley released his first collection, Jones published his second volume, *Jesus Only Nos. 1 and 2* (1901). Oddly enough, while *Songs of Zion* included twelve pieces by Tindley, it contained none by Jones, whose hymns are particularly well known and loved by black Holiness and Pentecostal worshipers. What this omission suggests is that *Songs of Zion* was more denominational and less ecumenical than it initially appeared to be, and that it peculiarly reflected the composite personality of black Methodists in general and black United Methodists in particular.

Doubtless, Tindley was a pivotal figure in the hymnic history of the black church. Cleveland was correct in stating, in his prefatory essay on black hymnody, that Tindley "bequeathed to all Methodism and to Christianity a legacy that will live on through his hymns." Tindley's hymns, which condemn the world of unjust inequalities and portray the beauties of the Kingdom of

Heaven, have long been comforting to black worshipers of every denominational persuasion. In his hymn "Some Day," for example, Tindley characterizes the human domain as a "world of sin" and a "world of tears," a "wilderness" from which, he wrote, "I shall be free some day." In one of his most celebrated songs, "We'll Understand It Better By and By," he identifies impoverishment as one of the principal dilemmas of his day:

> We are often destitute of things that life demands,
> Want of food and want of shelter, thirsty hills and barren lands,
> We are trusting in the Lord, and according to his word,
> We will understand it better by and by.

The world Tindley depicts in song is also a place in which decent persons are rare commodities and so-called friends are never available when help is needed. His response to these "trials dark on ev'ry hand" and to being "tossed and driv'n on the restless sea of time" is to turn away from the world toward his heavenly "home":

> By and by when the morning comes,
> When the saints of God are gathered home,
> We'll tell the story how we've overcome:
> For we'll understand it better by and by.

Finally, in his hymn "What Are They Doing in Heaven," Tindley says that those who are already enjoying heaven are the oppressed who "lived and suffered in the world" and the "poor and often despised" who "looked to heaven through tear-blinded eyes." Conversely, in "Stand By Me," he exhorts those who still live in the world to persevere amid the storms of life:

> When the storms of life are raging, Stand by me (2×)
> When the world is tossing me, like a ship upon the sea,
> Thou who rulest wind and water, Stand by me.

A large segment of the hymns in this section are traditional evangelical pieces that black worshipers, from the mid-nineteenth to the early twentieth centuries, adapted and have sung ever since. While some black hymns, such as Thomas A. Dorsey's "There'll Be Peace in the Valley Someday," have been more popular among white worshipers than black, some white gospel hymns, such as Charles D. Tillman's setting of M.E. Abbey's "Life's Railway to Heaven," have been more popular among black worshipers. In his introduction to this section, Cleveland explains the means by which black worshipers adapted white hymnody:

> When blacks began to establish their own churches, they did not discard the sophisticated hymns learned from their experiences in White Christian worship; rather, many of these hymns were adopted and converted into original Black songs. These "made-over" White hymns were the results of diverse influences including: (1) African religious music, (2) the African call-and-response song, (3) European or American religious or secular songs, and (4) various African and Afro-American dialects. And how were they made over? The melodies were often improvised to fit the needs of the Black worship service. On the other hand, many of these melodies were kept intact, but the rhythms and harmonies of these hymns and songs were changed to reflect the Black worship experience; consequently, many hymns from Watts, Wesley, Sankey, and other hymnals were molded into a strictly Black idiom.

Some of the old favorite evangelical pieces in *Songs of Zion* are "Jesus, Keep Me Near the Cross" by Fanny J. Crosby, "It Is Well with My Soul" by Horatio G. Spafford, "His Eye Is on the Sparrow" by Civilla D. Martin, "No, Not One" by Johnson Oatman, "In the Garden" by C. Austin Miles, "Throw Out the Lifeline" by Edward S. Ufford, "Savior, Lead Me, Lest I Stray" by Frank M. Davis, "I Surrender All" by Judson W. Van de Venter, and "Love Lifted Me" by James Rowe. Also included are a couple of hymns arranged melodically and rhythmically to be lined-out and sung in the customary slow and embellished "Dr. Watts" fashion. One such piece is Cleveland's arrangement of Wesley's "Father, I Stretch My Hand to Thee."

Of special historical interest in this section is "Prayer for Africa," a Zulu hymn written and set by Enoch Sontonga. The footnote to the piece explains its origin and significance:

> Nkos Sikele'i Afrika was composed in 1897 and first publicly sung in 1899. The composition has a somewhat melancholy strain. The black folk around Johannesburg were, at the time, far from happy. The piece was commonly sung in native day schools and further popularized by the Ohlange Zulu Choir that visited the Rand giving concerts.
>
> When the African National Congress flourished, its leaders adopted this piece as a closing anthem for their meetings, and this soon became a custom in the other provinces in connection with all types of Bantu organizations. Of late the black races of the Union and the Protectorates have somehow by tacit assent adopted it as their recognized national anthem, sung before royalty and on big public occasions.

The single verse to the hymn appears in the original Zulu language, with Swahili and English translations:

> Bless, O Lord, our country, Africa,
> So that she may waken from her sleep.
> Fill her horn with plenty, guide her feet.
> Hear us, faithful sons.
> Spirit, descend, Spirit descend,
> Spirit descend, Spirit divine.

The second section in *Songs of Zion*—"Negro Spirituals"—naturally is the lengthiest, for spirituals probably still constitute the largest body of black sacred music in the history of the American black church. In the historical introduction to this section, Cleveland and McClain figured that there are approximately six thousand extant spirituals which have been handed down to the present generation. Among the ninety-eight spirituals comprising this section are pieces that reminded black Christians of the wide range of sentiments felt by the enslaved: songs of joy such as "Ev'ry Time I Feel the Spirit," songs of thanksgiving such as "Free at Last," and songs of praise such as "Ride On, King Jesus." As well, spirituals expressed with unyielding faith the belief that God would repeat in behalf of the Africans enslaved in America the liberating act performed for the Hebrews subjugated in Egypt: "Didn't My Lord Deliver Daniel," "Freedom Train a-Comin'," "Go Down, Moses," "Joshua Fit de Battle of Jericho," and many others. On the other hand, there were the "sorrow songs"—the cries of the homeless, troubled, and sunken-down—which seemed to be individual rather than communal expressions: "I Been in de Storm So Long," "Nobody Knows the Trouble I See," and "Sometimes I Feel Like a Motherless Chile." Most of the "sorrow songs" actually were not as mournful as they initially appeared, for, while they commenced on a low note of dejection, they typically concluded on a high pitch of praise. For instance:

> Nobody knows the trouble I see,
> Nobody knows my sorrow;
> Nobody knows the trouble I see,
> Glory, hallelujah!

Two of the very few exceptions to this characteristic of the "sorrow songs" are "Were You There" and "He Nevuh Said a Mumbalin' Word," both of which show no glimmer of hope, in that Christ is left crucified rather than resurrected.

There also are in this work spirituals complementary of every phase of the church year; spirituals arranged to be sung by choir, congregation, and solo voice; spirituals of a range of formulaic types, from the call-and-response format to those with either syncopated melodies cast in short phrases or slow lyrical melodies cast in long phrases. All of the pieces attempt to recapture the original dialect, and the prefatory "Keys to Musical Interpretation, Performance, and Meaningful Worship," written by Verolga Nix, advises worshipers neither to change the dialect into correct English nor to exaggerate its diction.

While these instructional "keys" complement the historical essays in the volume, detracting from the latter's historical reach is the absence of spirituals arranged by the renowned black composers who devoted their careers to the documentation and performance of this music: R. Nathaniel Dett, H.T. Burleigh, Hall Johnson, William Dawson, Edward Boatner, Samuel Coleridge-Taylor, Lena McLin, Undine Smith Moore, and many others (all of whom are mentioned in the historical essay prefacing this "Spirituals" section of *Songs of Zion*). Instead, nearly all of the spirituals included were arranged by Cleveland and Nix. Of the fifty-four pieces composed or arranged by Cleveland, thirty-five are spirituals (nineteen arranged in collaboration with Nix), and of the forty-eight pieces composed or arranged by Nix, thirty-three are spirituals (nineteen arranged in collaboration with Cleveland). Aside from these, there is one spiritual each arranged by Delores Lane, Fredrika R. Young, and the acclaimed John W. Work, Jr., with the remaining spirituals simply denoted "traditional."

The section on spirituals is listed in the volume's classification index as "Negro Spirituals and Afro-American Liberation Songs." This section includes the anthem of the Civil Rights movement, "We Shall Overcome," and several spirituals adopted and popularized during the movement (for example, "Amen" and "Free at Last"). As Cleveland and McClain explain in their preface, "Out of the reservoir of Negro spirituals were created the freedom songs of the nonviolent movement in the South during the peak of the demonstrations for social justice and human dignity." Although the anthem of the movement was not an adopted or adapted spiritual, it was, like numerous Civil Rights songs, a synthesis and adaptation of extant hymnody. Combining the tune to the old Baptist hymn "I'll Be Alright" and the text of the Tindley gospel hymn "I'll Overcome Someday," the piece is emblematic of how the oral tradition adapts hymns to meet new social needs. Observe a side-by-side comparison of the two choruses:

I'll overcome some day.	We shall overcome,
I'll overcome some day,	We shall overcome,
I'll overcome some day;	We shall overcome someday.
If in my heart I do not yield	If in our hearts we do believe,
I'll overcome some day.	We shall overcome someday.

The third section of *Songs of Zion*—"Black Gospel"—contains thirty-one pieces from the traditional and contemporary eras of gospel music. The inclusion of this section functioned to document and give credence to this widespread yet often controversial form of religious music. While black gospel music has, from its inception, met with some opposition from a substantial faction of sophisticated black worshipers and theologically trained clergy, McClain's preface to *Songs of Zion* gives a positive theological explanation of the significance of this body of black song:

> The gospel song expresses theology. Not the theology of the academy or the university, not formalistic theology or the theology of the seminary, but a *theology of experience*—the theology of a God who sends the sunshine and the rain, the theology of a God who is very much alive and active and who has not forsaken those who are poor and oppressed and unemployed. It is a *theology of imagination*—it grew out of fire shut up in the bones, of words painted on the canvas of the mind. Fear is turned to hope in the sanctuaries and storefronts, and bursts forth in songs of celebration. It is a *theology of grace* that allows the faithful to see the sunshine of His face—even through their tears. Even the words of an ex–slave trader became a song of liberation and an expression of God's amazing grace. It is a *theology of survival* that allows a people to celebrate the ability to continue the journey in spite of the insidious tentacles of racism and oppression and to sing, "It's another day's journey, and I'm glad about it!"

Whether because it embodies theologies of experience, imagination, grace, and survival, or because it features enlivening rhythm and memorable rhetorical texts which today's youths enjoy, Cleveland (in his historical introduction to this section) estimates that gospel music is present in approximately 95 percent of all black churches in the country.

In this section of the volume, the traditional period or golden age of gospel (1930–69) is well represented by the songs of such composers and arrangers as Doris Akers, J. Herbert Brewster, Lucie E. Campbell, James Cleveland, Thomas A. Dorsey, Theodore Frye, Roberta Martin, Kenneth Morris, Clara Ward, and many others. Together these musicians transformed the congregational *gospel hymn* of the transitional period (1900–1930)— the C.A. Tindley and C.P. Jones era—into the solo, quartet, and choral *gospel song* of the traditional period. The contemporary period, or modern gospel era, has been, from its inception in 1969, dominated by Pentecostal artists of the Church of God in Christ. Among them, Walter Hawkins and Andrae Crouch both have songs included in this collection.

The remaining two sections in *Songs of Zion* are "Songs for Special Occasions" and "Service Music" (neither of which is arranged according to genre like the previous sections). "Songs for Special Occasions," containing the more intricate arrangements of familiar spirituals and hymns, was intended for church musicians and choirs who read music. Included among the thirteen pieces of this group are anthems, ensemble music (quartets, trios, and duets), and arrangements for solo voice. Two eminent black composers represented in this section are R. Nathaniel Dett, with his anthemic arrangement of the spiritual "We Are Climbing Jacob's Ladder," and Lena McLin, with her setting of Thomas Ken's doxology, "Praise God from Whom All Blessings Flow."

The thirty-four pieces comprising the section on "Service Music" include amens, benedictions, chants, communion music, introits, offertories, and responses. Among these hymns is a complete musical setting of the communion service by William Farley Smith, entitled "Communion Music for the Protestant Church." Its eight parts are "Introit," "Gloria in Excelsis," "Hymn—Hungry and Thirsty, Lord, We Come," "Doxology," "Sanctus," "Agnus Dei," "The Lord's Prayer," and "Benediction." This section also contains pieces by Roland M. Carter, the celebrated choir director, formerly of Hampton University, and Odell Hobbs, the distinguished choir director of Virginia Union University.

Songs of Zion, in sum, was a hymnbook and historical document of real distinction. Its function, however, went far beyond its use, for it also served as a strong retort to the leaders of the African Methodist denominations, who long had chided those blacks who remained members of the white Methodist churches. Probably unintentionally, *Songs of Zion*, as the most public and popular document produced by black United Methodists, did more than anything else to counter that criticism. More African-American than any black Methodist (or Protestant) hymnbook published in the history of the black church, it is the paradigm of black religious self-awareness, after which future black denominational hymnals must be measured and modeled. However, more important than the fact that other black denominations must now take account of the racial content of their hymnals is that *Songs of Zion* finally showed the black church that there is more in common between black United Methodists and their black Protestant counterparts than between black United Methodists and the majority race of their own denomination. McClain (a black United Methodist) gave a fitting example of this contention in his book, *Black People in the Methodist Church:*

> Even in those places where there was the emulation of the white
> churches and their worship style, "Amazing Grace" never sounded
> the same, and there was a bit of a "bounce" in the choir's procession.
> The black religious experience had meticulously placed some chords in
> the soul that were responsive to its familiar beat. No yearning thought of
> assimilation could totally drown out the sound of the pulsing jungle;
> faint, perhaps, but still there.[13]

In comparison to both the 1939 Methodist hymnal, containing no racial representation in the hymnody, and the 1964 UM hymnal, containing a mere six pieces from the extensive corpus of black hymnody, the present 1989 hymnal contains a fairly suitable representation of the hymnody of all four of the church's major ethnic groups. *Songs of Zion* not only had a direct impact on the inclusiveness of the 1989 hymnal, it also was a stalwart statement of self-determination by a people who had been repressed by nearly three decades of legal segregation within the Methodist Church. When, at the General Conference of 1939, the white delegates voted to form a separate jurisdiction for the entirety of their black membership, they then arose and sang "We Are Marching to Zion," while the black delegates remained seated, some weeping.[14] But when black Methodists later turned to the third hymn in *Songs of Zion* and sang "We Are

Marching to Zion," it was indeed emblematic that they had made large strides, not only in the life of Methodism but also in reconciling the races in North America. "It is true that at times the black members of the U.M.C. have had to struggle for equal participation in their predominantly white Church," said Harry V. Richardson. "But the struggle in their Church was simply part of the struggle that Blacks were waging in every phase of American life."[15]

Hence, just as the black Methodist denominations remain an inescapable critical commentary on the historic failure of the Methodist Episcopal churches to deal prophetically with the "race problem," so was the publication of *Songs of Zion* a discriminating critique of the initial inefficacy of the United Methodist Church in remedying the causes that had led to the institutionalization of the Black Methodist Church within United Methodism. Had the southern and northern branches of the Methodist Episcopal Church not been exclusionary, then the black Methodist denominations probably never would have come into existence. Had the 1964 Methodist hymnal not been exclusionary, then *Songs of Zion* perhaps never would have come into existence. Notwithstanding, these racial entities and artifacts do exist for these reasons, which is why this brief survey of the composition and content of *Songs of Zion* is so historically revealing.

CHAPTER 5

The National Baptists

The Home Mission Board was constitutionally established in September, 1895. But in 1896 it brought into existence one of the most notable heritages the Negro Baptist ever did, or ever will have, in that our Publishing House was then established. This enterprise was started with nothing save faith in God and the justice of the cause, backed by Negro brain and ambition. And to-day ten thousand dollars' worth of printing material and machinery, an average monthly distribution of nearly two thousand dollars' worth of periodicals, sixty-eight ardent workers and writers of our own race, causing a pay-roll amounting to one hundred dollars per day, speak out in one tremendous voice and tell whether or not we have made progress. The sun has forever gone down on any race of people who will not encourage and employ their literary talent. How could the Negro Baptists ever hope to be or do anything while they were committing literary suicide?

—Elias C. Morris,
first president of the National Baptist Convention[1]

This chapter examines the hymnody of three black Baptist denominations that are so closely related with respect to their origin, doctrine, and theology that their hymnic history is best addressed as a single entity. The three denominations are the National Baptist Convention, USA (founded in 1895), the National Baptist Convention of America (formed schismatically from the original body in 1915), and the Progressive National Baptist Convention (formed under protest against the National Baptist Convention, USA in 1961). The interrelatedness of these three Baptist conventions is exemplified by the fact that there is greater commonality among the hymnodies of these three Baptist conventions than there is among those of their three Methodist counterparts—the African Methodist Episcopal (AME), African Methodist Episcopal Zion (AMEZ), and Christian Methodist Episcopal (CME) churches.

The first black Baptist national connection was formed in September of 1895, upon the merger of the Baptist Foreign Mission Convention of the United States, the American National Baptist Convention, and the National Baptist Education Convention. The inaugural hymnal of the fledgling National Baptist Convention, USA, was *The National Baptist Hymnal*, published in 1903 by the National Baptist Publishing board in Nashville. Rev. R.H. Boyd, the founding secretary of the Publishing Board, served as the hymnal's editor, and William Rosborough as its musical editor.

In the "Publisher's Note" prefatory to the hymnal, Boyd documented the series of events that had preceded its publication:

> At a meeting of the National Baptist Convention in September, 1900, a paper was read by Dr. Harvey Johnson, of Baltimore, Md., on "Distinctive Literature for the Colored Baptists of the Country; for Sunday Schools, Societies and Churches." In this paper, he referred to the great need of a hymnal peculiarly adapted for use in Negro Baptist churches. After a careful and full discussion of the subject, a resolution was unanimously adopted, ordering the National Baptist Publishing Board to publish a hymn and tune book, containing familiar hymns and tunes such as would be useful in our churches, both in cities and rural districts.

Boyd proceeded to explain that the Publishing Board initially postponed publication of the book until 1901, due to its exorbitant production cost. That year, the board's attempt to purchase extant printing plates of hymns from senior publishers in order to bypass the expense of manufacturing their own was unsuccessful. "These publishers refused to show the Board any courtesies," wrote Boyd. Finally, in March of that year, at a joint meeting of the Home Mission and Publication boards, it was decided that the hymnal would be published regardless of cost:

> It was there decided to fully undertake the work regardless of cost, and the editor in chief and musical editor at once addressed letters to one hundred leading pastors, asking them to make choice of three or more of the popular old songs used in their congregations and forward them to the Secretary of the Publishing Board. A great number of them re-

sponded, but a few failed to give any reply. A second letter was addressed to the same brethren, asking those who had not sent in their songs to do so, and at the same time mark their songs, first, second and third choice.

It will be seen that the editors and committee on publication in selecting the songs contained in this volume were not guided alone by their own choice, but were greatly helped by these pastors. The editor in chief and musical editor, with the advice of the committee on publication, have gone over the songs carefully, both words and music, making such revisions as were necessary to build up the faith and doctrines of the Baptist churches composing the National Baptist Convention. This work has been in progress for more than two years.

Published in 1903, *The National Baptist Hymnal* turned out to be closely modeled after *The Baptist Hymnal*,[2] which was published in 1883 by the American Baptist Publication Society located in Philadelphia. Its table of contents employed subject headings very similar to those of its model,[3] and identical hymnists predominated. As was typical of its model and other Protestant hymnals of the turn of the century, *The National Baptist Hymnal* contained a great quantity of hymns by Watts (146), Wesley (37), and other British composers, such as Horatius Bonar, William Cowper, Philip Doddridge, James Montgomery, John Newton, Anne Steele, and Samuel Stennett. It is likely that the fledgling hymnal contained chants (17) merely because its model contained them (61), and that its author index was likewise a modernism copied from its model (an author index is present in no subsequent black Baptist hymnal).

The Baptist Hymnal (1883) was, almost without question, the collection after which *The National Baptist Hymnal* (1903) was to some degree modeled. What editors R.H. Boyd and William Rosborough apparently did was to delete a select number of the hymns from their model hymnal in order to replace them with others that would give their resultant collection a black Baptist bent. Among the added selections were nearly all of the sixty-five pieces comprising the "Supplement" section that had been at the end of the hymnal. While no spirituals were added, among the supplemental works were seventeen hymns either written or set by Rosborough. Among those seventeen was his setting of "Hear the Savior Calls Thee Now" by former Baptist (turned Holiness) preacher Charles Price Jones.

It is not unusual that the inaugural hymnal produced by black Baptists was closely modeled after one compiled and published by their white denominational counterparts, for, as we have seen, the same pattern typified the nascent hymnals of the black Methodist denominations. What was distinctive about *The National Baptist Hymnal*, however, was that it was published in its entirety within the National Baptists' own publishing facility. In fact, the first books both printed and bound on their premises had appeared four years earlier, in 1899.[4] Thus, in his report to the convention of 1900, Boyd was able to make much of the fact that the National Baptist Publishing Board was "the first Negro institution known to us on American soil to enter upon the task of real book making." Continuing, Boyd warned, "But if our pastors, missionaries, and Sunday school workers, could be able to see the importance of having their people use in their churches and Sunday schools our own song books, and read only literature manufactured and handled by ourselves . . . it would not be long until our Publishing House would be a great factor in the denominational and religious work."[5]

The book department of the National Baptist Publishing Board was partitioned into three divisions concerned with (1) the sale of books purchased from other publishers in order to supply the needs of the board's patrons, (2) the manufacturing and sale of volumes published by the board for the exclusive use of its convention members, and (3) the manufacturing and sale of books written by black Baptist authors. Categorized under the second department was *The National Baptist Hymnal* (1903) and the numerous songbooks published by the board,[6] while categorized under the first division was the volume after which the hymnal was modeled, *The Baptist Hymnal* (1883). Because the latter was published by the preeminent American Baptist Publication Society, which black Baptists had patronized prior to the founding of their own company, it is likely that *The Baptist Hymnal* was in use among them prior to the publication of their own hymnal in 1903.

Indeed, we gather from Boyd that there were some leaders among the nascent National Baptists who maintained that the convention ought to continue employing *The Baptist Hymnal* and patronizing the American Baptist Publication Society, rather than to enter into competition with it. As R.H. Boyd explained:

"The general idea was that . . . the American Baptist Publication Society of the North was engaged in this work, and it had done so much for the Christianizing and evangelizing of the Negro Baptists of the South, that in case the Negroes went into this commercial and manufacturing business they would become competitors and thereby appear in the light of ingrates to these great Northern societies."[7] Boyd knew all too well, however, that the officials of the American Baptist Publication Society would neither publish material by their black patrons nor allow them to contribute written lessons to the very Sunday school literature blacks purchased for their churches. Moreover, *The Baptist Hymnal* did not contain so much as a single piece by a black hymnist. Still, there remained those leaders of Boyd's convention, even after nine years of the Publishing Board's successful operation, who held that publishing was not genuine Christian work. On the other hand, Boyd rejoiced, there stood churchmen of a more prophetic vision: "But there has always been from the time Negro Baptists begun organization, state or national, a great number of those who believed that the Negro Baptists could never succeed in being a distinct and separate denomination without having religious literature that was adopted to the peculiar needs, and that this religious literature should be written, published and printed by the Negro Baptist people for themselves."[8]

Although it was the year 1900 when a hymnal was first petitioned for by the convention, Boyd identified 1897 as the year of the hymnal's true beginnings:

> The National Baptist Publishing Board began the publication of a hymn and tune book in 1897, when publisher's rights were secured on its first song books, "Gospel Voices" and "Choice Songs." In 1898 the publication was extended by the addition of another hymn book called, "National Tidings of Joy." The same rights were secured for the publication of "Celestial Showers," song book No. 1, and two years later, "Harp of Zion," or "B.Y.P.U. Hymnal." Again, "Celestial Showers," song book No. 2, and "Pearls of Paradise" were added to these publications in 1901. All of these books, except "Celestial Showers," were examined by a committee appointed by the National Baptist Publishing Board before they were adopted for the use of our Sunday Schools and Young People's Societies.[9]

In his report to the convention's annual meeting of 1900, Boyd listed the above five song books with the following annotations:

The National Tidings of Joy,
Is a choice selection of hymns, and contains the rudiments of music.
The National Gospel Voices,
Is an excellent book for Sunday school and prayer meeting use. It is full
of good music.
Celestial Showers, by Prof. Wm. Rosborough,
Is another excellent Sunday school music book. We cheerfully commend
this excellent work.
The National Harp of Zion or B.Y.P.U. Hymnal,
Is a new book worthy of the consideration of all music lovers and
B.Y.P.U. workers.
Choice Songs,
Is a collection of hymns, prepared for those who may want a cheap
singing book.[10]

A year later, in his report to the 1901 convention assembly in
Cincinnati, Boyd listed two new books with annotations:

Pearls of Paradise.
A collection of Song Gems, by W.G. Cooper and D.E. Dortch.
Celestial Showers, No. 2.
A choice selection of Sacred Songs, by Prof. Wm. Rosborough.[11]

As a result of these additions to his publication line, R.H.
Boyd became even more confident about the company whose
growth he alone had nurtured: "We have the best and most
thoroughly equipped publishing plant in America owned and
operated by Negroes," he exulted.[12] Following the publication
of *The National Baptist Hymnal* in 1903, Boyd was able to report
the following year to the convention assembled in Austin: "This
has become one of the most important of our book departments.
We are now making about fourteen song books of our own.
These are all printed and bound by us. A number of them are
edited by the best Negro Baptist composers of music, some,
however, are edited by white composers; but all have been carefully selected by a committee appointed by our Publishing
Board."[13] Always the shrewd businessman, Boyd, in an apparent effort to promote the songbooks of his company, made a
doctrinal assertion in his report:

It is most alarming when we take into consideration the great variety of
song books that are being used to-day in our Sunday-schools, and most
of these claim to be undenominational. This works greater damage than
can possibly be imagined by unthinking people—to put undenominational literature in our Sunday schools. . . . The greatest mistake that

> Baptists are making now, is the using of undenominational literature,
> and especially this is true in the use of song books. Doctrine can be more
> easily taught in poetry set to music than it can be by dry prose. When we
> sing skepticism into our children, with beautifully arranged verse and
> poetry set to the sparkling and mellow sound of sacred music, it makes
> indelible impressions on their memories and are there to stay. We,
> therefore, call special attention to this department.[14]

In spite of the numerous songbooks on the Baptist market,
there were repeated calls for a hymnal specifically designed for
liturgical use.[15] Yet, not long after the publication of the hymnal,
which had been arranged to serve equally well as a word edition,[16] there arose a petition for a pocket-size hymnbook (words
only). It did not take Boyd long to respond. In 1904 he informed
the convention, meeting in Austin, of the preparation of a word
edition of its hymnal:

> Our Baptist Hymnal was completed and brought to the Convention
> one year ago, and met with such flattering success in the form of sales,
> that we have had nothing but praise and joy for the undertaking. So well
> has the Board been satisfied with the music edition that we now have
> about completed a Baptist Hymn Book, pocket edition, of words only.
> This book will contain between 800 and 1,000 of the old, endeared,
> familiar songs with meter tunes. We believe that this book will fill a long
> felt want. We are making it into plates at a very great expense, but this
> will enable us to put the book on the market at a very small retail price,
> such as will justify our pastors in recommending it to their congrega-
> tions.[17]

A short time afterward, *The National Baptist Hymn Book* (1905)
was released. In its prefatory "Publisher's Note," Boyd justified
its production: "The pastors, deacons, prayer meeting leaders,
and other Baptist church members continued to call for a Baptist
Hymn Book of the old style pocket edition, as each member
desired to have his or her own pocket hymn book, and select and
sing the old metered songs of his or her choice."

Regarding the selection of hymns in *The National Baptist Hymn
Book*, Boyd said this in his prefatory note: "The Publishing Board
has not attempted to publish or set forth this book as a new
collection of songs, but felt that in attempting to respond to this
call precludes the attempt of offering any new songs whatever,
but to select from among the old ones dear to the people's
heart." What he meant was not only that there were no hymns of
contemporary composition (such as those by William Rosborough), but also that, in terms of content, the hymnbook was

largely identical to the 1903 hymnal. The principal distinctions were that the hymnbook contained only 622 of the 704 pieces in the hymnal, plus an additional 10 pieces in its supplement (for a total of 632), and that the chants were omitted altogether. The 10 hymns comprising the hymnbook's supplement (5 of which were by Wesley and 1 by Watts) replaced the numerous pieces by Rosborough in the hymnal's supplement. The headings and pagination of the table of contents remained the same as in the hymnal, but within the hymnbook, the pieces (which retained their original numbering) were rearranged (the hymn numbers were literally out of sequence).

In the years following the publication of the 1905 hymnbook, more songbooks were released by the Publishing Board. An advertisement at the back of R.H. Boyd's semiautobiographical *Story of the National Baptist Publishing Board* (ca. 1915) listed all of the song- and hymnbooks released by the Publishing Board to date, with details of price and the like. The volumes not yet listed above were the following:

> **National Baptist Hymn Book.** Word Edition. A collection of old meter songs, selected for use in home, prayer-meetings, and other religious services. . . .
> **National G.V. Hymnal.** Contains 447 songs; new and old selections. . . .
> **National Hymns of Victory.** This book contains some of the choicest songs ever published for Sunday-schools, Churches and prayer meetings. . . .
> **Choice Songs No. 2.** One hundred and twenty-five New Songs. . . .
> **National Temperance Songs.** New and old selections for temperance leagues or societies. . . .
> **National Songs of Praise.** A New Song Book by Carter and Rosborough.

Also listed with the above, with no description other than price, were *The National Baptist Hymnal, National Gospel Voices* Nos. 1, 2, or 3, *National Gospel Voices Nos. 1 and 2 Combined, National Anthem Series,* and a book titled *Short Talks on Music or Rudiments of Vocal Music.* The songbooks were described in an advertisement closing the published minutes of 1916:[18]

> **National Gospel Voices, No. 1.**—Prepared especially for Baptist churches, Sunday schools and Young People's meetings, with music. . . .
> **National Gospel Voices No. 2.**—Especially prepared for Baptist meetings. . . .

National Gospel Voices No. 3.—A selection of the songs not heretofore offered. . . .
National Gospel Voices, No. 1 and 2 Combined.—Published in round
or shaped notes. Try this one and you will be satisfied. . . .
National Anthem Series.—A series of anthems for choirs, concerts
and young people's meetings, by Wm. Rosborough and J.H. Carter.

The last on the list, the *National Anthem Series,* constituted a
distinctly different kind of production on the part of the National Baptist Publishing Board. Released in 1906, the collection
contained fourteen anthems by William Rosborough, J.H. Carter, and J.W. Tobias, each of whom, R.H. Boyd said in the "Publisher's Note," held the position of chorister in the church of
their membership. The publication of this series was no mere
venture, continued Boyd, but the consequence of real need
among the convention's churches:

> They found, after publishing more than fifteen song books, that our
> churches, especially our church choirs, were generally attracted by
> anthems, and after further looking over the field, the Publishing Board
> decided to encourage the use of such anthems as are doctrinally sound,
> of high-class music and spiritually inspiring.
>
> It was noticed that there were among the colored Baptists but few
> sacred song writers and comparatively no anthem writers. In order to
> encourage anthem writing they set out first to induce our few sacred
> writers among the Baptists to write anthems and publish the same in
> sheet music form. After publishing and circulating a few sheets from the
> pen of the late Prof. William Rosborough, author of *Celestial Showers* No.
> 1 and 2, it was decided to ask him to prepare a book of anthems but
> before this task could be accomplished, he was called from labor to
> reward. The Board, therefore, decided to gather up the few anthems
> written by him, together with those of Prof. J.H. Carter and Prof. J.W.
> Tobias and compile them into one volume for the benefit of our church
> choirs.

After September 1915, any published material bearing the
appellation of the National Baptist Publishing Board was the
production and property of one (and only one) of what now
became two National Baptist groups. Resolving a ten-year dis-
pute over the ownership of the Publishing Board, R.H. Boyd, on
9 September 1915, mobilized a separate connection, the National Baptist Convention of America (unincorporated). Because, prior to this time, the inaugural National Baptist Convention, USA, was not an incorporated organization and the
Publishing Board was legally incorporated in Tennessee, Boyd

and his followers (designated the "Boyd Convention") were able to prevent the larger convention from securing ownership of the board. Hence the longtime complaint regarding the fact that the Publishing Board's liturgical and catechetical publications all were copyrighted in Boyd's name turned out to be a valid concern;[19] following the schism, the initial convention was left without access to these resources. Having learned a tough lesson, the original group not long afterwards became incorporated—the National Baptist Convention, USA, Inc.

In the years immediately succeeding the schism, the National Baptist Publishing Board (under the "Boyd Convention") published three more songbooks—*The National Jubilee Melodies, New Victory,* and *Golden Gems. New Victory* (1918) was a collection of 165 pieces edited by Emmett S. Dean (21 of the hymns are set by Dean). While Dean's compilation included neither spirituals nor hymns by black writers, the ensuing *Golden Gems,* released sometime during T.B. Boyd, Jr.'s, twenty-year tenure as publisher (1959–79), contained a fair representation of pieces by such black hymnists as Lucie E. Campbell, Thomas A. Dorsey, Charles H. Pace,[20] and James E. Gayle.[21] *The National Jubilee Melodies,*[22] however, was the most significant of the songbooks published by the "Boyd Convention" during the immediate postschism years. We shall examine it further below.

An advertisement closing the printed minutes of the 1916 meeting of the unincorporated National Baptists stated the following regarding *The National Jubilee Melodies:* "This is the only book of songs of Negro origin in the world. Every song of the Ante Bellum days will be found in this book." With respect to the distribution of the volume, the announcement read, "*The National Jubilee Melodies* had an excellent run of its first edition, and became very popular." The collection was dedicated to the memory of black ancestry and published to the end that people would understand the means by which the enslaved had expressed their thoughts to God. In this regard, the "Publisher's Note" is worth reproducing in its entirety, as it may be seen as a manifesto of the Baptist worldview regarding its historical relationship to slavery:

> THE NATIONAL JUBILEE MELODIES is a collection of old plantation songs the words and music of which were composed and sung by the African slaves in the United States of America during the days of slavery.

Those have been kept alive by tradition and are now compiled in book form and are accepted for many reasons:

FIRST: It is and should be the idea of the present generation to keep alive the great religious achievements of our ancestors and hand them down to posterity as a legacy of noble sires to their sons.

SECOND: It is known throughout the length and breadth of this country that every people, from the early Jews, or Hebrews, down to the present day, have expressed their peculiar religious emotions, thoughts and deep meditations in proverbs, poetry and rhythm.

THIRD: It is the belief of the Publishing Board that these melodies express the emotion of the soul of the Negro race as no other collection of music—classically or grammatically constructed could possibly do.

FOURTH: It is the purpose of the Publishing Board in publishing this collection in book form to build a monument to the memory of our Negro ancestry and show the rising generation who may yet become a great and educated people that they sprang from a deep and prayerful religious race, whose religious convictions and faith in their God towered above any other race in a like condition.

FIFTH: In publishing this collection of melodies the Board wishes to give due credit to Mr. K.D. Reddick, of Americus, Ga., and Mr. Phil V.S. Lindsley, of Nashville, Tenn., for their faithful and painstaking work in collecting these songs, rhythms and melodies from the various rice, cane and cotton plantations of the South—just as they were handed down by tradition on the old plantations and kept alive by the offspring of these old slaves.

While nearly all of the 160 pieces in *The National Jubilee Melodies* were collected by K.D. Reddick and arranged by Phil V.S. Lindsley, several of them were arranged by W.H. Sherwood, and an original hymn by William Rosborough was included. The footnotes to the spirituals themselves are of real historical interest. The note to "Sing Aho that I Had the Wings of a Dove," for example, illustrates the way in which spirituals often were composed extemporaneously during the preaching of slave worship and subsequently were maintained and refined through oral transmission:

When the preacher has worked his auditors up to a high degree of excitement, he will often break off and extemporize some song, with his text as its basis, in which the audience joins, and then at the end of it will go on "exhorting" again. This song which is one of the most beautiful of our collection, was composed in this way in Robertson County, Tennessee. It seemed at first crude and unavailable but as it was sung over and over again gradually reached its present musical form.

The note to "Camp-Meeting," arranged by Sherwood, informed readers: "This is one of the Characteristic pieces that used to warm the Camp-grounds when the meetings had been turned over to the slaves, in the days of oppression and indeed is powerfully warming yet to those who love religious heat." The note to Sherwood's notation of the early version of "Nobody Knows the Trouble I See" rendered a poignant narrative regarding the creation of the familiar old sorrow song: "A poor old negro slave who had been a model Christian but who had a most cruel master, sat and sung this refrain one day after he had been given a most merciless whipping."

While R.H. Boyd was trumpeting the recent release of *The National Jubilee Melodies*, the rival National Baptist Convention, USA, Inc., was without a publishing board and so without hymnic and catechetical literature. With little hesitation, however, it set out to establish its own publishing house, for which beginnings onetime secretaries S.P. Harris and William Haynes are due recognition. The substantive development of the Sunday School Publishing Board, however, was the work of its longtime secretary, Arthur Melvin Townsend—Baptist minister, amateur musician, and physician (a 1902 graduate of Meharry Medical College). Townsend became secretary in 1920 and singlehandedly raised the money needed to build the edifice that today remains the Publishing Board headquarters. The grand old building that looms large on a plot of ground, once the location of a slave auction,[23] stands as a symbol of the progress of black Baptist proprietorship in the twentieth century.

The year after Townsend accepted the position of secretary of the Sunday School Publishing Board, a song collection titled *Gospel Pearls* (1921) was released. The Townsend Convention's nascent effort resulted in what musicologist Eileen Southern ranks as one of the most significant songbooks published by the black church:

> The year 1921 brought a milestone in the history of black-church hymnody. In my opinion, *Gospel Pearls*, published that year by the Sunday School Publishing Board of the National Baptist Convention, U.S.A., ranks with Richard Allen's hymnal of 1801 in terms of its historic importance. Like the Allen hymnal, it is an anthology of the most popular black-church music of its time. The Music Committee that compiled the hymnal . . . included some of the nation's outstanding

composers and performers of religious music . . . and the result was truly a "soul-stirring, message-bearing song-book."[24]

Referencing *Songs of Zion* (1982), compiled by the black United Methodists, Southern concludes, "It would be more than fifty years before the black church would produce a hymnal of equal power, musical worth, and emotional appeal to black Christians."[25]

The music committee responsible for compiling *Gospel Pearls* was chaired by Willa A. Townsend (A.M. Townsend's wife)[26] and included the two Work brothers (John, Jr., and Frederick), Lucie E. Campbell,[27] and several others who soon afterwards served on the committee to compile a hymnal: J.D. Bushell, R. Alwyn Austin, Carie Booker Person, Geneva Bender Williams, John H. Smiley, and W.M. Nix. Acclaiming the distinguished qualifications of several of its members, the music committee said in its preface that *Gospel Pearls* is "a boon to Gospel singers" in that it includes songs that have been sung most effectively by Smiley, Nix, and Williams, as well as by other prominent singers.

Left without access to the hymn- and song books published by the National Baptist Publishing Board and copyrighted in R.H. Boyd's name, the Sunday School Publishing Board wisely intended, as the preface stated, this new collection of standard hymns, popular songs, and spirituals to serve a broad variety of uses: "Notwithstanding the large number of song books in circulation, no apology is offered for the advent of 'Gospel Pearls'; for its name tells the story, coming as it does to supply the present needs of the Sunday school, Church, Conventions and other religious gatherings, with 'Pearls' of song suitable for Worship and Devotion, Evangelistic services, Funeral, Patriotic and other special occasions." These "pearls of song" were divided into three categories: worship, revival, and spirituals. Aside from the few "standard" hymns by such British songsters as Watts and Wesley, the mass of the volume was comprised of "popular" songs by such American gospel hymnists as Fanny J. Crosby, Johnson Oatman, Philip P. Bliss, and C. Austin Miles, and by such black gospel hymnists as C.A. Tindley, C.P. Jones, E.C. Deas, Thomas A. Dorsey, and Lucie E. Campbell. Additionally, the collection contained nineteen spirituals arranged by such composers as John Work, Jr., Frederick Work, J.D. Bushell, and Willa Townsend.

While Eileen Southern ranks *Gospel Pearls* high among the musical pearls of black hymnic history, six years after its publication, secretary Townsend's 1927 annual report rather unexcitedly commented: "'Gospel Pearls' is yet holding its own, as the best book for all purposes on the market today . . . it commends itself wherever used."[28] Conversely, the proud publisher was filled with enthusiasm for a newer publication, *Spirituals Triumphant, Old and New* (1927). In the same report Townsend heralded:

> "Spirituals Triumphant" is our new book of spirituals, for choir use. The second edition, revised and enlarged, is just off the press. It is a new collection of slave melodies, or "Jubilee songs" as they are familiarly called. This book contains a hundred pages of the "favorites," that had their origin in the life of an oppressed, yet hopeful people. It was arranged by Prof. Edward Boatner, Chorister of the National Baptist Convention, U.S.A., assisted by Willa A. Townsend, Music Editor of the Sunday School Publishing Board, and as sung by the great National Baptist Convention Chorus. In the arrangement, the harmony and characteristic way in which these songs were originally sung are maintained. No choir can do its most effective singing of these favorite spirituals without this book.
>
> The Baptist Sunday School Board (Southern Baptist Convention) has requested us to furnish them with descriptive matter of our "Spirituals Triumphant," in order that they may list it in their catalogue. This is evidence of the merit, appreciation, demand and general worth of our collection of "Spirituals" or "Jubilee Songs."[29]

As a counterpart to *The National Jubilee Melodies* of the "Boyd Convention," *Spirituals Triumphant* doubtless stands in the musicological tradition of James Weldon Johnson's *The Book of American Negro Spirituals* (1925) and *The Second Book of Negro Spirituals* (1926) and R. Nathaniel Dett's *Religious Folk-Songs of the Negro* (1927). *Spirituals Triumphant* contained a total of eighty-four pieces—seventy-six spirituals and eight hymns. Of the spirituals, almost half (thirty-six) were arranged by Edward Boatner (an additional piece by him was a hymn). Arranged by Willa Townsend were eighteen spirituals and one hymn, by A.M. Townsend nine spirituals and one hymn, and by E.C. Deas five spirituals and two hymns. Among the remaining works were included one or two pieces each by J.D. Bushell, Lucie Campbell, the Work brothers, and W.H. Sherwood.

A third songbook was *Inspirational Melodies,* published by the convention's National Baptist Training Union Board sometime between the release of *Gospel Pearls* (1921) and *Spirituals Tri-*

umphant (1927). Rev. E.W.D. Isaac, Sr., the first and longtime secretary of the Baptist Young People's Union (BYPU) Board, was most probably the catalyst behind its publication. The collection appeared in several editions, but *Inspirational Melodies* (no. 2), later became the most readily accessible edition.[30] Compiled by Rev. Isaac, Sr., his son Rev. E.W.D. Isaac, Jr., and Lucie Campbell, the selections included five pieces by the distinguished woman among them, among which was her famous "Something Within." This piece by Campbell was possibly the first gospel hymn written by a black woman.[31]

While *Gospel Pearls* (1921) was the first hymnic collection released by the Sunday School Publishing Board, the complex task of preparing a hymnal for the convention long had been under way. In their book on the history of the National Baptists, Rev. Owen Pelt (at the time historiographer of the "Townsend Convention") and Ralph Smith claimed that the publication of a hymnal for the incorporated convention was Townsend's first great challenge.[32] The undertaking required him to draw from three distinct sources of hymnody, each involving their own hymnological problems. First, the "standard" hymnody required the compiler to be familiar with a vast corpus of music. Second, the black spirituals necessitated musical settings capable of capturing the authenticity of the slave songs while also being appropriate in a denominational hymnal. Third, the gospel music required a determination of whether even to include it alongside the standard hymnody.[33] Given the fact that the final product included a mere two spirituals and nine black gospel songs, it is curious that Pelt and Smith proceeded to describe as follows Townsend's resolve regarding the latter two music genres:

> Dr. Townsend believed that spirituals and gospel music *both* deserved an honored place in any hymnal. The decisive issue for him was the simple fact that the best songs in both categories were wonderful and deeply reverent religious music.
>
> With the spirituals, he and his wife, Mrs. Willa A. Townsend, listened to and studied inferior versions of the songs, then prepared new arrangements to rescue the full beauty and meaning of the originals. He felt that the songs were sufficiently beautiful to justify this special and invaluable effort.[34]

In 1924, nine years following the schism that left the National Baptist Convention, USA, Inc., without a publishing facility, the

Sunday School Publishing Board released its long-awaited hymnal. Although Townsend, in his report to the convention in 1924, could only claim for the year ending the release of two other books—a text on systematic theology and a collection of sermons—the quality of *The Baptist Standard Hymnal* no doubt compensated for the dearth in the quantity of publications. To the 1924 assembly, Townsend breathed this testament:

> And third, comes our own "Baptist Standard Hymnal." This book is the realization of a dream of nine years ago to arrange or see arranged a hymnal that would be spiritual and inspiring and especially adapted to church worship. I beg to confess that in the coming forth of this book, the travail of my soul has become satisfied, and like Simeon of old, I am almost ready to say: "Now Lord, lettest thou thy servant depart in peace." I regard this hymnal as the crowning effort of my life—and it is a glowing and lasting tribute to the musical ability and efficiency of the Music Committee that compiled it, and to Mrs. Willa A. Townsend who edited it, she standing by me and working laboriously on it for nearly two years—it is the zenith of the work of the Sunday School Publishing Board that made it a possibility and it will be an everlasting credit to my departing Executive Committee. And now all of us—the Publishing Board, the Executive Committee, Mrs. Townsend, and myself, with satisfied hearts pass on to the denomination this "Standard Baptist Hymnal," as our everlasting contribution and permanent legacy, which will be a source of soul comfort and inspiration, yea, the salvation to generations yet unborn.[35]

Three years later, in his annual report to the 1927 convention, Townsend delivered an enthusiastic progress report on the *magnum opus* of his publishing career: "Our 'Baptist Standard Hymnal' is having a rapidly increasing success. It seems to have met a large felt need in our churches. It is said by critics to be the best Hymnal ever printed."[36]

The Baptist Standard Hymnal was edited by Willa Townsend, professor of church worship music and pageantry for the Sunday School Publishing Board. Her assisting music committee included Dr. J.D. Bushell (chair), Rev. F. Rivers Barnwell, Katie C. Dickson, Emma J. Haynes, Jeannette Taylor Nickens, Carie Booker Person, Rev. J.H. Skipwith, Rev. T.W.J. Tobias, Geneva Bender Williams, and Professors Wellington A. Adams, R. Alwyn Austin, H.B. Britt, Theodore P. Bryant, W.M. Nix, and John H. Smiley. Selected were 745 hymns divided into sixty subject categories and followed by forty-seven biblical responsive readings and indexes of titles, first lines, subjects, tunes, and meters.

Because *The Baptist Standard Hymnal* was the first hymnal published by the incorporated "Townsend Convention" and only the second hymnal produced in all of black Baptist history, it is not surprising that it was a very traditional Protestant hymnal. As expected of a volume fashioned under the influence of these factors, the "standard" hymnal contained a sizable number of hymns by Watts (fifty-five) and Wesley (twenty-six), as well as a generous selection of works by classic British hymnists such as Joseph Addison, John Bowring, William Doane, Philip Doddridge, John Fawcett, Joseph Hart, Reginald Heber, James Montgomery, and Anne Steele, to name only a few. The hymnal committee may have styled the volume after *The National Baptist Hymnal* (1903) and, by association, its model, *The Baptist Hymnal* (1883). Indeed, *The Baptist Standard Hymnal* more resembled the latter, published by white Baptists forty-three years earlier (1883), than its counterpart of the "Boyd Convention," *The New National Baptist Hymnal* (1977), published by black Baptists fifty-one years later.

On the other hand, as a product of the first decades of the twentieth century, *The Baptist Standard Hymnal* was substantially less traditionally Protestant and culturally British than its nineteenth-century counterparts had been. It was evident that the Moody-Sankey era of late nineteenth-century American revival hymnody had had considerable influence on its contents. Among the favorite North American gospel hymnists represented were Philip P. Bliss, Fanny J. Crosby, Charles H. Gabriel, C. Austin Miles, Johnson Oatman, and Charles D. Tillman. Also giving the "standard hymnal" a less prescriptive quality were the ample number of hymns by several of the black Baptists on the music committee: the two Townsends, Adams, Barnwell, Bushell, Nickens, Person, and Tobias. Their contributions varied according to their musical tastes. While the five pieces by A.M. Townsend tended to be settings of hymns by such classic British writers as John Newton and Benjamin Beddome, all of Tobias's five pieces were original settings of his own hymns.

The conventionality of this early North American Protestant hymnal was clear in its rather scanty representation of spirituals and the growing corpus of black hymnody. The only pieces by well-known black hymnists were six gospel hymns by C.A. Tindley (three arranged by F.A. Clark) and three by C.P. Jones.

The three Jones hymns were the longtime gospel favorites "All I Need," "I'm Happy with Jesus Alone," and "Where Shall I Be." The equally familiar Tindley songs were "Go Wash in the Beautiful Stream," "Some Day," "Nothing Between," "I'll Overcome Someday," "We'll Understand It Better By and By," and "Stand By Me." In addition, a mere two spirituals were included—"Old Time Religion" (arrangement unattributed) and "Wade in Water" (arranged by Willa Townsend). Perhaps *Gospel Pearls* (with its nineteen spirituals) or the subsequent *Spirituals Triumphant* (with its seventy-six spirituals) were intended to supplement the hymnal in the pews of black Baptist churches. As "Townsend" historiographers Pelt and Smith commented in their Baptist history, "Each of these two books is unique in its kind, and, together with the hymnal, provide a full selection of great music in the three categories of standard hymns, spirituals, and gospel music."[37]

Today *The Baptist Standard Hymnal* unquestionably is outdated. In general, it fails to reflect the progressive consciousness of post–Civil Rights African-American Baptists. Evidence of its outdatedness is its inclusion of the old Social-Darwinist "From Greenland's Icy Mountains" and exclusion of "Lift Every Voice and Sing" (the Black National Anthem), not to mention the fact that it contains a mere two spirituals. Neither does it incorporate, in the modern mood of ecumenism, the newer works of contemporary black hymnists both inside and outside the "Townsend Convention."[38] While there are those who have been petitioning for a revised hymnal, there remain those unyielding Townsendites who insist that *The Baptist Standard Hymnal* still sets the "standard" for Baptist hymnody. One such disciple is J. Robert Bradley,[39] the current music director of the Sunday School Publishing Board, who was selected by A.M. Townsend for the position prior to the latter's death in 1959. In recent years, Bradley published this testament to the hymnal that Townsend designated "our everlasting contribution and permanent legacy":

> Singing has always been one of the keys to worship for us. Baptists are singing people. The *Baptist Standard Hymnal* came at a time when Black Baptists had no official printed collection of songs we could sing during worship. "Doctor" (as Townsend was fondly called) gathered people from the four corners of this country and gave them the outline for

putting together one of the finest hymnals in America. Dr. J.D. Bushell and his wife were serving at Abyssinian (Abyssinian Baptist Church of New York City) under Adam Clayton Powell, Sr.; Skipwith (Rev. J.H. Skipwith) was a renown tenor and was later called to preach . . . the entire Music Committee was composed of people who were musicians and were musically inclined. Dr. Townsend (who mastered the piano, drums, and organ) was in touch with and respected by the hymnologists of the world; most of the copyrights to the selections in our hymnal were *given* to him.[40]

Bradley is by no means the only partisan to remain faithful to the sixty-five-year-old hymnal, which was reprinted for continued use as recently as 1985. In an article titled "Standards in the Worship Music of Our People," Brenda Holland, director of public relations for the Sunday School Publishing Board, commented: "As it pertains to our denomination, the National Baptist Convention, USA, Incorporated, the standard for hymnody was firmly established in the early 1920's with the first-edition publication of the *Baptist Standard Hymnal.*"[41] Holland stated further that A.M. Townsend's hymnal set the "standard" for praising God through song, and that it remains the responsibility of the convention members to preserve this great heritage.[42]

Denominational pride aside, *The Baptist Standard Hymnal* still may be "standard" (in terms of the prevalence of classic British hymnody), but it is by no means the hymnal of the black Baptist populace. That enviable place of distinction belongs to *The New National Baptist Hymnal*, the hymnal most commonly found in the pews of member churches of the "Townsend" and "Boyd" conventions alike. *The New National Baptist Hymnal* is the paramount achievement of the postschism "Boyd Convention" and undoubtedly is historically one of the most significant black denominational hymnals of the twentieth century. First, as musicologist Eileen Southern discerned, it is the premier black church hymnal published during the post–Civil Rights era and one which, second, reflects the social awareness of Afro-Christianity awakened in the late sixties and early seventies: "Beginning in the late 1970s, the largely black denominations seem to have awakened to the necessity for publishing hymnals that would confront the demands of the radically changing lifestyles of black Christians in the last quarter of the twentieth century. The Baptists were the first, in 1977, with their denominational hymnal, *The New National Baptist Hymnal.*"[43]

Hymnal committee chairperson Ruth Lomax Davis[44] compiled the hymnal more or less singlehandedly. Her two principal aids were questionnaires regarding preferred hymn selections, which she sent to ministers, church musicians, and Sunday school teachers throughout the country; and the suggestions made by music committee members W. Elmo Mercer, Juanita Griffey Hines, Virgie C. DeWitty, A. Charles Bowie, and Marena Belle Williams, and by special contributors to the music committee Anderson T. Dailey, Margaret P. Douroux, Mamie E. Taylor, and Odessa Jackson.

The New National Baptist Hymnal clearly reflects the awakened social consciousness of post–Civil Rights black Christians, as well as the popular taste of the younger faction in the church. The book contains such favorites of the Civil Rights movement as "We Shall Overcome," "Oh Freedom," "Kum Ba Ya," and "Onward Christian Soldiers," plus twenty-seven black spirituals (arranged by such composers as John Work, Jr., Willa Townsend, and J.D. Bushell), and "Lift Every Voice and Sing." The hymnal also includes other social hymns (hymns of the Social Gospel movement), such as "O Master, Let Me Walk With Thee" and "In Christ There Is No East or West," plus the popular patriotic hymns of the day. In spite of such hymns, however, the volume is far more evangelical than social in nature. Accordingly, in constitution it is far more popular than classical, by which is meant that it is more akin to the songbook *Gospel Pearls* (1921) than to its "standard" progenitor, *The National Baptist Hymnal* (1903).

Demonstrating the popular character of *The New National Baptist Hymnal*, its mere eight "standard" hymns by Wesley and eleven by Watts are offset by a deluge of gospel hymns by such American hymnists as Philip P. Bliss, Fanny J. Crosby, B.B. McKinney, Johnson Oatman, and the contemporary gospel hymn duo William and Gloria Gaither. Also well represented are the gospel hymns of such black composers as Doris Akers, Lucie Campbell, E.C. Deas, Thomas A. Dorsey, Theodore Frye, C.P. Jones, Magnolia Lewis-Butts, Roberta Martin, Kenneth Morris, C.A. Tindley, and such contemporary black gospel songwriters as Andrae Crouch and Margaret P. Douroux.[45] Additionally, there are several hymns each by music committee members Anderson T. Dailey and Juanita Griffey Hines (one of

Hines's three is arranged by contemporary black hymn writer James Hendrix).

In 1979, the National Baptist Publishing Board released *Free Spirit* (1979), a songbook compiled for the use of both youth and adult choirs. The collection clearly contains music attractive to youths and young adults, for example, the nine gospel songs by Andrae Crouch, Edwin Hawkin's famous contemporary gospel arrangement of the old Baptist hymn "Oh Happy Day," and Danniebell Hall's "Ordinary People." As well, there are such popular songs as "Climb Every Mountain," such favorite spirituals as "Michael, Row Your Boat Ashore" and "We Are Climbing Jacob's Ladder," plus such entertaining pieces as the round on Psalm 23.

Doubtless, the publication of *The New National Baptist Hymnal* by the "Boyd Convention" thwarted any intention the "Townsend Convention" may have had to revise its hymnal. Because the Baptist conventions are rather discretionary associations of independent Baptist churches, the Sunday School Publishing Board has no authority to constrain its member churches to procure only the hymnbook bearing its appellation. A common hymnal published jointly by the two conventions or, better still, their full union would have solved this hymnological quandary—that is, if they had been able to succeed where the three black Methodist denominations failed in the second and third decades of the twentieth century.

Instead of pursuing such lofty ideals, the National Baptist Convention, USA, Inc., in November 1961, saw another faction of Baptists leave the fold. This schism was caused by the unusually long tenure of convention president Joseph H. Jackson, and his perceived social conservatism as reflected in the convention's lack of involvement in Civil Rights activism. Reflecting on the cause of the schism, Jackson defended his position, making allusions to Martin Luther King, Jr., one of the defectors involved in founding the Progressive National Baptist Convention, Inc.:

> There were some pastors and some lay people who felt the convention should become a direct action organization specializing in civil disobedience. But the convention's interpretation of the social gospel related the church to business, to economics, to politics, to the struggle for civil

rights, and to all the elements of human benefit, but this religious group did not so interpret the social gospel to mean that the church should give its wholehearted support to a program of civil disobedience. . . . The masses of the members of the convention remained loyal to the convention's tradition of a Christian ministry, a social concern, but primarily a gospel fellowship.[46]

What resulted from the schism late in 1961 was the 1962 founding of the Progressive National Baptist Convention, under the direction of Rev. L. Venchael Booth. A full fourteen years following the founding of the new convention, the Progressive Baptists published their first hymnal, *The Progressive Baptist Hymnal* (1976), edited by Rev. D.E. King, retired pastor of Monumental Baptist Church in Chicago.

The 1961 schism had hardly anything to do with the traditionalism of *The Baptist Standard Hymnal,* for *The Progressive Baptist Hymnal* was but a "special edition" of the thirty-six-year-old *Broadman Hymnal,* edited by gospel songwriter B.B. McKinney and published by the Broadman Press (of the Southern Baptist Convention) in 1940. Just as *The National Baptist Hymnal* (1903) had been essentially a revision of *The Baptist Hymnal* (1886) published by white Baptists seventeen years earlier, so was *The Progressive Baptist Hymnal* a slight modification of a hymnal compiled and published by white Southern Baptists thirty-six years earlier.

Replacing 41 of the 503 hymns in the *Broadman Hymnal* were four spirituals (all co-arranged by John W. and Frederick J. Work), six hymns by editor D.E. King, three pieces each by Lucie Campbell and Gordon Blaine Hancock,[47] two each by C.P. Jones and Kenneth Morris, and one each by E.C. Deas, J.D. Bushell, and L.V. Booth (the Progressive Convention's founder).[48] The inclusion of these pieces, however, did not compensate for the absence of a pervasive post–Civil Rights ethos. Hence, while in 1977 the unincorporated National Baptists published the inaugural post–Civil Rights black Protestant hymnal, the Progressive Baptists only a year earlier had published an edition of an outmoded hymnal. Most telling was that the *Broadman Hymnal* turned out to be a hand-me-down; the year following the Progressive Convention's adaptation of the aged hymnal, Broadman Press released *The New Broadman Hymnal* (1977). Moreover, the new Broadman Press hymnal contained a few pieces by black composers Doris Akers, C.A. Tindley, and H.T. Burleigh, none of whom were represented in *The Progressive Baptist Hymnal*. Too, *The New Broadman Hymnal* contained seven more spirituals than the mere three the Progressives added to their edition of the dated *Broadman Hymnal*.

After the National Baptist Publishing Board released *The New National Baptist Hymnal* in 1977, it, rather than *The Progressive Baptist Hymnal*, probably was to be found in the pews of the majority of Progressive Baptist churches. Thus, it was timely for the Progressives not long afterward to have D.E. King edit a new hymnal, one that not surprisingly turned out to be a "special edition" of *The New National Baptist Hymnal*. The foreword to *The New Progressive Baptist Hymnal* (1982) reads, "The Committee especially acknowledges indebtedness to Dr. T.B. Boyd III of the National Baptist Publishing Board who permitted the use of a voluminous collection of contents." In sum, the progressive Baptists repeated the procedure used to adapt the *Broadman Hymnal*: they replaced a number of hymns in *The New National Baptist Hymnal* with pieces apparently of special importance to them. Among the thirty-four substitutes, for instance, are seven hymns by editor D.E. King (set by such black musicians as H. Hortense Love, Charles Clency, and Edna Jordon) and a single hymn arrangement each by hymnal committee members Samuel L. Cosby, Jr., Robert E. Wooten, Sr., and H. Hortense Love. Also included is Elizabeth Maddox Huntley's setting of a hymn by the Progressive Convention's founder and hymnal committee member, L. Venchael Booth.

Eileen Southern ranks *Songs of Zion* (1982), compiled by black United Methodists, as equal in historical importance to *A Collection of Hymns and Spiritual Songs* (1801), compiled by AME Church founder Richard Allen, and to *Gospel Pearls* (1921), compiled by the "Townsend Convention." It appears that *The New National Baptist Hymnal* ought also to be ranked alongside these three. It is the first post–Civil Rights hymnal published, the preferred hymnal of both the "Townsend" and "Boyd Conventions," and the volume of which the Progressive Convention's hymnal is an adaptation. Moreover, it is the volume exactly duplicated by *The Hymnal of the Christian Methodist Episcopal Church* (1987). Finally, it is one of the hymnals most commonly seen sitting upon the organs and pianos in black Holiness and Pentecostal churches. Thus, if 1921 was a milestone year in black church hymnody, in that *Gospel Pearls* (published that year) is of exceptional historical import, then so too is the year 1976 a milestone, for *The New National Baptist Hymnal* is the *Gospel Pearls* of post–Civil Rights Afro-Baptists.

PART 2

BLACK HOLINESS AND PENTECOSTALS

CHAPTER 6

The Church of Christ (Holiness), USA

When I first gave myself to the Lord to be sanctified (this was in 1894 at Selma), I had no idea at all of taking up holiness as a fad, or an ism, or a creed, or a slogan of a "cult." I just wanted to be personally holy. I just wished to make my own calling and election sure to my own heart by walking with God in the Spirit.

One day as I staggered under the weight of this obligation, under the necessity of this ministry, I felt that I must be alone and especially talk with God about it. . . . The Spirit spoke within from the holy of holies of my redeemed spirit, and said, "You shall write the hymns for your people." This He said six or seven times till it was fixed in my mind. I got up and went to the organ in the corner of the room, wrote a song titled "Praise the Lord," ruled off a tablet, set it to music, and sang it before I left the room.

—*Charles Price Jones,*
founder of the Church of Christ (Holiness), USA[1]

The Holiness movement in North America officially commenced upon the convening of its first national convention in 1867. It was a full twenty-seven years later that Charles Price Jones organized a similar convention for the "colored" Holiness believers, due to dissatisfaction, said Jones, with the spiritual condition of the Baptists:

As a Baptist I had doctrinal assurance; I wanted spiritual assurance, heart peace, rest of soul, the joy of salvation in the understanding of a new heart, a new mind, a new spirit, constantly renewed and comforted by the Holy Ghost (Titus 3:5–8; John 14:15–20). But when I reached Jackson, Miss., I became convinced by the Lord that what I needed, all His people needed; that without following peace with all men and holiness, no man could see the Lord (Heb. 12:1–14); that no man could follow Christ in his

own strength; that therefore it was the privilege and duty of all to be
filled with the Spirit (Eph. 5:16–18) and walk by the Spirit (Gal. 5:15–26);
that Christ in us is the Hope of Glory (Col. 1:27, 28).[2]

Although Jones was convinced by the Lord that what he and
his people needed was holiness, he did not set out to found a
new denomination. Instead, the group was rejected by the Baptists. The contempt the Baptists felt toward this perceived fanati-
cism within their camp escalated when Jones joined the larger
Holiness movement, already in full progress, by mounting a
national campaign. Imitating the publication of Holiness periodicals which began appearing in 1866 and the convening of the
national Holiness Convention of 1867, Jones, exactly thirty years
later (in 1896 and 1897, respectively), began publishing a Holiness periodical titled *Truth* and holding an annual ecumenical
Holiness convention. The consequences, as Jones recorded
them, were corrosive and schismatic:

> Our ministers and churches who were fostering the glorious and
> scriptural doctrine that we are to follow peace with all men and holiness,
> without which no man shall see the Lord, submitted to persecutions of
> all kinds till after a few years when those churches and ministers who
> held forth the doctrine that the Holy Spirit was building a holy church as
> the body of a holy Christ, were put out of the churches as they then
> existed and of which most of us were members (the Baptist denomina-
> tion), and were compelled to build our church houses, beginning with
> Christ Temple on Grayson and Monument Streets in Jackson, Damascus
> at Hazlehurst, Miss., Church of God in Little Rock, Ark., and many
> others too numerous to mention here, that joined us in those glorious
> attempts to honor the Lord.[3]

Jones refused to accept any accusations that he and his Holiness devotees were "come-outers" or sectarians. Even when the
seedling movement within the Baptist church had grown into a
full-fledged denomination, Jones occasionally reminded his
members of the reality of this part of their history. In his annual
address to the 1930 Annual Holiness Convention in Los Angeles, for instance, he sounded a reminder that may have helped
fuel his members' resentment toward the Baptists (perhaps a
reason why Baptist hymnody was completely excluded from all
their denominational hymnals): "We only wanted to carry the
message to the churches," said Jones. "We did not want another
denomination. We are not sectarians. But the churches rejected
us. So we had to build for the Lord."[4] Similarly, in his 1935

autobiography, Jones suggested that the very first hymn he wrote failed to be published by black Baptist composer William Rosborough[5] because Jones had been dismissed by the Baptists as a Holiness fanatic. "This song I lost, to my regret," recalled Jones. "I sent it to a publisher, a Mr. William Rosborough, author of *Celestial Showers,* and he failed to bring it out. For it was his second book, *Celestial Showers No. II.* Before he brought the book out I was rejected by the Baptist people as a heretic."[6]

C.P. Jones built not only churches and the Church of Christ (Holiness), USA for the Lord, but also a vast and rich corpus of original hymnody—some one thousand hymns (including anthems), almost all of which he personally set to music. Two years following the inaugural Holiness Convention of 1897 (the official founding date of the denomination), Jones' first songbook, *Jesus Only* (1899), appeared. "*Jesus Only, No. 1*—For all religious services; songs of the higher Christ life a specialty," the advertisement read. "They express your soul's deepest devotion in catchy, yet most appropriate tunes."[7] *Jesus Only* proved to be only the first of a prolific production of songbooks. Two years later Jones published *Jesus Only Nos. 1 and 2* (1901). In the ensuing years, *Select Songs* appeared, "With some of the best songs of the editor and others; containing the African Hymn of Hope, 'Stretch Your Hand to God,' 'Wanted—Men,' a quartette, etc., for emancipation celebrations and other occasions."[8] Still later came *His Fullness* (1906), then *Sweet Selections,* both of which he described as "jewels . . . precious in the spiritual life of the church."[9]

In 1927, at the National Holiness Convention in Norfolk, Virginia, the Church of Christ (Holiness) instituted an episcopal form of church government; C.P. Jones, who had served the last thirty years as president of the Holiness Convention, became the first and senior bishop of the denomination. About a year later (1928), the newly elevated prelate published *His Fullness* (enlarged), "being *Sweet Selections* and *His Fullness* combined, with the addition of a few new and inspirational songs."[10]

His Fullness (enlarged) was the last songbook Jones compiled and published himself. Nonetheless, the numerous songbooks he published over a thirty-year period reveal that he viewed his music ministry as principally one of written documentation rather than of oral tradition. "This is the day of the printer's ink, of the picture, of the radio," he said in his 1930 address to the Annual Holiness Convention. "We are too poor to use the radio, but we can use printer's ink."[11] Jones clearly was quite a progressive leader for his time. If the founding secretary of the National Baptist Publishing Board, Rev. R.H. Boyd, found it difficult to convince the fledgling National Baptist Convention of the viability of a publishing ministry, then it is likely that such a ministry was viewed with even greater suspicion by the early Holiness folk, who were far more rooted in the oral tradition and less in touch with intellectual currents. If C.P. Jones' followers ever did grumble about his intellectual endeavors, they certainly were not alone. As Jones noted five years later in his autobiography, there were some whites in Jackson, Mississippi, who "could say, and did say, 'The idea of a Nigger printing books!' "[12]

In 1935, *Jesus Only Nos. 1 and 2 Combined* was reprinted by R.C. Cook of Bogalusa [sic], Louisiana, on behalf of the publishing board of the Church of Christ (Holiness).[13] Five years later, the first official denominational hymnal, *Jesus Only Songs and Hymns Standard Hymnal* (1940), was printed and released under the auspices of the Jones Foundation. The foundation was organized to carry on the publication program initiated by the denomination's venerable founder.[14]

While the Jones Foundation has been responsible for publishing all of the hymnals of the denomination since 1940, it is not clear how much of the hands-on work in publishing early songbooks Jones himself did. The title page of *Jesus Only Nos. 1 and 2* (1901) attributes its publication to C.P. Jones' privately-owned Truth Publishing Company, which was located in the church he pastored in Jackson, Mississippi. However, in his autobiographical essay, "The History of My Songs," Jones mentions the involvement of the National Baptist Publishing Board, as he recalls that his printing office was burned down in 1905 by a mob of white arsonists: "Our printing office with two thousand new *Jesus Onlies I and II* just shipped to me from the Baptist Publishing house at Nashville, and a new book of my own not quite finished, and a new issue of *Truth*, a paper I published more than 20 years, were all burned up, with thousands of dollars of office material, type and presses."[15] While it is not clear how much of the work Jones' Truth Publishing Company actually did in manufacturing his songbooks, what is particularly informative is that, in 1901, he was not considered such a pariah by the Baptists that the National Baptist Publishing Board, under Rev. R.H. Boyd, would not print his *Jesus Only Nos. 1 and 2*. In fact, many years later, after the Baptists themselves had split into separate conventions, Jones again turned to the National Baptist Publishing Board, now under Henry H. Boyd, to have his enlarged edition of *His Fullness* (1928) printed.[16]

What became of the new book that was left incomplete at the time it was lost in the church fire can only be surmised. Possibly it was one of two songbooks advertised on the back cover of *Jesus Only Nos. 1 and 2*, neither of which was ever again mentioned by C.P. Jones or his biographers—*Songs and Hymns* and *Popular Songs and Ballads*. The former volume Jones advertised as "A hymn book with above 300 selections, new and old, having an appendix with marriage and burial ceremony and Bible readings on Holiness, Church Discipline, etc. The thing for the religious worker's pocket. It will not only help devotions, but help search the scriptures on any point." *Popular Songs and Ballads* he merely advertised as "A ten cent song book with words only."

Although Jones lost to fire some two thousand copies of *Jesus Only Nos. 1 and 2*, evidently he had the volume reprinted. It was probably the success of *Jesus Only* (which today has all but disappeared) that encouraged him to print in larger quantity the combined volume (currently obscure but nonetheless extant). To this effect, his preface to *Jesus Only Nos. 1 and 2* reads:

> *Jesus Only No. 1*, has, by the grace of our Lord Jesus Christ, met a hearty reception; chiefly too, upon the merits of the new and original songs therein contained. For this we thank God in Christ, Who condescended to give this blessed work to do. Call has long been made for the Second Number combined with the First, which we have also long promised, but for reasons which He knows better than any of us, we have been delayed. But it is here at last, and we bespeak for it a much more gratifying reception than the first book had, though God has blessed *it* as he has.

Jones stated in conclusion: "We ask the prayers of those who love the Lord that the songs herein contained may, in that melody that the grace of the Spirit alone can impart, reach the hearts of men. Amen."

Jesus Only Nos. 1 and 2 was a meritorious compilation on the part of Jones, comparable to any songbook of the day. It contained 412 hymns, a little over one-third of which were unaccompanied (meters were given or tunes suggested). Of the 412 pieces, about half were composed by Jones himself, with the remaining half written by a broad representation of American gospel hymnists, such as Horatius Bonar, Fannie J. Crosby, William G. Fisher, William P. Mackey, Johnson Oatman, Jr., H.G. Spafford, and Charlie D. Tillman. Balancing off his own (then unknown) pieces were such familiar hymns as "What a Friend" (Bonar), "Rescue the Perishing" (Crosby), "No Not One" (Oatman), and "When Peace Like a River" (Spafford). The largest number of gospel hymns by a writer other than Jones were the fourteen by Elisha A. Hoffman, whom Jones acknowledged in the preface (along with Gertrude Harris) for his help in "criticising the work." Jones might have included the generous number of hymns by Hoffman as compensation for the assistance of this experienced publisher of the Hoffman Music Company, Cleveland, Ohio.

Also included in *Jesus Only Nos. 1 and 2* were a relatively small number of "standard" hymns by such British classicists as Watts and Wesley. Of the hundreds of hymns by these two that filled Protestant hymnals from the eighteenth to the early twentieth centuries, only about a dozen by each were adopted by nineteenth-century revivalism and its companion, the Holiness movement. The pieces by Watts and Wesley especially favored by the revival and Holiness movements customarily centered around the life and personality of Jesus, who was portrayed (as epitomized in Wesley's "Jesus Lover of My Soul") as an affectionate friend and divine protector.

Often these classic hymns were adapted to the gospel hymn movement by the customary practice of affixing a chorus. During nineteenth-century revivalism, for instance, the most popular rendition of Watt's "Alas, and Did My Savior Bleed" was Ralph E. Hudson's setting, which contained his original chorus, "At the Cross." For *Jesus Only Nos. 1 and 2*, however, C.P. Jones set this Watts hymn himself, giving it his own original chorus and titling the piece "I Surrendered at the Cross":

> Alas! and did my Savior bleed?
> And did my Sovereign die?
> Would He devote that sacred head
> For such a worm as I?

Chorus:
I surrendered at the cross, and my heart was cleansed from sin
By the precious blood the Savior shed for me;
I am living in His word, and it daily keeps me clean!
Hallelujah, from the pow'r of sin I'm freed.

Of the 412 hymns in *Jesus Only Nos. 1 and 2* (about half written by Jones), fully one-third had both text and music composed by Jones. An additional 40 of his hymns were unaccompanied. About a dozen more were set to music by Maud L. Washington, Mrs. M.F. Wilson, and Sallie M. Rather (to name the principal ones). Jones also included several of his anthems, an arrangement of the spiritual "Free at Last" (identified as an "old jubilee tune"), and original musical settings of about two dozen hymns by other writers. Several of the hymns set by Jones were written by his church associates—Elder Alexander J. Scarborough, Elder Daniel G. Spearman, and Amelia Gaynor Anderson. Elder Scarborough, who had 3 hymns in the volume (2 set by Jones and 1 unaccompanied), was one of the charter pastors of the Church of Christ (Holiness) who attended the inaugural 1897 convention organized by C.P. Jones.[17] Amelia Anderson, who contributed to the volume 2 hymns set by Jones, long was an active lay member of the church. Elder Spearman, who contributed 2 hymns set by Jones, was one of the ministers who left the church in 1907 to join Charles H. Mason's fledgling Church of God in Christ (COGIC).[18] Though Spearman defected to the Pentecostal movement, Ortho Cobbins, the longtime historiographer of the Church of Christ (Holiness), nonetheless spoke highly of him: "Rev. Spearman was a man of brilliant intellect, a deep thinker, an eloquent orator, a good singer, a diligent student, and could be ranked among the real forceful preachers of the land."[19]

The content of *Jesus Only Nos. 1 and 2* and C.P. Jones' other songbooks was typical of similar collections published by other gospel hymn writers of that era. The customary practice, which Jones probably observed in such gospel hymn collections as Charlie D. Tillman's *The Revival* (1891) and William Bradbury's *Fresh Laurels* (n.d.), was to supplement the compiler's original songs with the favorite gospel hymns of the period.[20] This was probably the most effective means by which an unknown gospel hymn writer could get his own works circulated among churches and traveling evangelists.

Jesus Only Nos. 1 and 2 was a product of its times in another sense. Akin to the Singing School songbooks of the eighteenth century, it contained an essay on the fundamentals of music. On the back cover of the songbook, C.P. Jones gave substantial space to advertising this feature:

> This book has a treatise on vocal music in the back, which will be valuable to both country and city choirs, as well as to music teachers. Get it, and learn to sing. Some of the songs (in the same book) are in shaped notes and some in the round; this gives an advantage to the one who wishes to master vocal music rather than merely know a note by its shape. To know vocal music sure enough is a great help to the mind, and gives great measure both to the singer and listener.

Titled "Inductive Lessons in Vocal Music," Jones' pedagogy contained two parts. The first part had fifteen practical pointers for amateur church musicians—from "Do not be late to choir rehearsal" to "Do not be afraid to sing with rejoicing." The second part was essentially a definition of such fundamental elements of music as clefs, time and key signatures, major and minor scales, and shaped and round notes. Although the second part of the lesson was proof of the musical aptitude of this prolific hymnist and self-taught musician, it was nothing more than a standard course in the fundamentals of music theory. Jones himself said at the outset that "this is not an exhaustive treatise on the subject, but it will give one sufficient knowledge to be a fairly intelligent reader of music."

On the other hand, the first part of Jones' essay on music was historically and theologically informative, in that it presented his personal thoughts on church music and musicianship. The writing naturally had a biblical bent characteristic of Holiness teaching and preaching, but it was by no means a doctrinal discourse intended only for a Holiness audience. Consequently, its concise and unpretentious points are timeless guidelines for music directors who wish their choristers to "sing with the spirit":

> (a) Unless there is music in one, it is hard to get it out with ever so much training; yet one does not know what he can do until he tries.
> (b) "I will sing with the spirit, and with the understanding also," said the inspired apostle; which showed that he believed in correct singing, but in the spirit of devotion as well. The heart of the church choir should

be prepared for singing as the heart of the minister is prepared for his sermon.

(c) "Be at peace among yourselves," would do admirably well as a choir motto, and with it such blessed divine instruction as, "Let all your things be done in charity" (1 Cor. 16:14). "In honor preferring one another" (Rom. 12:10). "Do all to the glory of God" (1 Cor. 10:31).

(d) While the singing practice need not be a funeral occasion, it should not be either an occasion of folly and fuss. God is present with His people everywhere; learn to "practice the thought of His presence," and respect Him.

(e) Sing full round tones. Do not blare like a file against a saw. If the voice at first be not sweet and musical, practice will bring it to be so. To this end, sing much when by yourself. Practice the scale; practice correct pronunciation. Yet so practice it as to let your heart be on what you sing, not how. Avoid any sort of "put on."

(f) Do not sound R in words where there is no R. That is affection or put on, and is objectionable to all refined people.

(g) Give all words their proper sound as nearly as can be done in singing. Teacher, see to this; but do not criticise to the point of discouraging your pupil.

(h) Do not be late to choir practice, only when compelled. Then be polite enough to render excuse and beg pardon.

(i) Why should you be late at the service, either? God, the Spirit, needs your help. Render it to Him so soon as you can. Good singing done by willing hearts and trained minds and voices is such help. In Solomon's temple certain of the Levites were especially appointed to this service. You have somewhat their place. Be humble and diligent and fill it well (2 Chron. 5:12–14).

(j) Practice so much to yourself that you can sing well at sight, but don't become puffed about it; that would take all the virtue and power out of an otherwise useful accomplishment.

(k) Do not be afraid to sing with rejoicing. Fastidiousness spoils much of the joy of life. Let us love God, love souls, love music—and sing. That's what we are here for—to sing! (Isa. 12). Many a soul has been converted by a song, and many a despairing one filled with renewed hope. We can live life but once; then, filled with the spirit of God's own holiness, let us do our best and sing.

(l) Get you a dictionary and learn what words which you don't know mean, so that you may be thorough and both study and sing with the understanding as well as with the spirit. Do not be too lazy to know. Ask those who know to help you. Expose your ignorance, if need be, and acquire knowledge. Do this and see how it will profit you in days to come.

(m) Invoke God's help in all things. Let your knowledge thus be sanctified and pay the debt of politeness to your Maker and Redeemer.

(n) In studying these lessons notice well the parts in larger type. Don't leave them till you get the sense of what is said so that you can give it in your own words. Let your mind master something; it will do you good. Whether people seem to appreciate it right away or not, they will some day.

(o) But sing; nothing will teach how to do this like doing. "Have grace and sing" (Heb. 12:28, 29).

The songbooks that followed *Jesus Only Nos. 1 and 2* were essentially vehicles for distributing C.P. Jones' more recent works and therefore were all of the same general character and quality: a selection of favorite gospel hymns of the day supplementing an abundance of Jones' own hymns. A cursory examination of three of these later volumes will illustrate the point.

1. The 1928 enlarged edition of *His Fullness* contains 144 hymns, 88 of which were composed by Jones. His arranged spirituals in this volume are "Die in the Field of Battle," "Going to Break Down Confusion," and "Preaching in the Wilderness." The remaining pieces include the customary classics by such British hymnists as Watts and Wesley and the favored gospel hymns by such writers as Elisha A. Hoffman, Will L. Thompson, A.B. Simpson, and C.A. Tindley (the latter's famous "We'll Understand It Better By and By").

2. *Jesus Only Songs and Hymns Standard Hymnal* was the denomination's first official hymnal, which appeared in nine editions between 1940 and 1966. It showed few differences from the earlier volumes compiled by Jones. The ninth edition (1966), for instance, was characteristically indistinguishable from *Jesus Only Nos. 1 and 2*, published sixty-five years earlier (1901). Of the 421 hymns in the ninth edition of the *Standard Hymnal*, 296 were carried over from *Jesus Only Nos. 1 and 2* and 108 from the enlarged edition of *His Fullness* (1928). This left only about 24 pieces that appeared in neither of these earlier volumes; and of those 24, about a third (8) were written by Jones. Furthermore, of the 108 carried over from *His Fullness* (Enlarged), two-thirds (75) were written by Jones. Hence, it is clear that the reason for publishing the *Standard Hymnal* was not to modernize the hymnody, but (a) to give the denomination its first official hymnal, and (b) to accumulate the hymns of its venerable founder, along with the old favorites of the gospel hymn repertoire.

3. *His Fullness Songs* (1977), the current denominational hymnal, is, according to its preface, a revision of the *Jesus Only Songs and Hymns Standard Hymnal*. Of the 512 hymns in *His Fullness*

Songs, approximately 310 in fact were carried over from the ninth edition (1966) of the *Standard Hymnal*. Of Jones' hymns, all but about 10 in the 1966 hymnal were carried over to *His Fullness Songs*, giving it a total of 241 hymns by the prolific prelate. This leaves about 183 pieces that were not in the 1966 hymnal. Clearly, the majority of the 183 "new" pieces are in fact not new at all, but simply different selections from the dated repertoire of gospel hymns and British standards.

With such modifications, the modernization in *His Fullness Songs* is insubstantial in terms of updating the overall character of the denomination's lineage of hymnbooks. (1) Included are two time-honoured hymns of the Social Gospel movement—"O Master, Let Me Walk with Thee" (Washington Gladden) and "Rise Up, O Men of God" (William P. Merrill). (2) For the first time in the denomination's lineage of hymnbooks, "Mine Eyes Have Seen the Glory" (Julia Ward Howe), rather than "Am I a Soldier of the Cross" (Watts), is listed as the "Battle Hymn." (3) The increased number of classic British hymns gives the hymnal an added air of sophistication and sublimity.

Conversely, the dearth of modernization in *His Fullness Songs* is all too evident. (1) There are no spirituals arranged by such renowned composers as John W. Work and R. Nathaniel Dett, but only those few arranged by C.P. Jones over his hymn-writing career. (2) There are no gospel hymns of the golden age of gospel (1930–69) by the celebrated black Baptist writers—Lucie E. Campbell, Thomas A. Dorsey, Roberta Martin, Kenneth Morris, and many more. (3) There is no contemporary gospel music of the modern age of gospel (1969–present) by performing artists affiliated with the Church of God in Christ (COGIC), such as Elbernita Clark (of the Clark Singers), Andrae Crouch, Edwin Hawkins, and Walter Hawkins. (4) While "My Country, 'Tis of Thee" is included, the Black National Anthem, "Lift Every Voice and Sing," is not. (5) There is only one gospel hymn by the eminent black Methodist minister, Rev. C.A. Tindley, "Nothing Between," leaving Tindley's even more celebrated "We'll Understand It Better By and By" curiously omitted. (6) Aside from the few aforementioned pieces, there is no social gospel hymnody such as is increasingly found in the twentieth-century black church hymnals of the mainline Protestant denominations.

With regard to the dearth of Social Gospel hymns in *His Fullness Songs*, it may be useful to note that the Holiness movement, which was evolving during the same period, was formed in part in reaction against the secularism, intellectualism, and theological liberalism of the Social Gospel. Although both Social Gospel hymnody and C.P. Jones gospel hymns were written during the same general timeframe (1895–1930), and although both were responses to the inadequacy of church and society in addressing social problems, what distinguishes Jones' hymns is their severe anticulturalism. Both the Holiness and the Social Gospel movements maintained that human beings were perfectible. However, Holiness doctrine maintained that society would only be perfected upon Christ's Second Coming and initiation of the millennium,[21] while the Social Gospelers were great champions of culture and believed that society could be reformed. This was the principal reason why there was no alliance between the movements even on hymnological grounds, and why there was a dearth of Social Gospel hymnody in Jones' songbooks. The underclass to whom black Social Gospelers Rev. Henry Hugh Proctor (Congregationalist), Rev. Reverdy C. Ransom (African Methodist Episcopal), and Rev. Gordon Blaine Hancock (Baptist) attempted to minister in their churches was the very class whose members rejected the Social Gospel as merely one more example of the church's ineffectual involvement in worldly matters. With Charles Price Jones, the masses began to turn to the Holiness churches.

Why a large quantity of white gospel hymns and selected British standards were included in *His Fullness Songs*, to the exclusion of black hymnody composed by the Baptists and Pentecostals (COGIC), is also explainable. The Holiness and revival movements which produced the white gospel hymns and adopted choice British hymns were interrelated crusades. The leading revival evangelists typically were advocates of the Holiness campaign, and many of their converts, swayed by the numerous gospel hymns strategically aimed at spurring on the conversion decision, became members of Holiness churches.

On the other hand, the exclusion of the black Baptist and COGIC brands of gospel was likely a result of historical antagonisms and doctrinal differences, rather than of denominationalism or separatism. First of all, C.P. Jones and his Holiness followers had been rejected by the Baptists, causing the former to form a separate denomination when they did not wish to be schismatic. Second, while Bishops C.P. Jones and C.H. Mason remained on amicable terms after their split, Jones nonetheless told the 1931 National Convention of the Church of Christ (Holiness) that he regretted the fact that they had lost members and churches to the COGIC: "The 'Tongues' Movement . . . went out from us," he complained, "we regret this wild fire that has really hindered us in pushing the claim of the Holy Ghost on the people."[22] For whatever reason, black Baptist and Pentecostal (COGIC) hymnody was excluded from *His Fullness Songs* (1977). The hymnal is, in the final analysis, by no means a modern one. As a matter of fact, it is doubtful if it contains many (if any) hymns written after World War II. Although it is one of the two earliest hymnals published during the black consciousness movement of the 1970s, it, unlike its counterpart *The New National Baptist Hymnal*, neglects to reflect the prevailing Afro-Christian social consciousness.

Reflecting the overarching milieu out of which *His Fullness Songs* came, Jones' hymns fail to mirror the progressive social views of the mass of modern Afro-Christians. They are religiously conservative and biblically centered pieces that are completely anticultural—Christ is not the sustainer or transformer of the world, but the disdainer of the world. In spite of this anticulturalism, which makes many of Jones' hymns theologically repulsive to mainline Protestants (probably the reason so few of his hymns are found in their hymnals), his poetry is often exquisite and always heartfelt. His hymns evolved, said Jones, out of real life experiences of trial and victory.[23]

C.P. Jones' songs teach Christian believers that they are weak, worthless, weary pilgrims struggling through an evil world. According to Jones' hymn "Praise Ye the Lord in Faith and Hope," the only means by which believers can be liberated from this toilsome pilgrimage is to keep their eyes on Jesus alone, so that the Holy Ghost will make them citizens of heaven while they yet dwell on earth below. This turning away from the world heavenward for citizenship in another world is what Jones' hymn "Saving Me Wholly By Grace" terms the "heavenly calling":

> I am so glad of the heavenly calling,
> Calling away from the world and its charms;

> I am so glad I have fled for a refuge,
> Into the Savior's strong arms.

One of the most important songs written by Jones is "Jesus Only," the opening hymn in *Jesus Only, Jesus Only Nos. 1 and 2, Jesus Only Standard Hymnal,* and *His Fullness Songs.* "Perhaps few songs I have been given the grace to write," said Jones, "are sung more among our people."[24] The song was conceived of, Jones recalled, when the Spirit revealed to him that the Baptists were glorying in their own name rather than in the name of Jesus:

> Between the Holiness convention in 1897 and 1898 I began to be impressed with the inconsistencies of our Baptist churches, being myself almost a fanatical Baptist. Our slogan was that we were the only scriptural people; the only people who preached the whole Bible without adding to or taking from—without changing the word of God to add the traditions of men. . . . We boasted of our scripturalness. If it was, "Thus saith the Lord," it was Baptistic; if not, it was the mere tradition of men and unworthy of authority. This was our claim as Baptists.
>
> But I was taken to account before God. "You Baptists are liars," said the Spirit. "You profess to love me, but you do not. You love yourselves, but you do not love *My Name.* You praise yourselves, but you do not praise *Me.* You glory in yourselves, but you do not *glory in My Name*" (Ps. 105:3).[25]

Jones concluded his recollection with the resolve that suggested to him the song's words and title: "It is the Name of Jesus alone that has salvation in it. . . . Christ must be all. Holiness belongs to God. Christ is the life. All else is failure."[26] Clearly bearing the Holiness insignia of zealous Christ-centeredness, "Jesus Only" interprets what it means to surrender oneself fully to the Lord:

> Jesus only is my motto,
> Jesus only is my song,
> Jesus only is my heart-thought,
> Jesus only all day long.
>
> Then away with ev'ry idol,
> Let my Lord be all to me;
> Jesus only is my Master,
> Jesus only let me see.

There are three theological threads in this hymn that all relate to the idea of surrendering to the Lord, which, in Holiness doctrine, is the prerequisite to appropriating holiness: (1) "the Name of Jesus" as the formula for summoning spiritual authority and power, (2) the belief that Jesus is "All," the source of that power and sustenance, and (3) the desire to see Jesus face to face.

One of C.P. Jones' most popular songs stressing the importance of Christian believers' surrendering all to Jesus is "I'm Happy with Jesus Alone." Jones recalled the real-life experience that led to his writing this hymn, one that expressed his determination to stay close to Jesus and the Holy Word. "Severe trials had beset me," he said. "My meetings had been shot into at Lexington. C.H. Mason had started his meeting, but that night the meeting had been turned into my hands and I had preached. Five people were shot—none seriously hurt."[27] Despite such unhappy episodes, Jones was determined to be happy with Jesus alone: "No name but His. No master but Him. No law but His word. No creed but Jesus." All else is "trash," he said; happiness lies with Jesus alone.[28]

> There's nothing so precious as Jesus to me;
> Let earth with its treasures be gone;
> I'm rich as can be when my Savior I see;
> I'm happy with Jesus alone.

In order to forsake earth's treasures, one has to surrender all to Jesus, by denying not only one's kindred, but also one's own life. Only the Christian believer who has denied self, says Jones' hymn "I Am Wholly Sanctified," can attain full sanctification.

All of the vital theological threads constituting Holiness doctrine converge in this single concept of sanctification. The reason Jones' songs are so permeated by this theme is that the desire to be holy was a heartfelt motivating factor in his life. Indeed, his spiritual journey often was a lonely one, for even Jones' wife had little sympathy with his "high spiritual aspirations."[29] One of Jones' most popular gospel hymns, expressing his commitment to live the arduous and lonely life of holiness, is "Deeper, Deeper." It is a song, he recalled, that evolved out of deep dissatisfaction with his own imperfection:

> The Savior had said, "He that believeth on me the works that I do shall he do also, and greater works than these shall he do because I go to my Father." Not understanding thoroughly the oneness of the Christ body as revealed in I Corinthians 12, and Ephesians 4, I did not see how anyone could do greater works than the Savior had done. I felt that nevertheless I was coming short of my highest privileges of service in Christ. I wonder

if I was not right. Nevertheless I prayed in that song for deeper grace, deeper wisdom, more perfect conformity to and willingness to do God's will.[30]

The words to this hymn suggest that the sojourn toward sanctification—deeper grace, wisdom, and perfection—requires a deeper embracing of the love of Jesus through a higher knowledge of the Holy Word he embodies:

> Deeper, deeper in the love of Jesus
> Daily let me go;
> Higher, higher in the school of wisdom,
> More of grace to know.
>
> Chorus:
> O deeper yet, I pray,
> And higher ev'ry day,
> And wiser, blessed Lord,
> In thy precious holy word.

Another well-loved hymn by C.P. Jones is the resplendent "I Will Make the Darkness Light," which Jones recalled grew out of a desperate experience. Around the year 1907, while down in Louisiana preaching a revival, Jones became stricken with fever, and the Spirit gave him a song that encouraged him at his lowest moment of faltering faith:

> I had distressing fevers every day and sleep was taken from me at night. I would go and preach, for the Spirit of truth teaches me to walk by faith rather than by feeling. One day I said, "Well, Lord, I guess that the end has come." That was about twenty-eight years ago. I walked down the road praying and contemplating the end. When I got back into my room and knelt, as I usually was compelled by the Spirit to do, He said, "Write a song." And there upon my knees I wrote the words, then went to the organ and set them to music. And God has fulfilled every word of it to me. O how many have been helped and blessed by it![31]

The poetic words born out of this experience further attest to Jones' spiritual sensitivity and to his surrender to the impulsion of the Spirit:

> I will make the darkness light before thee,
> What is wrong I'll make it right before thee,
> All thy battles I will fight before thee,
> And the high places I'll bring down.
>
> Chorus:
> When thou walkest by the way I'll lead thee,

> On the fatness of the land I'll feed thee,
> And a mansion in the sky I'll deed thee,
> And the high places I'll bring down.

> With an everlasting love I'll love thee,
> Tho' with trials deep and sore I'll prove thee,
> But there's nothing that can hurt or move thee,
> And the high places I'll bring down.

The concomitant of turning fully toward the Lord, who alone is able to make the darkness light and the wrong right, is, according to Holiness belief, complete divorce from the world of human culture. The appropriate response for the Holiness believer, says Jones in "I Have Surrendered to Jesus," is to abandon human traditions and surrender to the Lord:

> I have surrendered to Jesus,
> Conquered by weapons of love;
> I have forsaken earth's treasures
> Seeking a treasure above.

While the worldly are the enemies of holiness, the holy citizens of heaven are, reciprocally, the enemies of the world and necessarily forsake the world in order to turn fully to Jesus and serve him. The sanctified must be willing to flee not only from wealth and earthly honor but also from friends and relatives; all else but Jesus is counted as loss. Divine love is not familial, but Christ-centered in a most anticultural way:

> Should father and mother forsake me below,
> My bed upon earth be a stone,
> I'll cling to my Savior, He loves me I know,
> I'm happy with Jesus alone.

In addition to the propositions that human traditions are unworthy of honor and human relationships are untrustworthy, life as a whole, as Jones' songs portray it, is constantly troubled by unexpected problems created by the worldly. Jones' hymn "I Will Hide" thus exhorts the sanctified to "come out" from among such wretchedness and hide away from the temptations of the world:

> From the malice of the wicked I will hide,
> From their tongues' deceitful slander, from their pride;
> From the evil that they do, From their worldly pomp and
>   show—
> In Thy presence I will happily abide.

C.P. Jones' songs speak of eluding the world rather than attempting to transform it because human culture is believed to be incapable of being transformed. Sin in the world, his songs claim, will remain untransformed until the Lord returns to initiate the Apocalypse. Hence, Jones' hymns teach Christian believers simply to endure until the end. Their vocation in life is not to make the world a better place, but to erect the barricade of faith to protect them from evil embodied in the world:

> There are cities great and high, Hallelujah!
> Strong and wall'd up t'ward the sky, Praise the Lord!
> But by faith we'll bring them low, Hallelujah!
> And Jehovah's pow'r we'll show, Praise the Lord!

While the children of Jesus faithfully endure the ways of the world, waiting for the victorious Last Days, says Jones' hymn "Come Unto Me," the Lord lovingly gives them rest from life's drudgery:

> Have you cares of business, cares of pressing debt?
> Cares of social life or cares of hopes unmet?
> Are you by remorse or sense of guilt depressed?
> Come right on to Jesus, He will give you rest.

Ultimate rest is, of course, the reward of heaven, which is seen by Holiness believers as the Christian's central goal in life. While the world is unjust and unhappy, heaven is a place of justice and joy, says Jones' hymn "There's a Happy Time a-Coming":

> There's a happy time a-coming,
> There's a happy time a-coming,
> When oppressors shall no longer sit on high,
> When the proud shall be as stubble,
> For their sins receiving double;
> There's a happy time a-coming by and by.

The themes that coalesce in Jones' songs clearly define him as a product of the gospel hymn movement. The selected gospel hymns in his songbooks were probably those he first heard sung in revivals during his upbringing in Texas Valley, Georgia, and which later his parishioners sang in the Baptist churches he pastored in Arkansas, Alabama, and Mississippi. However, far more than the gospel hymns of the Protestant writers, Jones' songs bear the distinct insignia of Holiness religion: biblicism, perfectionism, separatism, antisecularism, and anticulturalism.

CHAPTER 7

The House of God Church

We believe all human beings should know that it is the
will of God that all true people should have a rule to walk
by in any matter of business, both spiritual and temporal
and they should have their rules written up in books.

—*"Church Decree," The House of God*[1]

But if I tarry long, that thou mayest know how thou
oughtest to behave thyself in the house of God, which is
the church of the living God, the pillar and ground of the
truth. And without controversy great is the mystery of
godliness.

—*1 Tim. 3:15–16a*[2]

The House of God, Which is the Church of the Living God, The
Pillar and Ground of the Truth, Without Controversy, Inc. was
founded in 1903 by Mary L. Tate. The original congregation of
this Holiness denomination, in Chattanooga, Tennessee, was
probably initially associated with another black Holiness group
founded in 1889—the Church of the Living God (Christian
Workers for Fellowship). This older fellowship was organized in
Wrightsville, Arkansas, by William Christian, who "by virtue of
a divine call, created the office of chief."[3]

The reason such sects as the House of God Church became
permanent entities in Christianity, rather than remaining mere
passing inspirations, is due, claims Joseph R. Washington, to the
interacting roles which suffering and music played in the lives of
church members.[4] Less than half a century removed from slavery, those who gravitated to Holiness churches were indeed "the
least of them," people who suffered most severely from social
and economic repression, even at the hands of some of the more
privileged blacks of the Methodist and Baptist churches. But
they sang their hymns of faith and perseverance and gleaned the

power needed to live on. "The truth is," explains Washington, "these Holiness types are under so much oppression in the midst of so much obvious affluence until what is generally assumed to produce emotional stress really produces emotional power, which really guarantees mental health in an unhealthy society."[5]

The hymns that contributed to the maintenance of Mother Tate's church beyond her death in 1930 were documented in the denomination's first hymnbook, *Spiritual Songs and Hymns.* Privately published in Chattanooga around 1944,[6] the paperback volume indicated on its cover that its content was "Composed and Compiled by Bishop M.L. Tate and Edited by Bishop M.F.L. Keith." On the reverse side of the page containing Bishop Tate's photograph was the preface of her successor, Bishop Keith, which said, "This Hymn Book represents the work and labor of our Dear Mother M.L. Tate." Bishop Keith then proceeded to address the claim that Mother Tate "composed" the hymns in the volume and that these were in fact the pieces sung by the members of the House of God Church from its inception: "Its contents were composed by Mother M.L. Tate, the founder of the herein named church. They were first written up in ballard [ballad] form and sung that way for years in the church. Finally, she requested that those ballards be rewritten in book form and be used in the church. She further requested that those songs be written with music when convenient and finance can be provided by the church for the work to be accomplished."

Although no authors were attributed for the 254 hymns of the volume, Mother Tate by no means "composed" all or even most of them. That Bishop Keith perhaps meant that Mother Tate "composed" the hymnbook and not each and every hymn therein was suggested when she later omitted the claim and simply wrote that her predecessor "compiled" the volume. Furthermore, Bishop Keith remarked that "the composer of this song book always confessed that the author was God."

Following this preface was a photograph of Bishop Keith, beneath which she told the story of the hymnbook's fruition:

> I, M.F.L. Keith, rewrote this song book in Bishop Tate's lifetime. I, M.F.L. Keith, was the general secretary of the entire church during Mother Tate's lifetime. I rewrote this book by her orders, but due to lack of finances she was not able to have the book printed for the church. She

commanded me to have this book printed for the church if I lived the longest in life. I promised her I would do so if I could.

The Lord blessed me to come in possession of $350.00 last November, although it happened by meeting with an accident for which I am very regretful, because it has caused me much pain. I may suffer from the effects of it as long as I live. I am determined to use the money to the glory of God. I have rewritten the book and am now editing it.

At the close of this testament, Bishop Keith confessed that the hymnbook is not all that Mother Tate would have had it to be: "I am very sorry that I am unable to print all the songs that Mother Tate composed and compiled in this publication; due to a shortage of finance is the hindrance. But I hope that the church will be able to edit its full edition some day." The contents of this hymnbook therefore are but a representation of the hymns that this Holiness denomination used to sing and which, as responses to their suffering, helped sustain the denomination beyond its first generation.

The major part of Bishop Keith's foreword consists of information regarding her career in the House of God Church. The brief bit that she recalls about herself is valuable, since it is the only available information on the extremely clandestine and separatist church she helped build:

I, M.F.L. Keith, was appointed to the Bishopric, 1921, ordained as Bishop, 1923, by Bishops M.L. Tate, F.E. Lewis, and the General Assembly. I served the church at large, as general secretary, and state Bishop of the diocese over which I was appointed by the guidance of the Holy Ghost through the Chief Apostle, M.L. Tate, for ten years.

After the death of Mother Tate, I, M.F.L. Keith, was and am, anointed with the powers of God to lead the church on with God and Jesus in the Holy Ghost, and in the doctrine of Jesus in true holiness until I am called from labor to reward. I was also ordained in 1931 by the General Assembly and placed in office as Chief Overseer, that is why I am printing this book; I am in authority to do so. I pray God's blessing upon every one that uses this book. The Lord has given me many songs which I hope to bring out some day in music form.

Within this autobiographical segment, Keith also comments on her building (both spiritual and material) career as Chief Overseer. "The Lord saved many souls through me," she asserted. "I have also bought church lots and built several church houses while serving in my capacity as a Bishop." Among the "church houses" built under Bishop Keith's administration was the magnificent brick edifice erected in Nashville in 1948. Now vacant, it still stands in a black neighborhood adjacent to Fisk University. The cornerstone of the old church reads: "Founded by Bishop Mary Madgelena Tate, 1903. Bishop Mary F.L. Keith is one of the Successors to the Founder, Ordained and Appointed to Office, June 1931." Adjacent to the church is a set of buildings or dormitories, the cornerstone of which reads: "Saint's Home for Girls, founded 1943 by Bishop Mary F.L. Keith, Erected Here 1952." Keith was in fact such an entrepreneur that, probably after her death, the name "Keith Dominion" was made an addendum to the already lengthy denominational name: The House of God, Which Is the Church of the Living God, The Pillar and Ground of the Truth, Without Controversy, Inc., Keith Dominion. The abbreviated name of the church is the House of God Church, Keith Dominion.

Also to be recognized among Bishop Keith's accomplishments is the editing and publishing of *Spiritual Songs and Hymns.* As suggested earlier, her statement that the contents of the hymnbook were "composed" by Mother Tate might not have been intended as a claim that she actually wrote each and every hymn. Indeed, many of the gospel hymns were longtime favorites by known composers—"Nearer My God to Thee" (Sarah F. Adams), "Blessed Assurance" (Fanny J. Crosby), "He Leadeth Me" (Joseph H. Gilmore), "Leaning On Jesus" (Elisha A. Hoffman), "Since Jesus Came Into My Heart" (Rufus H. McDaniel), "His Eye Is On the Sparrow" (Civilla D. Martin), "In the Garden" (C. Austin Miles), "Lift Him Up" (Johnson Oatman, Jr.), and "What a Friend We Have in Jesus" (Joseph M. Scriven). Among the favorite gospel hymns by black composers were "Deeper, Deeper" and "I Will Hide and Abide" (Charles Price Jones); "We'll Understand It Better By and By," "Stand By Me," and "Nothing Between" (Charles Albert Tindley); "He'll Understand and Say 'Well Done'" (Lucie E. Campbell); and "He Knows How Much We Can Bear" (Roberta Martin). Also in the collection were several spirituals: "I Got a Hiding Place," "When the Saints Go Marching In," "Were You There," and "We Will Rise and Shine." The last was actually composed of two spirituals—the verses of "We Are Climbing Jacob's Ladder" and the refrain of "Rise and Shine Give God the Glory":

> We are climbing Jacob's ladder, ladder, (3×)
> Soldiers of the cross.

Chorus:
We will rise and shine, and give God the glory, glory,
Rise and shine and give God the glory, glory,
Rise and shine and give God the glory, glory,
Soldiers of the cross.

Each day brings me one round higher, higher, (3×)
Soldiers of the cross.

Jesus cleanseth all who trust Him, trust Him, (3×)
Soldiers of the cross.

Don't you wish you had this blessing, blessing, (3×)
Soldiers of the cross.

Jesus died that you might have it, have it, (3×)
Soldiers of the cross.

Whereas most spirituals explicitly or implicitly make reference to the desire of the enslaved for freedom in the present world, not one of the spirituals in this volume emphasizes such an aim. Moreover, it is likely that, whatever spirituals the House of God "saints" might have sung over the years, such references had been reinterpreted to refer to spiritual liberation (from sin) upon the Second Coming of the Lord. During the first half of the twentieth century, the Holiness churches and their Pentecostal successors indeed preserved the musical legacy of the enslaved Africans in North America, while the black Methodists and Baptists rejected it, but the Holiness and Pentecostals also led the way in reinterpreting these songs of longing for this-worldly liberation as having otherworldly meaning. Even the traditional gospel hymn, "Jesus, I'll Never Forget," became a favorite among them because it followed the New Testament lead in construing the biblical exodus as a spiritual event (liberation from sin) rather than as a physical event (freedom from human forms of bondage):

Jesus, I'll never forget when way down in Egypt's land,
How you brought me out with a mighty outstretched hand,
Broke the bonds of sin and set me free,
Gave me joy and peace and victory.

Chorus:
Jesus I'll never forget what you've done for me,
Jesus I'll never forget how you set me free,
Jesus I'll never forget how you brought me out,
Jesus I'll never forget, no never.

In a quantitative analysis of the theological themes in the hymnody of this volume, Hugh J. Roberts found that its entire hymnic corpus comprised this very sort of polarity toward the other world:

> The major theological themes in the hymn book are salvation (soteriology), found in 125 pieces, and the last days (eschatology), found in 112 pieces. In general the 60 untitled hymns (by the classic evangelicals) are more eschatological than soteriological (30:22), while the reverse is true for the titled pieces (82:103). The most frequent soteriological motifs are personal testimony regarding one's salvation and consequential pledges for service (together a total of 52 instances). Another frequent soteriological strain is that of challenge to sinners to turn to Christ and accept salvation (35 instances). Appearing less frequently are such keynotes as atonement (20 instances), and petitions for salvation (7 instances).
>
> The most frequent eschatological reference is to heaven (44 instances), also referred to as "the promised land," "glory land," "the golden city," "the golden strand just beyond the river," "a home where no dark clouds can rise," and "that perfect day." A closely related eschatological theme is the desire to see the Lord face to face (13 instances). The subject of death and resurrection occurs in 21 pieces, realized eschatology (the presence of God's kingdom in the present life) in 15 pieces, and the Parousia (return of Christ) in four pieces.[7]

Typical of gospel hymnody, the pieces in *Spiritual Songs and Hymns*, as Roberts' figures show, emphasize the spiritual world and the afterlife, as exemplified in such familiar songs of this collection as "Golden Crown" and "I'll Fly Away" (Albert E. Brumley). The first verse and chorus of the former reads:

> Watch ye therefore, you know not the day,
> When the Lord shall call your soul away;
> If you labor, striving for the right,
> You shall wear a golden crown.
>
> Chorus:
> I shall wear the crown
> When the trumpet sounds
> I shall wear the crown,
> I shall wear the golden crown.

Similarly, the first verse and chorus to "I'll Fly Away" reads:

> Some glad morning when this life is o'er
> I'll (fly away) fly away (fly away).
> To that home on God's celestial shore,
> I'll (fly away) fly away (fly away).
>
> Chorus:

I'll . . . fly away, Oh, glory, fly away;
I'll . . . fly away, fly away in the morning,
O when I die, hallelujah, by and by,
I'll (fly away) fly away (fly away).

Although most of the hymns in this collection have a strong leaning toward the heavenly realm, many of the gospel hymns make references to everyday experiences (albeit in order to clarify their spiritual teachings). In "Death Is a Police," for instance, the metaphors might be interpreted in part as having some relation to the problems blacks faced with the legal system in the South: while "Death is a police going through the land,/Serving notice on every woman and man," the belief is that "Jesus is a lawyer, He never lost a case." Another example is "I Don't Know What I'd Do without the Lord," which typifies how the "saints" give God the glory for bringing about benefits in this present life:

When the banks all had their holidays
And the factories all closed down
And the poor were in mourning
Almost the whole world around,
He said go down to the welfare,
I have plenty down there to spare.

An additional feature of the hymns in this collection is that many apparently were notated according to the way the "saints" of Mother Tate's church sang them over the years. The version of C.A. Tindley's famous "We'll Understand It Better By and By," for example, probably is evidence not of Mother Tate's carelessness in transcribing, but of how she and her church members had learned these songs through the oral tradition. A comparison of the first verse of the original Tindley hymn with the version found in *Spiritual Songs and Hymns* shows several textual differences. The original reads:

We are often tossed and driv'n on the restless sea of time,
Somber skies and howling tempests oft succeed a bright
    sunshine,
In that land of perfect day, when the mists have rolled away,
We will understand it better by and by.

Here is Mother Tate's version (with textual modifications noted in italics):

> *Here we're* often tossed and driven on *this* restless sea of time,
> *Rolling clouds* and howling tempests oft succeed a bright
>   sunshine,
> In that land of perfect day, when the *mist is* rolled away,
> We will understand it better by and by.

Similarly, in Mother Tate's transcription of the chorus to the traditional gospel hymn "A Closer Walk with Thee," the original phrase "is my plea" has been replaced by the colloquialism "if you please":

> Just a closer walk with Thee,
> Grant it, Jesus, *if you please;*
> Daily walking close to Thee,
> Let it be, my Lord, let it be.

Midway through *Spiritual Songs and Hymns* is a group of sixty untitled pieces with the old-fashioned meter indications—S.M. (short meter), C.M. (common meter), L.M. (long meter), and so forth. This might be the section Bishop Keith added (as she noted in the preface) to "expand" the collection. Most of these hymns are the works of such classic British writers as Watts ("Alas! And Did My Savior Bleed," "Am I a Soldier of the Cross," "O God, Our Help in Ages Past"), Wesley ("A Charge to Keep I Have," "Father, I Stretch My Hand to Thee," "Oh, For a Thousand Tongues to Sing"), Horatius Bonar ("I Heard the Voice of Jesus Say"), William Cowper ("O For a Closer Walk with Thee," "There Is a Fountain Filled with Blood"), Philip Doddridge ("Grace! 'Tis a Charming Sound"), John Fawcett ("Blest Be the Tie that Binds"), John Newton ("Amazing Grace"), Samuel Stennett ("On Jordan's Stormy Banks I Stand"), and Samuel J. Stone ("The Church's One Foundation"). These and many other "standard" hymns of this section were pieces long adopted and adapted by the black church.

While these "old standards" of British hymnists have long carried a healing and encouraging word to Holiness believers, it is the gospel hymns of the late nineteenth and early twentieth centuries and the black gospel songs of the golden age of gospel (1930–69) that especially have characterized the music of the black Sanctified Church. Gospel music in the Sanctified Church, it has been said, is far more sacred than in the other mainline Protestant churches.[8] The black Sanctified or Holiness churches differ from the Protestant churches, explains Joseph Washington, in the seriousness with which they practice their religious beliefs.[9]

The seriousness and sincerity of Sanctified religion is reflected in the puritanical mores observed by Holiness folk and by the doctrinal themes lyricized in their hymns. Prayer, faithful perseverance, and sanctification (holiness) are among the theological tenets Hugh Roberts observed in the selections of *Spiritual Songs and Hymns:*

> There are 26 pieces that either focus on prayer or are in themselves prayers for divine sustenance. While there are only three references to the holy trinity, there are 13 pieces (all titled) in which . . . reference is made to the Spirit (also referred to as Holy Ghost and Holy Spirit), and in three of those thirteen pieces reference is made to speaking in tongues. And while the aspects of sanctification and holiness are specifically referred to in only four pieces each, these important doctrines are intimated in a substantial number of the pieces.[10]

One hymn that exemplifies the extent to which Holiness mores were thematized in song is "Stop Now! It's Praying Time." The purpose of this piece is to warn the "sinner man" about the spiritual liabilities of dancing and "pooling dice," and to exhort the "saved and sanctified" to make sure they are living "the life" (of holiness). The song reminds those who were converted long ago of the necessity of appropriating the Holy Ghost, of which, the last verse reads, the gifts of tongues and divine healing were signs:

> Now these are the signs of the Holy Ghost,
> Speaking in tongues ain't no idle boast,
> Laying on hand the devil come out,
> That's what the children are shouting about.

Supporting this sung affirmation was the church decree that says, "We believe and do firmly preach that the Bible evidence of receiving the baptism of the Holy Ghost and fire is speaking with tongues as men of God giveth utterance as on the day of Pentecost."[11]

The very doctrinal and theological beliefs thematized in the old gospel songs that continue to be sung by the "saints" to this day are affirmed by the members of the House of God Church in various historical and creedal statements: "We believe our founder and First Chief Overseer found the church in 1903 and that our Church Decree is based on the Bible, ordained of God and inspired by the Holy Ghost."[12] One of these church decrees based on the Bible is: "Harken to my instructions, you forever abide in the doctrine that were taught you by the founder and first Chief Overseer of this church, in person Bishop M.L. Tate."[13] Another dictum, always appearing above the picture of Bishop Keith in the printed programs of the church's annual General Assembly, is: "Stay in the Faith and Doctrine" (Hebrews 6:1). All of these beliefs and affirmations were captured in one of the hymns in *Spiritual Songs and Hymns*, "The Church of the Living God," which may have been the anthem of the church (perhaps "composed" by Mother Tate or Bishop Keith):

> Built on the Rock, without spot or wrinkle,
> In the Church of the Living God;
> Born of the Spirit, filled with His glory,
> 'Tis the way the Apostles trod.

> Built on the Rock, on the Solid Rock,
> Is the Church of the Living God,
> The gates of hell can never prevail,
> For 'tis built on the Solid Rock.

> Built on the Rock, Rock revealed to Peter,
> It will stand every raging storm;
> Jesus the head, we the living body,
> We are safe from all earthly harm.

> Built on the rock, and 'twill stand forever;
> It is God's earthly government;
> To shine on earth, and draw saints together,
> Holy Spirit to earth was sent.

> Built on the Rock, and in the One Body,
> 'Tis the Bride of the Lamb once slain;
> The Church of God, the pure, spotless Virgin,
> She will forever with Him reign.

Another identifying peculiarity of Holiness faith is its biblicism. Even Bishop Keith's preface to *Spiritual Songs and Hymns* reflects the Holiness belief in the inerrancy of the Bible: "It is hoped that these song books will prove of interest and help both to those who believe in the Divine origin of the Bible and to those who do not." Moreover, a substantial number of the hymns in the collection actually incorporate scriptural references in a fashion that is typical of Holiness preaching and teaching. The unusual nature of this practice in hymnody led Hugh Roberts to suspect that these might be among the pieces "composed" by Mother Tate.[14] It is also possible that some of these scripture-citing hymns might be the work of Bishop Keith, for one of the closing statements in her autobiographical foreword affirms that the Lord had given her many songs that she hoped someday to bring out in music form.

Whether composed by Mother Tate or Bishop Keith, or by neither of these female church leaders, these scripture-citing hymns are worth examining in terms of the manner in which they typify the catechetical and homiletical style of the Holiness clergy and laity. One of these eccentric pieces was given a title nearly as long as the name of the church, "You Had Better Not Work on Sunday (The Seventh Day, Which is the Sabbath Day)":

> Now listen unto me and understand what I say!
> God is the very Man who instituted the Sabbath Day.
> Read Genesis 2 and 2. Now you know God's word is true, yes.
> It's written in the law you see, and it's not too old for me,
> It's just like not drinking wine. Acts 13 and 27, you will find,
> Now you had better not work on Sunday, it's a sin and a shame.
>
> Chorus:
> You must not work on Sunday, it's a shame, it's a shame;
> You should not work on Sunday, it's a shame, it's a shame;
> I don't have to work on Sunday, it's a shame, it's a shame.
>
> Read Exodus 20th Chapter, beginning at the third verse,
> Surely if you work on Sunday it's the Sabbath, you will surely
>   be cursed.
> Read Hebrews 4 and 4, if you don't want to read no more,
> Read Acts chapter 16 and verse 13, tells how and where the
>   Saints convened to meet on the Sabbath day
> To teach and hear what the word of God did say;
> And they did not work on Sunday, it's a sin and a shame.
>
> I am working in the vineyard where I am sure to get my pay,
> This is the only kind of work for me to do on the Sabbath day.
> I work the work of Him that sent me, and let the people hear
>   the words of God,
> God's yoke is easy and His burden is light, but the way of the
>   transgressor is hard.
> So you had better stop your work on Sunday, it's a sin and a
>   shame.

The spirit tells us in Titus, chapter 3, and one.
To be subject to principalities and powers, so let God's will be
    done.
And be subject to magistrates, to be ready to every good work.
They all OK's Sunday for Sabbath. See Acts 13 and 14 verse,
I regret that I did not know the Sabbath all the way from my
    birth,
Then I never would have worked on Sunday, it's a sin and a
    shame.

Monday, Tuesday, and Wednesday are half the working days we
    see,
So Thursday, Friday and Saturday, these make the other three;
And Sunday is the seventh day, it shall ever be Sabbath to me.
Read Exodus the Twentieth verse of chapter 23,
And you better not work on Sunday, it's a sin and a shame.

Several hymns in the collection illustrate what outsiders might view as contradictory to the biblical and puritanical nature of the Sanctified Church—a kinship with what the sanctified called "the devil's music," the blues. These two longtime warring factions of the black southern community—the Sanctified Church and partisans of the blues—were evolving simultaneously during the first half of the twentieth century. In fact, the advocates of Holiness religion came out of the Protestant denominations for reasons similar to those the blues people had for coming out of the Sanctified Church and its Baptist and Methodist precursors: dissatisfaction with (1) the self-righteousness and hypocrisy of the churched and (2) the inability of the church to respond sufficiently to the repressive conditions afflicting the black oppressed in this land. The response of some black Christians was to travel spiritually toward a more intense Christian faith—Christian sanctification as mediated through the Holiness church—from which locale they sat in judgment on mainline Protestantism. The counter-response of the blues people was to move toward the periphery of doctrinal Christianity, from which locale they sat in judgment on the entire church, particularly its so-called sanctified "saints."

The piece in the hymnbook titled "When I Take My Vacation in Heaven" included the very sort of claims to which blues people took exception: "I will spend my vacation with Jesus/In the place He went on to prepare." Former blues singer Rev. Rubin Lacy felt not only that blues songs and church songs were similar, but moreover that the blues were truthful, while church songs were often untruthful. With reference to this hymn, he admonished the congregation he pastored:

> Sometimes I preach now and I get up and tell the people now that . . . I used to be a famous blues singer and I told more truth in my blues than the average person tells in his church songs. . . . The blues is just more truer than a whole lot of the church songs that people sing. Sometimes I think the average person sings a church song just for the tune, not for the words. . . . But the blues is sung not for the tune. It's sung for the words mostly. . . . Now you get out here to sing a church song about "When I take my vacation in Heaven." That couldn't be the truth. That's a lie in the church, because a vacation means to go and come. You don't take a vacation in heaven. But now if you're playing the blues, you say "I never missed my water 'til my well went dry." That's the truth. . . . That's the difference in a church song and the blues.[15]

One of the gospel hymns in *Spiritual Songs and Hymns* was particularly reminiscent of numerous verses of blues lyrics that criticized the ministers and members of the church for their intemperance and arrogance. "Do You Call That Religion?" made just such a commentary:

> Some men are out a-preaching
> Just for a preacher's name,
> Their doctrine and their teaching
> Is scand'lous and a shame.
>
> Chorus:
> Do you call that religion? O, no. (3×)
> It's scand'lous and a shame.
>
> Some deacons in the churches
> Are living with two wives.
> When you tell them about true virtue
> You see their temper rise.
>
> Some deacons in the churches
> Are sitting in the deacon's chair,
> They drink their beer and whiskey
> And say they don't care.
>
> Some members in the churches
> Love to dress and put on airs:
> They are getting full of evil
> They won't bow their knees in prayer.
>
> If you can't dress up with them
> And wear the finest clothes,

They will not associate with you
Nor ask you to their doors.

Some members in the churches
Love to talk and grin,
And when you start the services
Won't open their mouths and sing.

Since you have been converted,
Why don't you stop your lies.
Stop drinking your beer and whiskey
And be more civilized.

Some preachers will come in your home
You may ask him to rest his hat,
Then he will begin to laugh and grin,
Say, Sister, where is your husband at?

Some members talk so charming,
Saying I am growing weak, you know;
They say I am doing no harm
But tattling from door to door.

Some men, while up a-preaching,
Their voices sound so sweet,
But the reason they don't like holiness,
They want to court every sister they meet.

Though blues-like, this "hymn" obviously was written from the purview of the Holiness church, and seemingly by a woman. However, there are segments of it that easily could have originated in the blues singer's caustic criticisms of the church. Compare its eighth verse above with a verse of blues found in Will Shade's "I Can Beat You Plenty":

Now the preacher will come to your house; your wife will ask
    him to rest his hat
Next thing he want to know, lady where is your husband at.

Many blues singers recognized this very kind of kinship between church songs (gospel songs and spirituals) and the blues. "Blues is so close to religious music that you can play a blues in the church now and they think's one of them good old swingin' hymns," commented bluesman Lowell Fulson. "All you have to do is just keep out 'baby,' and other sweet stuff you put in there."[16] Blueswoman Flora Molton similarly recalled a woman bishop of the Holiness Church who regularly gave blues songs religious words. "It's Tight Like That," said Molton, became "He

Was Done Like That."[17] The early gospel songs by Thomas A. Dorsey and Robert Wilkins, too, were little more than religious lyrics set to blues music. As Joseph Washington explains, "Black Holiness people were of the street and the people they engaged were of the street. It was natural for them to bring this music of the street into the church and make a 'joyful noise unto the Lord.' "[18]

"Do You Call that Religion?" was not the only piece in *Spiritual Songs and Hymns* that criticized those who had an aversion to holiness. A similar gospel song was "No Grumbler There," by C.P. Jones, the founding bishop of the Church of Christ (Holiness), USA. The first and last verses of his gospel hymn read:

> In every town and city, some people may be found,
> Who spend their time in grumbling at everything around,
> Especially of holiness, some curious things they say,
> But if we're true to Jesus, we're sure to win the day.
>
> . . .
>
> We know that they'd never grumble, if they could understand
> The precious truth of holiness, the theme of Beulah land,
> But some for lack of knowledge will turn from us away,
> And still keep up their grumbling while here on earth they stay.

That the blues had many musical and thematic features in common with black church hymnody is not surprising given the religious nature of the blues. A true peculiarity of *Spiritual Songs and Hymns*, however, is the considerable number of hymns about "mother," pieces that help identify the compilation as clearly the work of women presiding over a matriarchy. To the exclusion of the old greybeard of mainline Protestantism, "Faith of Our Fathers," were "Will My Mother Know Me There," "If I Could Hear My Mother Pray Again," "You Know Your Mother Always Cares," "I Hear My Mother Call My Name," "Please Shake My Mother's Hand," and "Meeting Mother in the Skies." "If we can say only one thing about women in the Sanctified Church," sociologist Cheryl Gilkes believes, "we should be able to say that they are prophets in this tradition."[19]

Whether these six pieces about "mother" were "composed" by Mother Tate or Bishop Keith, or simply selected by one of these two matriarchs, the mere fact that the familial was viewed positively rather than negatively here set these hymns apart from the anticulturalism of Holiness belief and from gospel music in the aggregate. Most gospel hymns which refer to the family exhort that human relationships are carnal and not to be trusted. Indeed, they teach that mothers, fathers, brothers, and sisters will forsake their own kindred, and that Jesus is the only one to be trusted. However, in these six special hymns, "mother" is portrayed as a saint, even while, as "Please Shake My Mother's Hand" illustrates, the other family members are depicted as sinners:

> My brother turned his back on Jesus,
> Sister sinful as can be;
> My father did not seem to want me,
> Please shake my mother's hand for me.

The hymn that best portrays mother as a sort of religious madonna was "You Know Your Mother Always Cares." Perhaps its words of compassion were in reference to Mother Tate's love for her parishioners, her "children":

> Your mother is your friend and she'll be to the end
> And if her hope and dreams will just come true.
> No bitterness or strife will even touch your life,
> You know your mother always cares for you.
>
> You know her heart beats thru shade and sunshine too
> There's not a day she does not think of you.
> She grieves when you are sad, rejoices when you are glad.
> You know your mother always cares for you.
>
> When trouble in the home and things going wrong,
> Poor mother sits and wonders what to do.
> And with a mother's care she kneels in prayer,
> You know your mother always cares for you.

During Mother Tate's lifetime, these hymns may have been sung in her honor, or after her lifetime in her memory. In either case, it is likely that Mother's Day was a special occasion for the great "watchwoman on the wall,"[20] and that selected hymns were sung in obeisance to her church leadership.

These hymns about "mother," in short, exemplify the manner in which the House of God Church affirmed womanhood and the religious freedom of women. No other hymnal of any Protestant denomination, nor of any patriarchal Holiness or Pentecostal denomination, has ever affirmed womanhood in this way. This is true of the numerous hymnals produced by the Church of Christ (Holiness), USA, founded by C.P. Jones; the Church of God in Christ, founded by C.H. Mason; and the Fire Baptized Holiness Church, founded by W.E. Fuller, Sr. The fact that churches founded and governed by men neglected to affirm womanhood and grant complete religious freedom to women was perhaps the reason Mary L. Tate left William Christian's Church of the Living God (if in fact she ever was part of his Christian Workers for Fellowship). However, the foundation of womanist affirmation that Mother Tate and Bishop Keith built during the first fifty-eight years of their denomination's life was partly (albeit unintentionally) overturned when, in 1962, Bishop James W. Jenkins succeeded the late Bishop Keith and became the third chief overseer of the House of God Church.

Currently Bishop Jenkins presides over approximately seventeen bishops of the House of God Church, about half of whom are women. Although he is the senior prelate in a denomination still numerically dominated by women, Bishop Jenkins is a highly venerated man. Probably akin to the testimonies given during the tenures of Bishops Tate and Keith, testimonies currently commence by "giving honor" to the chief overseer. Just as hymns of praise were probably sung to honor Bishops Tate and Keith, so are songs sung on occasion in recognition of Bishop Jenkins. One such hymn (printed in the program bulletin of the 1988 Annual General Assembly) was sung to the tune of "America":

> God bless our Overseer,
> One we all love.
> Stand beside Him,
> As he guides us thru
> The House of God Church of the Living God.
> In Alabama, in New Jersey,
> Down in Nashville, Tennessee.
> God bless our Overseer,
> Thru life and eternity.

More is revealed about the reigning patriarch of the House of God Church in the prefatory matter of the new *Spiritual Songs and Hymns*, which was compiled under his administration. The biographical statement beneath Jenkins' photograph (which follows a picture of Bishops Tate and Keith) is very similar to that beneath Keith's photograph in the first volume. It hardly provides substantive empirical data, but, compared with the manner in which the "saints" of the church customarily are historicized with religious platitudes, the minutia here is informative:

> Bishop James W. Jenkins received the Baptism of the Holy Ghost and began preaching at the age of twelve. He began pastoring at age 17, and served the Church at large as secretary of Keith Dominion for many years. He was appointed to the Bishopric by the late Dr. M.F.L. Keith in 1934. In September 1962 he was elected third Chief Overseer of Keith Dominion.
>
> Churches have been built and bought under his administration. Souls have been saved through his teachings, and he has labored in every possible way to contribute to the progress of God's House.

The principal church "house" erected under Bishop Jenkins' administration is the large modern brick facility that serves as the denominational headquarters and the site of the annual General Assembly. Completed in 1981, the building is located a few blocks from the old church headquarters built by Bishop Keith in 1948.

In terms of the direction the church is taking under Bishop Jenkins' leadership, it is significant both that the position of chief overseer is, for the first time, held by a man and by a college-educated individual. Thus both the longtime matriarchy and some of the anti-intellectual currents long embedded in the Holiness tradition are being undermined. Both of these trends are clearly reflected in the new *Spiritual Songs and Hymns.*

The new hymnal, rather than being a means by which Bishop Jenkins could intentionally assert his masculinity and his education, supposedly was published to fulfill the mandate left to Bishop Keith by Mother Tate. "She further requested"—Keith's exact words in her preface—"that those songs be written with music when convenient and finance can be provided by the church for the work to be accomplished." Bishop Jenkins claims in the preface to the new *Spiritual Songs and Hymns* that this mandate of Mother Tate now has been fulfilled:

> The desire to publish a hymnal for the House of God Which is the Church of the Living God the Pillar and Ground of the Truth was expressed by the Late Mother M.L. Tate, Founder and First Chief Overseer. The first hymnal was compiled by the Late Dr. M.F.L. Keith,

second Chief Overseer. Due to financial limitations the original hymnal did not fulfill all of the founders hopes for the best in hymnology.

The present Chief Overseer, Dr. J.W. Jenkins, obtained permission and suggestions from the son of Dr. Keith, Professor R.D. Lewis to produce a hymnal which would consummate the initial desires of the founder. To this end, Dr. Jenkins appointed a committee who accepted the sacred task of compiling this hymnal.

Perhaps it would be of some consolation to Mother Tate that most of the 164 hymns in the new *Spiritual Songs and Hymns* are in fact set to music. However, the new volume is comprised of an almost entirely different corpus and character of song. All of the hymns Mother Tate or Bishop Keith might have "composed" are omitted. Indeed, the new hymnal has been so standardized that it could easily have been one of the many songbooks published by the black Baptists during the fifties or sixties. There are no more hymns about "mother," which helped identify the church as matriarchal; no more scripture-citing hymns in the manner reminiscent of Holiness preaching and teaching, which helped identify the church as steeped in biblicism; and no more hymns specifically highlighting Holiness doctrine, which helped identify the church as Sanctified. Although it would be difficult to go so far as to conclude that this hymnal is no longer authentically Holiness, it is clear that it is no longer Mother Tate's "composition," as Bishop Keith claimed the first volume, under her editing, was.

Although the new hymnal, like the old hymnbook, contains a few spirituals and a substantial number of gospel hymns (many carried over from the first volume and now set to music as Mother Tate had willed), the peculiar Holiness character of the original hymnbook has been lost. Replacing the distinctive hymns of the initial hymnbook (some of which may have been composed by Bishops Tate and Keith) are more recent gospel songs by Lizzie M. Cheatham and Rev. Bobby Jean Moore. A major shift from the original hymnbook is the unusually large number of hymns by the old-line British writers. Certainly it has long been customary to include choice pieces by Watts and Wesley and a select few by their compatriots, but not in such quantity as here. Represented are John Bowring, Philip Doddridge, Timothy Dwight, Frederick Faber, John Fawcett, Francis

Havergal, John Keble, Henry F. Lyte, Samuel Stennett, and Augustus M. Toplady, to name only a few. Too, not far removed from these British "standard" hymns are the equally Anglo-Saxon classics of the American literati Harriet Beecher Stowe and John Greenleaf Whittier. Further, it is not so much the thirteen Christmas carols as it is the thirteen hymns by Wesley alone that begin to give the volume the flavor of a mainline Baptist or Methodist hymnal.

Further evidence of the evolving sophistication and seasoning of the House of God Church is the overarching milieu of the new *Spiritual Songs and Hymns*. Significantly, each of its three sections opens with a rather philosophical, nonbiblical statement that hardly reflects the common religious tongue of the Holiness folk masses. The first section on "Christian Life" opens uncharacteristically with a bar of music from the "Kyrie Eleison" of an unidentified Catholic Mass, beneath which is a rather refined maxim: "Spiritual music is one of the fairest and most glorious gifts of God, to which Satan is a bitter enemy. Why? Simply because it washes away from the soul the dust of every-day life; it removes from the heart the weight of sorrow, and the fascination of evil thoughts." The quotation opening the second section on "Christian Hope" is a saying of that British reform poet of the Social Gospel, Harriet Martineau (whose inclusion here is an anomaly in that the Holiness movement arose partly in opposition to the secularism and intellectualism of the Social Gospel): "Ballads and popular songs are both the cause and effect of General morals; they are first formed, and then re-act. In both points of view they are an index to public morals." The third and last section commences with an unattributed aphorism that is also uncharacteristic of the folk truisms of the Sanctified church: "The best days of the church have always been its singing days. A well composed song will outlive all sermons in the memory." What these three prefatory epigrams help illustrate is that the second and third generations of a sectarian church begin to reintegrate some of the attributes of the denominations from which that church initially separated.

Looking at the rather cosmopolitan nature of the epigrams prefacing the three sections of the hymnal and at many of the hymnic selections therein, it is not surprising that all but one of the four persons on the committee that compiled the hymnal are

college graduates. Neither is it surprising that two of them—
Bishop Jenkins and committee chair Dovie Shuford—hold graduate degrees. Therefore, what is actually reflected in the increased sophistication and standardization of the new *Spiritual
Songs and Hymns*, as compared with the first volume's vernacular
quality, is the higher educational level and socioeconomic status
of its compilers, who in turn mirror the evolution of the church
toward middle-class Protestantism.

As the church considers reprinting the current hymnal, many
of the older "saints" are calling for a reissue of the original
hymnbook compiled by Mother Tate and edited by Bishop Keith.
It appears that, for many of the church members, the "best days
of the church" are the "singing days" captured in the original
volume—for instance, in Thomas A. Dorsey's hymn "Little
Church on the Hill." Perhaps Dorsey's old gospel song is reminiscent of the "old-time religion" that filled the little wooden
House of God church in Chattanooga when Mother Tate, and
later Bishop Keith, served as its pastor.

CHAPTER 8

The Church of God in Christ

> The sound of a mighty wind was in me and my soul
> cried . . . and soon I began to die. It seemed that I heard
> the groaning of Christ on the cross dying for me. . . .
> Then the sound broke out in me again. Then I felt
> something raising me out of my seat without any effort of
> my own. . . . Then I gave up for the Lord to have His
> way within me. So there came a wave of glory into me,
> and all of my being was filled with the glory of the
> Lord. . . . When I opened my mouth to say glory, a flame
> touched my tongue which ran down to me. My language
> changed and no word could I speak in my own tongue.
> Oh, I was filled with the glory of the Lord.
>
> —*Charles H. Mason,*
> *founder of the Church of God in Christ*[1]

Pentecostalism originated in April 1906 with the protracted Los Angeles revival at 312 Azusa Street, led by black Holiness preacher William J. Seymour. Charles H. Mason, also a Baptist preacher of Holiness persuasion, attended the Azusa Street revival for approximately five weeks, and in March 1907 he was baptized by the Holy Ghost, as shown by his speaking in other tongues (glossolalia). Converted to the belief that tongues alone is the initial evidence of Spirit baptism, Mason returned to Lexington, Mississippi, where he had been working with his partner, C.P. Jones, in the Holiness crusade and pastoring a Holiness church. Because Jones would not accept Mason's newly adopted belief that tongues is the sole initial evidence of Spirit baptism, the two longtime friends went their separate ways. Mason's wife, Elsie W. Mason, recalled that year when her husband's search for a fuller relationship with God resulted in a break in his relationship with Jones:

Elder C.P. Jones, Mason's dearest friend, offered further information and insight concerning the baptism of the Holy Ghost (over which doctrine they were later destined to part company). But as did Charles Mason, C.P. Jones contended that every saint should receive that spiritual baptism. This he believed would "complete" the believer-in-Christ by a "third work of grace" to empower him/her for effective service. However, Charles Mason and C.P. Jones were to finally dissolve their ministerial partnership and friendship because Jones did not agree that tongue-speaking was necessary and Mason felt that it was biblical and therefore necessary.[2]

In August 1907, Mason called a meeting of Pentecostal believers in his hometown, Memphis. At this meeting he was made the "chief apostle" and "general overseer" of what became the officially chartered Church of God in Christ (COGIC). During the ensuing months, Mason and his ministerial colleagues diligently built up their constituency. Writing back to the Azusa Street Mission from Lexington on 28 November 1907, Mason informed the Azusa "saints" of the success of his work in Mississippi:

Dear ones, it is sweet for me to think of you all and your kindness to me while I was with you. My soul is filled with the glory of the Lord. He is giving great victory wherever He sends us in His name, many being baptized with the Holy Ghost and speaking in tongues. Praise the Lord. The fight has been great. I was put out, because I believed that God did baptize me with the Holy Ghost among you all. Well, He did it and it just suits me. Glory in the Lord. Jesus is coming. Take the Bible way, it is right. The Lord is leading me out of all that men have fixed up for their glory. Be strong in Him.[3]

The Pentecostal movement took not only most of its members and its leaders from the Holiness churches, but also its hymnody—the gospel hymns, spirituals, and selected favorites of the Watts and Wesley tradition. About William Seymour's role in bringing spirituals into the worship experience at the Azusa Street revival, scholar Walter Hollenweger says: "Seymour affirmed his black heritage by introducing Negro spirituals and Negro music into his liturgy at a time when this music was considered inferior and unfit for Christian worship, for he had drunk from 'the "invisible institution" of black folk Christianity' with its themes of freedom, equality and community."[4] Among the gospel and "standard" hymns sung at the Azusa revival were familiar pieces that were actually rendered in tongues and subsequently interpreted in English: "Must Jesus Bear the Cross Alone," "Praise God from Whom All Blessings Flow," "Holy, Holy, Holy," "Jesus Is Tenderly Calling You Home," "Under the Blood," "Heavenly Sunlight," "Down Where the Living Waters Flow," "Beautiful Beckoning Hands," and "The Comforter Has Come."[5] Drawing themes from such favorites as these, Hollenweger characterized the hymns preferred by Pentecostals as being Christ-centered:

> Apart from the classical themes (the church year, revival hymns, hymns of the world to come, etc.) the most striking group consists of the numerous hymns which sing of Jesus as the friend of the soul. . . . These hymns (which are not sung in the Pentecostal movement alone) use the imagery and key words of popular songs, and apply them all to the one true friend who never leaves us, to the "lover of my soul" who "sought me in tenderness" and who "leads me in the dark." For a long time he "stood at my heart's door," but now the Pentecostal asks "Draw me nearer!" For he wants "to go deeper and deeper into the heart of Jesus."[6]

There is one type of song (manifested earlier among African peoples and other such religious groups as the Shakers and Mormons) that burgeoned anew at the Azusa Street revival—tongue-song (known among the primal Pentecostals as "singing in the spirit").[7] When the Second Pentecost (Pentecostalism) commenced at 216 Bonnie Brae Street in Los Angeles on 9 April 1906, a young black woman named Jennie Moore gave evidence of her Spirit baptism by "singing in the spirit." About a month later her written testimony appeared in *The Apostolic Faith*, the newspaper of the Azusa Street Mission: "I sang under the power of the Spirit in many languages, the interpretation both words and music I had never before heard, and in the home where the meeting was held, the Spirit led me to the piano, where I played and sang under inspiration, although I had not learned to play."[8] Hence, when the "latter rain" of the Spirit first fell upon those early Pentecostals, Spirit baptism was revealed by singing in tongues, making tongue-song one of the first and certainly one of the most theologically important forms of music manifested in primal Pentecostalism and (by divine succession) in Mason's newly founded Church of God in Christ (COGIC).

Although tongue-song perhaps occurred among some of the members of Mason's church, the early music of the COGIC was principally comprised of hymns inherited from the Holiness movement. From the point of the church's founding in 1907, it was a long three-quarters of a century before the COGIC departed from its sacred oral tradition and amassed these beloved hymns into a single printed source—*Yes, Lord!: Church of God in Christ Hymnal* (1982). Like its Holiness predecessors, the Pentecostal churches viewed musical expression spontaneously prompted by the Spirit as more authentic than the singing of songs from a hymnbook. Testimony after testimony published in *The Apostolic Faith* indicated that singing had to be prompted by the Spirit rather than by the flesh, and that formality, including the use of hymnals, was disparaged. "Many times we do not need these song books of earth," said one Azusite, "but the Lord simply touches us by His mighty Spirit."[9] Some early Pentecostals actually feared "grieving the Spirit" if they were to depend on such worldly props as a hymnbook: "No one dared to get up and sing a song or testify except under the anointing of the Spirit. They feared lest the Holy Ghost would cut them off in their song or testimony. We would wait upon God expecting Him to use whom He would. . . . No one dared to say, 'We will now have a song by Brother or Sister so and so,' and then as they would come to the front to sing, for the congregation to clap their hands and laud them for their singing."[10]

The earliest collection of hymnody produced prior to *Yes, Lord!* by a member of the COGIC was *The Jackson Bible Universal Selected Gospel Songs,* the work of Elder H.C. Jackson, probably published during the forties.[11] According to the caption beneath his picture on the inside cover, Elder Jackson was from Bishop Mason's hometown, Memphis, and had come to Mississippi to pastor two small churches, in New Albany and Aberdeen. While residing in New Albany, the caption reads, Jackson became the state evangelist of Mississippi Churches of God in Christ and the founding president and dean of a Bible school bearing his name, the Jackson Bible Universal, Inc.

The cover of the volume suggests that the songbook was published by Elder Jackson solely as a means of raising funds for his school (hence the volume was not really breaking with the Pentecostal oral tradition): "Will You Help The Bible School By Taking a Book. The Songs Are A Penny Each. 'A Donation Of 35c.'" This was persuasively followed by a reading from Second Corinthians 9:7, which included the familiar passage, "God loveth a cheerful giver." Whatever the reason for its publication, this little songbook of thirty-five hymns is a rare and valuable document. Commenting on its historical value in a critical study of the songbook, one of the elders of the COGIC, Garry Seabron, is enthusiastic:

> This obscure song book is an important historic document, particularly for the Church of God in Christ. It reveals much about the life and ministry of one of its workmen, Elder H.C. Jackson, whose diligence led him to found and preside over a Mississippi Bible school. The volume reflects COGIC doctrine and theology, which since the publication of this volume nearly a half century ago has remained relatively constant, and it documents many of the songs apparently favored by black Pentecostals in the deep South during the first four decades of the relatively nascent religious movement.[12]

Pursuant to his comment that the songbook reflects COGIC doctrine past and present, Seabron says, "Elder Jackson not only reflected his Pentecostal orientation by including the favorite gospel songs of the church and excluding the traditional Protestant hymns of Wesley and Watts, but also by highlighting such themes as divine healing, eschatology, the Holy Spirit, perseverance, dependence on Jesus, and perfection, clearly reflecting the theology and doctrine of the denomination."[13]

Most of the thirty-five songs in the volume do not acknowledge authorship. Among the few hymnists credited are Thomas A. Dorsey ("The Little Wooden Church on the Hill"), Kenneth Morris ("My Life Will Be Sweeter Some Day"), and J.H. Brewster ("I'm Leaning and Depending on the Lord"). Other popular gospel hymns not attributed, but recognizable, are "Stand By Me" and "Farther Along," by C.A. Tindley, and "Take My Hand Precious Lord," by Thomas A. Dorsey. Additional traditional pieces are "Just a Closer Walk with Thee," "Just a Little Talk with Jesus," "I'll Fly Away," and "I Know the Lord Will Make a Way, Yes He Will" ("As Sung by Myrtle Jackson, Radio Gospel Singer").

Also included in Jackson's songbook are three original hymns by Jackson himself. One of these understandably is devoted to the subject of divine healing, for the four written testimonies prefacing the volume claim that Jackson was a "God sent man" and a "God man," through whom the Lord healed all manner of diseases and afflictions among the multitudes. "The Elder has favors with God in prayer," reads the caption above his picture, "and is widely known in the United States by the Lord healing through him, and throughout the Church of God in Christ." One of the testimonies prefacing the volume boasts of the time Jackson healed the assistant church mother of his New Albany congregation. One evening when Elder Jackson was away from the church, she became very ill. By the time he returned (apparently for an evening service), the woman was "lying out" stiff, seemingly with no respiration or pulse. "He walked in and said, 'she will not die,' and rebuked us for being afraid, saying that we were of a little faith, and he took our hands off her, and began to slap her in the face and talk to her, but got no reply. Then he groaned in the Spirit and began to call on the Lord. And the woman that I said was dead got up, and began to rejoice in a dance, and is still healed."

With reference to one of Jackson's songs in the collection, Seabron comments that divine healing was then and remains a viable aspect of COGIC ministry:

> The idea of divine healing has always been an important component in the doctrine of Jackson's denomination. Even today the official manual states: "The Church of God in Christ believes in and does practice Divine Healing. It is taught by the Founder, Bishop C.H. Mason, who was known widely for his practices of Faith Healing." By incorporating the distinctly COGIC slogans—"The blood is prevailing," "Woman you are healed," and "Man you are healed"—Elder Jackson's song, "Jesus is Healing Today," further documents the character of a tradition going as far back as Bishop Mason himself.[14]

Seabron further suggests that Jackson himself might have sung his original "Jesus Is Healing Today" as he healed the afflicted who flocked to his revivals.[15] This is quite likely, for two of the unattributed pieces in the songbook have the footnote "As sung by Elder H.C. Jackson," implying that Jackson was indeed a singing evangelist. In the following chorus and verses to his "Jesus Is Healing Today," each couplet is repeated:

> Chorus:
> Oh, Jesus is healing, Jesus is healing,
> I feel the kingdom coming.
>
> Stretch out your hand,
> I feel the kingdom coming.

> The blood is prevailing,
> I feel the kingdom coming.
>
> Thy presence is mighty,
> I feel the kingdom coming.
>
> Own thine own, Lord,
> I feel the kingdom coming.
>
> God is anointing with the oil of gladness,
> I feel the kingdom coming.
>
> Woman, you are healed,
> I feel the kingdom coming.
>
> Man, you are healed,
> I feel the kingdom coming.

As Seabron examined *The Jackson Bible Universal Selected Gospel Songs* for its COGIC doctrines, he found that the most prominent theological theme in its hymnody was the "last things" (eschatology). Of thirteen hymns more or less thematizing eschatology, one was Jackson's own "The Crown of Life":

> Blessed is the man that endureth temptation;
> For when he is tried, he shall receive the Crown of life
> Although you may be burdened, although you may get tired,
> But just keep on traveling, for the way is right.
>
> Chorus:
> Lord, keep me in thy path for the Crown of Life,
> Lord, keep me in thy path for the Crown of Life.
> For thy way is love, and thy path is light,
> Lord, keep me in they path for the Crown of Life.
>
> Let no man say when he is tempted, I am tempted of God,
> For God cannot be tempted with evil, neither tempted he any
>   man:
> Lord, keep me in thy path till I reach that happy land,
> For without Him, there's no one can stand.
>
> If you don't mind your own sins will find you out,
> If you don't mind your own sins will find you out,
> Some may laugh when you shout, but let me tell you, you better
>   watch out;
> If you don't mind your own sins will find you out.

Another original song in the collection was written by Elder S.R. Chambers, probably a fellow churchman of Jackson. Elder Chambers apparently was a singing evangelist as well, for one of the other pieces in the collection has the footnote "As sung by

Elder S.R. Chambers." The original song by Chambers, "Me and the Devil Had a Tussle but I Won," reflects the denomination's doctrine of demons. "It can well be said that the Christian Church believes in demons, Satan, and devils," says the COGIC manual. "We believe in their power and purpose. We believe they can be subdued and conquered as in the commandment to the believer by Jesus. (St. Mark 16:17)."[16] That Satan can be conquered was the very message in Elder Chamber's hymn:

> O the devil he try to steal my joy (2×)
> Me and the devil could not agree
> I hates the devil and he hates me,
> Me and the devil we had a tussle but I won.
>
> Chorus:
> Me and the devil we had a tussle but I won. (2×)
> Me and the devil could not agree,
> I hate the devil and he hates me.
> Me and the devil we had a tussle but I won.
>
> Everytime I have a talk with Jesus the devil try to hinder me
>   (2×)
> Me and the devil could not agree,
> I hate the devil and he hates me.
> Me and the devil we had a tussle but I won.

It is feasible that these were only the initial two verses of a song that was extemporaneously extended at will. With such a repetitive format (easily learned by rote), it would have been characteristic of the oral tradition, within which evangelist Chambers functioned, for him to have simply "lined-out" new opening sentences for additional verses to be sung by his congregations.

Following *The Jackson Bible Universal Selected Gospel Songs*, the next collection of COGIC hymnody was the denomination's first official hymnal, *Yes, Lord!* (1982). Prior to this, however, the Fire Baptized Holiness Church (FBH), a black Pentecostal denomination founded in 1908 by the late Bishop W.E. Fuller, Sr.,[17] began the practice of publishing a small collection of hymns as part of their denominational discipline. The hymnbook, titled *Hymnal of the F.B.H. Church*,[18] is the second part of the nearly pocket-sized book. The majority of its seventy-nine unaccompanied hymns (containing meter indications) were the time-honored works by Watts and Wesley. Along with a few additional classics by William Cowper and Joseph Hart were such gospel hymn favorites as "Nearer My God to Thee" (Sarah F. Adams) and "What a Friend We Have in Jesus" (Joseph M. Scriven). While this collection of hymns appears to be but a small addendum to the FBH discipline, it is nonetheless a sufficiently genuine hymnbook to prevent us from making the potential error of identifying *Yes, Lord!* as the first hymnal published by a black Pentecostal denomination. *Yes, Lord!* is, of course, a far more important work for several reasons: As the product of the oldest, largest, and fastest-growing black Pentecostal de-nomination in the world, it is a much larger compilation of 525 hymns and consequently is more representative of the broad hymnic tradition of black Pentecostalism in general.

Yes, Lord!, the official hymnal of the COGIC, was published in 1982, the denomination's diamond jubilee year, by the church Publishing Board, located in Bishop Mason's hometown, Mem-phis.[19] The hymnal project was conceived of by Bishop Nor-man N. Quick and commissioned by the late senior prelate, Presiding Bishop J.O. Patterson. The publication of *Yes, Lord!*, two years in the making, constituted a large leap forward into modernity for the COGIC and a momentous milestone in the history of black church hymnody. As Eileen Southern enthusi-astically comments, "For scholars of black-church music, per-haps the biggest event of the 1980s was the publication, for the first time, of an official COGIC hymnal."[20] Even though the *Yes, Lord!* hymnal is rarely, if ever, found in the pews of COGIC churches, perhaps that day will come. In the meantime, its pub-lication demonstrates that the second and third generations of a sectarian and separatist church eventually come full circle, to reintegrate into society, and their church now begins to resemble the churches from which it originally separated. Whereas Pen-tecostals initially disparaged the use of hymnbooks, the increas-ingly mainline COGIC has published its first official hymnal, now nearly a decade old.

Many of the older "saints" of the church were (and probably remain) opposed to the modernism of publishing a hymnal, seeing this as a transgression against the spontaneity and au-thority of the Spirit. However, there were and are those in the COGIC who have long seen a need for the denomination to modernize. One musician affiliated for a while with the

COGIC, black sacred music scholar Donna Cox, suggests this very viewpoint with a tacit reference to the progressive pastor of the West Angeles Church of God in Christ, Bishop Charles E. Blake. Cox says,

> The black Pentecostal church is ever evolving with the needs of its members and . . . any ministry wishing to remain viable must shift with the times. Clearly the quality of life for many blacks has greatly improved over that of our recent Pentecostal predecessors who attended storefront churches during the first half of the twentieth century. Today we are generally better educated and more gainfully employed and consequently not confronted with the same existential plights.[21]

The *Yes, Lord!* hymnal is symbolic of, if not hard evidence of, the evolution of the COGIC from a separatist institution consisting largely of storefront churches housing the "least of them" into an increasingly integrationist institution comprised of numerous grand edifices housing a multiplying middle-class membership.

The content of the hymnal also points to a progressively integrationist denomination that is not at all restrictive in terms of hymnody, including all manner of works from the classic British standards to modern gospel music, without limitations as to the hymn writers' denominational affiliation. This broad selection of hymnody reflects the religious outlook of the entire denomination—from the hymnal's compiler, COGIC musician Iris Stevenson, to the clergy and laity of the church. Although Stevenson basically selected the hymns to include in *Yes, Lord!*, her decisions were shaped by her extensive involvement in the music ministry of the church as the assistant to Mattie Moss Clark, longtime international director of the COGIC Music Department. In addition, her selections were informed by the suggestions of a cross-section of COGIC music ministers and clergy who submitted for consideration favorite hymns sung by their local congregations and choirs. From the suggested pieces, Stevenson selected hymns that were theologically consistent with COGIC doctrine. Many of the longstanding favorites, necessarily included because of their popularity, were not doctrinally problematical. Apparently they had survived in the church over the years precisely because they did concur with COGIC belief, making *Yes, Lord!* a codification of the black Pentecostal worldview of the COGIC.

Stevenson did more than select and organize the 525 selections in *Yes Lord!*, however. She also contributed five original hymns to the volume, as well as twelve arrangements, fifteen transcriptions of oral tradition hymns, and three call-and-response accompaniments. Hymnal Task Force chairman Bishop Norman Quick gave this compliment to Stevenson in the hymnal's preface:

> Foremost among them [the dedicated and competent members of the Church of God in Christ] was Iris Stevenson who worked diligently to create a comprehensive body of selections that were musically sound and reflected accurately the richness of the Church's past, Her present and Her hopes for the future. That *Yes, Lord!* is uniquely representative of the Church of God in Christ is due to the artistic sensitivity and the deep spiritual commitment of this gifted and tireless servant of God and the church. We are all in her debt.

Because of the work of Stevenson, who sensitively gauged the musical mood and tradition of her people, the *Yes, Lord!* hymnal is unmistakably stamped "COGIC." Paradoxically, because the hymns are arranged in universal doctrinal categories, the hymnal is equally ecumenical. Though Pentecostalism is often viewed by mainline Protestants as a religion strikingly different from their own, the headings in the table of contents of *Yes, Lord!* disclose no theological inconsistency with what Protestants define as Christian orthodoxy: "Worship and Adoration" (hymns 1–69), "Comfort" (70–87), "Assurance" (88–128), "God's Grace, Mercy and Forgiveness" (129–142), "Refuge" (143–152), "Heaven and Everlasting Life" (153–184), "The Holy Spirit" (185–202), "Christ's Birth" (203–217), "Life and Ministry of Jesus Christ" (218–236), "Christ's Crucifixion" (237–260), "Christ's Resurrection" (261–269), "Second Coming of Jesus Christ" (270–274), "Commitment and Devotion" (275–350), "Aspiration" (351–372), "Peace" (373–380), "Guidance" (381–404), "Renewal and Revival" (405–418), "Testimony, Witness and Evangelism" (419–490), "Missions" (491–498), "Patriotic and World Peace" (499–506), "Calls and Responses" (507–521), and "Amens" (522–525).[22]

The foregoing are universal doctrinal categories. It is only after applying the Pentecostal perspective to the doctrine of the Holy Spirit that Pentecostalism and Protestantism disengage theologically. Actually, the section on "The Holy Spirit" does not contain any hymns that would not be found in black Protestant hymnals—for example, Watts' "Come, Holy Spirit, Heavenly Dove," Frank Bottome's "The Comforter Has Come" (the favorite hymn of the Azusa Street revival), and Doris Akers' "Sweet, Sweet Spirit." Moreover, Charlie D. Tillman's "Old Time Power," which poeticizes the first Pentecost (Acts 2:2–4), is, surprisingly, the only one of these eighteen hymns specifically mentioning the crucial Pentecostal doctrine of tongues. The second verse and the chorus read:

> Yes, this pow'r from heav'n descended,
> With the sound of rushing wind;
> Tongues of fire came down upon them,
> As the Lord said He would send.
>
> Chorus:
> O Lord, send the pow'r just now, (3×)
> And baptize ev'ry one.

Although these hymns are found in Protestant hymnals as well, distinguishing factors are the frequency in which such hymns as "The Comforter Has Come" are sung among the Pentecostals, and the meanings they carry. When Pentecostals sing this hymn, they are acknowledging that the appropriation of the gift of tongues, as in the day of Pentecost, requires that believers wait upon God to fulfill Christ's promise that the Comforter (i.e., the Holy Ghost) would be sent by God in the Lord's name (John 14:26). Because, for instance, that promise was fulfilled daily at the Azusa Street revival, as proven by spoken and sung tongues, the primal Pentecostals gathered there sang this hymn at every gathering.[23] "The Comforter Has Come" is therefore of such historic import to Pentecostals that, in contrast to Protestant hymnals, it was necessarily included in *Yes, Lord!*:

> O spread the tidings 'round, wherever man is found,
> Wherever human hearts and human woes abound;
> Let ev'ry Christian tongue proclaim the joyful sound:
> The Comforter has come!
>
> Chorus:
> The Comforter has come, The Comforter has come!
> The Holy Ghost from heav'n, The Father's promise giv'n;
> O spread the tidings 'round, Wherever man is found,
> The Comforter has come!

Additional theological headings fundamental to Pentecostalism are (1) the "Second Coming of Jesus Christ," which is the essential doctrine of its premillennial eschatology; (2) "Testimony, Witness, and Evangelism"; and (3) "Missions," that is, the commissions worshipers receive from the Lord upon Spirit baptism (Acts 1:8). The "Missions" section of *Yes, Lord!,* the penultimate subject heading in the table of contents, contains eight hymns that actually neglect the crucial part evangelism traditionally has played in Pentecostalism. The archaic Social-Darwinist hymns of early evangelical Christianity are excluded. However, such muted mission hymns as "Bringing in the Sheaves" and "If Jesus Goes with Me, I'll Go" hardly capture the enthusiasm felt by numerous primal Pentecostals who, upon Spirit baptism, heeded the Spirit's commission to be witnesses of Jesus "unto the uttermost part of the earth" (Acts 1:8).

Also excluded, along with the Social-Darwinist missionary hymns, is the bulk of "standard" British hymnody that elite black Protestants perceive as more cultured, and therefore more orthodox, than the gospel hymns. Longtime favorites such as Martin Luther's "A Mighty Fortress Is Our God" naturally are included, as are the beloved Christmas carols. The "shocker," notes Eileen Southern, is Handel's "Hallelujah Chorus," which covers a full six pages in the hymnal. It is included because it is sung each Christmas season in the local churches and by the National Choir. Southern says: "I became aware several years ago that the black folk-church had adopted this work, that members of the congregation sang along with the choir when it was performed as naturally as if they were singing a hymn or spiritual, taking whichever voice-part they preferred and missing not a single note. The inclusion of the 'Hallelujah Chorus' in a hymnal legitimizes the establishing of yet another black-church-music tradition."[24]

Not unlike most modern black denominational hymnals, *Yes, Lord!* contains a mere nine hymns by Watts and a mere eight by Wesley. With the COGIC, in particular, there simply was no historical impulse to include in *Yes, Lord!* a large number of the Watts and Wesley hymns (both especially favored by the Methodists). After all, this Pentecostal church has its own rich musical legacy that is inherited partly from its Holiness precursors and partly created anew by its own composers and performing artists.

If the works of Watts and Wesley and their British compatriots are peripheral to COGIC hymnody, the hymns arising out of the Social Gospel movement are essentially nonexistent in *Yes, Lord!* This is altogether characteristic, for the Holiness and Pentecostal movements arose in part in reaction to the secularism, intellectualism, and racial exclusivism of this middle-class Protestant reform movement. What is unfortunate, however, is that there is no hymnody of a social nature that reflects the church's own version of social involvement—its concern for poverty, unemployment, broken homes, family maladjustment, antisocial behavior, physical, mental, and emotional handicaps, racial tension, limited recreation opportunities, inadequate housing, and insufficient family income.[25] Hardly any of the hymns in *Yes, Lord!* lyricize and assert in the crucial context of congregational singing these issues central to the survival of the COGIC people in this tempestuous world. Much more of its hymnody falls under the heading "Heaven and Everlasting Life" and is comprised of songs of worship and praise.

Evincing even further the removal of the COGIC hymnal and people from the theology of the Protestant Social Gospel, the heading "Patriotic and World Peace," far from having top priority, is the last subject category in the table of contents. Moreover, this section (subheaded "Brotherhood") contains a mere seven hymns, five of which were necessary inclusions found in practically every modern hymnal: "The Star-Spangled Banner," "America, the Beautiful," "My Country, 'Tis of Thee," "Battle Hymn of the Republic," and "God of Our Fathers," plus a sixth one found in every modern black denominational hymnal—"Lift Every Voice and Sing" (the Black National Anthem). The remaining two pieces of this section—"O Freedom" (the spiritual), and "Let There Be Peace on Earth," by Sy Miller and Jill Jackson—hardly compensate for the thematic imbalance caused by the preponderance of hymns of "Heaven and Everlasting Life."

On the positive side, joining "Lift Every Voice and Sing" to give the hymnal a strong ethnic leaning are a substantial thirty-two black spirituals, six gospel hymns by C.P. Jones, eight by

C.A. Tindley, and a total of twenty-one gospel songs written or arranged by the leading black artists of the golden age of gospel (1930–69): Doris Akers, Lucie E. Campbell, Mattie Moss Clark, Thomas A. Dorsey, Roberta Martin, Kenneth Morris, and Clara Ward. From the modern age of gospel (1969–present) are songs composed by COGIC performing artists Andrae Crouch and Elbernita Clark.

An equally large part of *Yes, Lord!* is comprised of white gospel hymns that became popular in the black church during the period of urban revivalism. It is not at all surprising that, among the gospel hymnists, Fanny J. Crosby is best represented in *Yes, Lord!*, with fifteen hymns. Other white gospel hymnists well represented, with five or more pieces, are Philip P. Bliss, William B. Bradbury, William H. Doane, Charles H. Gabriel, Eliza E. Hewett, Elisha A. Hoffman, William J. Kirkpatrick, Robert Lowry, and Johnson Oatman, Jr. Those with fewer than five hymns included are Homer A. Rodeheaver, Ira D. Sankey, George C. Stebbins, John R. Sweney, and Charlie D. Tillman. Among the contemporary gospel hymns are eight pieces by the well-known Gloria and William Gaither duo, and five by Lanny and Marietta Wolfe. Hence, while *Yes, Lord!* is distinctly stamped "COGIC," with its inclusion of white gospel hymnody and a cross-section of black hymnody by Methodist, Baptist, and Holiness writers, it is by no means exclusivist or separatist.

While there are several hymns expressing pride in the history and ministry of the COGIC, this is no more a statement of separatism than similar denominational expressiveness in any other black Protestant hymnal is. Insofar as *Yes, Lord!* is the official hymnal of the denomination, the inclusion of such hymns as "This Is the Church of God in Christ" and "Women of the Church of God in Christ" is fully understandable. The former is a congregational hymn sung in some of the churches immediately following the invitation to Christian discipleship. The latter (popularly called the "Women's Theme Song") was composed by COGIC Elder Wallace M. Cryor for the annual Women's Convention of the Church of God in Christ.

Among the renowned COGIC performing artists who have contributed to the hymnal are Mattie Moss Clark, the famed gospel songwriter, performer, and recording artist (five selections), and her daughter Elbernita Clark, the talented songwriter of the Clark Sisters (two selections). Also represented with five compositions is Andrae Crouch, whose father, Ben Crouch, is a bishop in the church. Other COGIC members with pieces included in *Yes, Lord!* are Betty Nelson, Elder Henry V. Reed, and Jerome Taylor. In addition, there are three pieces by the esteemed church founder, C.H. Mason—"Yes, Lord," "My Soul Loves Jesus," and "My Soul Says, 'Yes.'" All of these pieces by COGIC members add to the unique denominational and Pentecostal thrust of *Yes, Lord!*, making it a real contribution to the general corpus of black church hymnody. As Eileen Southern remarks: "*Yes, Lord!* makes a sharp break with the past. In its collection of 506 songs, the handling of the accompaniment, in particular, reflects the importance given to instruments and polyphonic textures in the Pentecostal tradition. Except for the old standard hymns (which retain their conventional, four-part harmonizations) the accompaniments are lively and imaginative, promising an extra dimension of richness and excitement to the performance of the songs."[26]

Especially giving *Yes, Lord!* its flavor of Holiness, which is still very much a part of Pentecostal doctrine, are two hymns by the esteemed white Holiness leader Albert B. Simpson, and six hymns by C.P. Jones, founder of the Church of Christ (Holiness), USA. Most of these Holiness hymns promote the doctrine of sanctification, which, according to COGIC belief, is "that gracious and continuous operation of the Holy Ghost, by which He delivers the justified sinner from the pollution of sin, renews his whole nature in the image of God and enables him to perform good works."[27] Of the three hymns by Jones that clearly thematize sanctification, none of them does so as zealously as "I've Believed the True Report":

> I've believed the true report,
> Hallelujah to the Lamb!
> I have passed the outer court,
> O glory be to God!
> I am all on Jesus' side,
> On the altar sanctified,
> To the world and sin I've died,
> Hallelujah to the Lamb!

The second part of stanza three proceeds to identify "the blood" as the crucial purifying agency in the work of redemption:

> But the blood has brought me in
> To God's holiness so clean,
> Where there's death to self and sin,
> Hallelujah to the Lamb!

These "Blood songs," particularly popular when the "latter rain" first precipitated on the Azusa Street revival in 1906,[28] still hold a privileged position in Pentecostal theology. Jones' hymns are among several in *Yes, Lord!* to voice the primal doctrine.

A substantial part of *Yes, Lord!* is comprised of anonymous gospel hymns that have long been traditional in the black church. Among these are the testimony hymns, which Donna Cox defines thus:

> Testimony hymns . . . are of course congregational songs which have long been traditional to the black church. Often sung at prayer meetings or as congregational songs during worship service, they have also functioned in the same manner as the standard church hymns. These songs emphasize personal experiences with the Lord, particularly the way in which God has delivered the persecuted from various kinds of bondage. Typical lines are "You don't know like I know what the Lord has done for me," or "He picked me up and turned me 'round, placed my feet on solid ground." In this respect the songs reflect the same love for freedom which characterize the spirituals.[29]

One of the favorite testimony hymns in *Yes, Lord!* is "Jesus, I'll Never Forget" (arranged by Stevenson):

> Jesus, I'll never forget what you've done for me.
> Jesus, I'll never forget how you've set me free.
> Jesus, I'll never forget how you've brought me out.
> Jesus, I'll never forget, no never.

Such songs are called testimony hymns because they are used by the "saints" to commence their testimonies during testimony services. Opening one's testifying in this way is a longstanding tradition that flourished in postbellum black Protestant and Holiness churches, later finding its way into Pentecostalism. In testifying, a worshiper stands, sings a verse or two (or the chorus) of a favorite hymn, and then gives her or his spoken testimony using the theme and language of the song. The fact that testimony typically begins with and is built thematically upon a hymn illustrates what an essential source of theology these songs have been for laity over the years of struggle.

Another group of hymns found in *Yes, Lord!* consists of the kindred praise and worship hymns. "Unlike the testimony songs," says Cox, "the *praise* and *worship* hymns focus not on individual experiences with God but on the praise and adoration of Jesus Christ."[30] Discussing the worship songs, Cox says:

> The worship songs, which are more intimate and devotional than the praise songs, extol the various attributes of the Lord. They laud the worthiness and majesty of God and awaken human awareness to God's presence, and provide worshipers access to the Lord so that wholeness and holiness of the Spirit can displace their unholiness and unwholeness. Worship songs, then, provide worshipers with an opportunity to obtain an infusion of God's traits through the presence of the Holy Spirit. . . . Unlike testimony songs, these works are "composed" (written out), a large number being written by musicians and ministers for use in their church services and by such well-known composers as Bill and Gloria Gaither and Andrae Crouch.[31]

Familiar examples of worship songs in *Yes, Lord!* are "We Have Come Into this House" (Bruce Ballinger) and "Bless His Holy Name" (Andrae Crouch). Crouch's song, based on Psalm 103, has this single verse of worshipful adoration which is generally sung repeatedly before moving on to the chorus:

> Bless the Lord, O my soul, and all that is within me,
> Bless His holy Name.
>
> Chorus:
> He has done great things, (3×)
> Bless His Holy name.

The third category of congregational songs found in *Yes, Lord!* is the praise song. "The praise songs," as defined by Cox, "are usually cheerful and positive declarations of exaltation to the Lord which provide worshipers with access to God and welcome the Lord's presence into the life of the believer."[32] In the singing of praise, often it is only the chorus of a hymn that is sung repeatedly. Of the three verses to Mrs. C.H. Morris's "Let All the People Praise Thee," for instance, frequently the chorus alone is rendered as a hymn of praise:

> Let all the people praise him (2×)
> Let all the people praise the Lord.
> Forever and forevermore.

Either during or following the singing of such a praise song, COGIC worshipers respond by giving the Lord a "wave offering" by means of the "lifting of hands," or by giving "hand praise" (applause in gratitude for the Lord's blessings). Describing this sort of activity in his own Pentecostal denomination, the United Holy Church of America, black church scholar William C. Turner says, "This sort of collective worship, often yielding tumultuous moments of praise in which an entire congregation is enraptured, is described metaphorically by the people as the 'falling of fire.' "[33]

The anthems of praise par excellence for COGIC worshipers are "Yes, Lord" and "My Soul Says, 'Yes'," both composed by their revered church founder, C.H. Mason. The former (the denominational anthem) precedes the table of contents in *Yes, Lord!*, functioning as a thematic prelude to the hymnal. At its foot is this stirring annotation:

> Yes, Lord! The sound of this phrase bespeaks a high exaltation found in God. Since the inception of The Church of God in Christ, the praise, "Yes, Lord," has carried a wealth of spiritual meaning.
>
> Bishop C.H. Mason sang this quite free, dynamic and spiritually lifting praise to pull the congregation together in commitment and spiritual communion. When the saints sing, "Yes, Lord!," we are saying "Yes" to God's will; "Yes" to God's way; and "Yes" to God's direction in our lives.

Typical of praise songs, "Yes, Lord" is very repetitive, commencing with the chorus which iterates the exaltations "Yes" and "Yes, Lord." The ensuing verses are reiterations of (1) "My soul says yes," (2) "Yes to Your will," (3) "Yes to Your way," (4) "Yes, I'll obey," (5) "We praise you, Lord," (6) "We thank you, Lord," (7) "Come the more," and (8) "In my soul."

While "Yes, Lord" is attributed to Bishop Mason, the late Arenia Conelia Mallory told a different story regarding its evolution.[34] Mallory, a protege of Mary McLeod Bethune and a devoted COGIC member, was invited by Mason to the Mississippi Delta area to teach music at the Saints Industrial School. Accepting the position, she arrived there from Jacksonville, Illinois, in 1926; later she would be elevated to the post of president as the school became Saints Industrial Junior College. While in Mississippi, according to her story, Mallory erred, according to the "standards" of the church, when she married a man who was not a COGIC member. During the thirties, a member would be "disfellowshiped" for such behavior and barred from testifying in the church until public repentance and intercessory prayer had been made. In seeking a church in which to confess and repent publicly, Mallory found many a sanctuary door closed to her, until finally she found a willing congregation in New York City. It was there, claimed Mallory, that the "Yes, Lord" praise was born. Retelling her story in a chapter titled "The 'Yes, Lord' Hymn (As it was told by the late Dr. Arenia Conelia Mallory)," her biographers stated forthrightly, "God . . . gave Sister Mallory the hymn, 'Yes, Lord' ":

> Certainly, the Lord was with Arenia Mallory on that day as she stood before the congregation in New York City. When she arose to speak, she repented and confessed her sin according to Acts 3:19. The presence of the Lord came upon her as she lifted her hands to God. Suddenly, the Lord spoke through her with a praise of "Yes, Lord." The whole church caught on fire and started singing the praise—"Yes, Lord"—speaking with other tongues as the spirit gave them utterance according to Acts 2:4.
>
> The refreshing spread near and far, all over the U.S. and abroad. Later, a hymn was born of that outpour of the spirit; "Yes, Lord; Yes to thy will; Yes, I'll obey," etc. Years later, the "Yes, Lord," hymn was called "The Church of God in Christ Anthem." From that, at the 75th Diamond Jubilee Celebration of the Church of God in Christ, the first C.O.G.I.C. Hymnal was presented, and it was entitled, *Yes, Lord*.[35]

This incident, Mallory's biographers suggested, occurred in the thirties. However, a book published many years earlier, in 1924, contains transcriptions of seven praise hymns created and sung extemporaneously by Bishop Mason. What is revealing about several of these hymns, heard and documented by COGIC Elder C.G. Brown, is the appearance of the "yes" exultation and other similar affirmative responses to God's summons. Elder Brown prefaces his transcriptions with a recollection of Bishop Mason's devout and stalwart singing of these praise songs:

> Spiritual singing is another manner in which God expresses Himself through him [Mason]. By it evil spirits are driven away and souls are called to repentance. When he [Mason] arises to sing under the influence of the Spirit, the glory of God envelops him and his soul is consumed in the sweetness of God's love. The music is so melodious and full of harmony, the thought is so blessed and full of inspiration . . . that those who know Christ and have been baptized into His body, realize that God has furnished His servant with an invisible song book upon whose pages are written songs to subdue every human passion; to extol the name of Jesus; to exalt the way of God, and to supply a balm for every wound

and a cordial for every fear. Very often the power of God is so gloriously manifested through the singing that the assemblies of saints are aroused with the same fire of enthusiasm and take up the theme and sing together with him till they are carried to heights unknown to the natural mind. . . . Very often his [Mason's] songs of assurance, consecration, devotion, guidance, invitation, loyalty and praise evoke the expression of, "that's just what I need, and just why I was blessed of the Lord to be here for He knows the desire of my heart."[36]

One of the praise songs among Brown's transcriptions distinctly employs the "yes" affirmation in the first of its three verses:

> Let your heart say *yes* to God, this hour,
> And let me know.
> Let your heart say *yes* to God, help me.
> Help me, Lord, more.
> Help my love and tenderness.
> Help the little ones, help the rest.[37]

Typical of praise songs, including the "Yes, Lord" praise, the following one-verse piece is replete with repetition, variation, and permutation, and phrases that imply an affirmative "yes" to the divine behest:

> Lord, O Lord, *I'm yielding* to Thee,
> Right, right here;
> O Lord, *I'm waiting* on Thee,
> Right, right here.
> O Lord, Thy goodness shall in me dwell,
> Right, right here,
> O Lord *I am ready* to tell,
> Right, right here.
> O Lord, Thy help shall come to me;
> Right, right here.[38]

A third praise hymn by Mason also captured the *yes*ness of his desire to surrender unconditionally to God's call. The poetic patterns in this hymn and Mason's other praise songs render all of these pieces akin to those lyrics and melodies that burgeon spontaneously during the chanted "celebration" in black sermonry (a customary mode of delivery in black Pentecostal preaching):

> Help me, help me.
> Every day, every day Lord help me.
> I ask my Lord for help in mind.

To be like Jesus now.
Help me, help me, Lord; I am thine;
Help me, help me, Christ, God's friend.
Help me, help me, Jesus I am thine,
Help me say, the Lord is mine
Help me say, Lord, I am thine.
Help me, help me, O Lord.
Help me to come to Thee when you call.
Help me to say, Lord, thou art all.[39]

Long before Elder Brown even documented these praise songs, Mason customarily uttered the word "yes" as an expression of spiritual surrender to the will of God. Several times during his 1907 visit to the Azusa Street revival, he uttered "yes" to the Lord as he opened himself up for Spirit baptism. One night, God communicated to him that Jesus refused to attempt to solve the world's problems until he had been overshadowed with the Holy Ghost, and that Mason too must disregard the burdens of his people until imbued with the power of the Spirit. "I said," recalled Mason, "I am no better than my Lord, and if I want Him to baptize me I will have to let the people's rights and wrongs all alone, and look to Him and not to the people. Then He will baptize me. And I said 'yes' to God, for it was He who wanted to baptize me and not the people."[40] Similarly, during his second night of steady prayer, Mason gave in to the divine impetus when God informed him that, if he fully turned his attention heavenward, he would be baptized. Said Mason, "I said 'yes' to Him."[41] It was Mason's saying "yes" that eventually led to his being baptized by the Spirit, as shown by speaking with other tongues. When he wrote back to the Azusa Mission in November 1907 from Lexington, he informed the people that the Lord had been singing hundreds of songs in Mississippi and that he had not had the time to go back and rehearse them: "The Lord is casting out devils, healing the sick, and singing the sweetest songs. He has sung hundreds of songs. I do not have the time to go back over one to practice it, for the next will be new. Praise His name. I sit under His shadow with great delight. His banner over me is love."[42]

What these early praise songs and testimonies of Bishop Mason illustrate is that many years before Mallory sang the words "Yes, Lord" before a New York congregation, Mason had long been speaking and singing a laudatory "yes" to God's will.

Though Mason did not live to witness the publication of *Yes, Lord!*, its title and hymnic content are a testament to his life of saying "yes" to the leanings of the Spirit. Just as "Yes, Lord" is vintage Mason, *Yes, Lord!*—which has adeptly recorded the historical and theological experience of its black Pentecostal constituency—is vintage COGIC.

PART 3

BLACK EPISCOPALIANS AND CATHOLICS

CHAPTER 9

The Episcopal Church

Now be it known to all the world and in all ages thereof, that we, the founders of said house, did on Tuesday, the 12th day of August, in the year of Our Lord one thousand seven hundred and ninety-four, resolve and decree to resign and conform ourselves to the Protestant Episcopal Church of North America, and we dedicate ourselves to God, imploring His protection; and our house to the memory of St. Thomas, the Apostle, to be henceforth known and called St. Thomas African Episcopal Church of Philadelphia; to be governed by us and our successors.

—*Saint Thomas African Episcopal Church*[1]

Brethren—After some deliberation in my own mind upon the call you have given me; I sensibly feel that it is of such serious nature as to cause me to tremble at the thought of such an undertaking. But, on my looking to Him who is the sovereign ruler of all things, the recollection of Jacob's going over the brook unfurnished, with nothing but his staff and crook; and seeing what great things were done for him, and how his fears were banished, I was led to put my trust in God, and become your servant in Christ; and in all things begun, continued and ended in his name, I hope He will be glorified, and our souls eternally profited.

—*Absalom Jones,*
pastor of the first black Episcopal parish

Born into slavery in 1746, self-educated, manumitted in 1784, and ordained the first black Episcopal priest in 1804, Absalom Jones represents the genesis of black Episcopalianism in North America. Although the first black Episcopal church, historic Saint Thomas African Episcopal Church, was dedicated on 29 July 1794, its beginnings really date back to about 1787, when, as

Richard Allen recalled, Absalom Jones and he withdrew from Saint George's Methodist Episcopal Church in Philadelphia:

> Meeting had begun, and they were nearly done singing, and just as we got to the seats, the elder said, "Let us pray." We had not been long upon our knees before I heard considerable scuffling and low talking. I raised my head up and saw one of the trustees . . . having hold of the Rev. Absalom Jones, pulling him up off of his knees, and saying, "You must not kneel here." Mr. Jones replied, . . . "Wait until prayer is over, and I will get up and trouble you no more." With that he beckoned to one of the other trustees . . . to come to his assistance. . . . By this time prayer was over, and we all went out of the church in a body, and they were no more plagued with us in the church.[3]

Within six weeks of this 12 April incident, Jones and Allen had founded the Free African Society,[4] a benevolent alliance that oversaw the spiritual welfare of its members. The society first met for devotional services in 1788 and for formal worship in 1791, and a few years later a church was built. But when in 1794 its members voted to associate their parish with the Episcopal church, Richard Allen departed and proceeded to build his own church, Bethel African Methodist Church (dedicated on 17 July 1794). Jones became the rector of the first black Episcopal congregation, named Saint Thomas African Episcopal Church, dedicated on 29 July 1794. The following year, Jones was ordained a deacon and nine years later a priest. Now honored with a feast day in the Episcopal calendar (13 February), Absalom Jones, who was once bound but then set free, is the icon of African-American Episcopalianism. "He belongs to black Episcopalians," says Ann Lammers, "as an image of Christ in their history."[5]

In the postbellum years, many other prominent and cosmopolitan black Episcopalian churches were founded—Saint Philip's Church in New York, organized in 1819 by its founding rector, Rev. Peter Williams (ordained a priest in 1826); Saint Mary's in Washington, D.C., organized in 1873 by its founding rector, Alexander Crummell (ordained a priest in 1844); and Saint Luke's in New Haven, Connecticut, where the great African-American scholar, W.E.B. Du Bois, was baptized. As in Absalom Jones's parish, the style of worship in these churches probably discouraged impulsive vocal and physical responses to the music being sung. Although there is some historic evidence that black Episcopalians occasionally sang Methodist hymns and that the oral tradition persisted to a degree well into the twentieth century, the genteel tradition of refined musical expression, according to Episcopal music scholar Irene Jackson-Brown, continued in the postbellum years: "Music in Black Episcopalian churches had become, by the post-bellum period, a 'cultivated' or 'genteel' tradition, as distinct from a 'folk' or 'vernacular' tradition."[6] Hence, from the time Saint Thomas African Episcopal Church was dedicated in 1794, it was over 170 years before black Episcopalians began to reappropriate their musical heritage of the spirituals and to integrate the developing genres of black gospel music into their worship.

The single most important factor that contributed to the formation of this new racial awareness was the conscious-altering revolution of the Civil Rights and Black Power movements. Some of the tangible results of the new consciousness within the Episcopal Church were the formation of the Episcopal Society of Cultural and Racial Unity, the General Convention Special Program in 1967 (intended to meet the needs of black self-determination), the Union of Black Episcopalians in 1968, and the Absalom Jones Theological Institute in 1972 (located at the Interdenominational Theological Center in Atlanta). It was the Union of Black Episcopalians that led the 1973 General Convention to form the Commission for Black Ministries "as the new focal point for Black concerns within the National Church."[7] Rev. Franklin D. Turner, a black priest, served as its first director.

Five years after the formation of the Commission for Black Ministries, Turner had the idea of documenting the sacred musical heritage of black Episcopalians in a hymnbook. His theological statement for the Commission for Black Ministries that initiated the project said, "Our theological perspective must be drawn not only from the tradition of our Church, but also from the culture of our people." Therefore, continued Turner, "we need to develop an Afro-American Hymnal that draws heavily on the wealth of Negro spirituals and gospel music." The time was right, and black Episcopalians responded favorably to this new impetus. One such response came from Episcopalian Professor Robert Bennett. In an article published in 1979, Bennett proudly claimed the spirituals as part of his religious heritage, firmly asserting that these songs of liberation have special meaning for him as an Episcopalian just as they have meaning for other black Christians.[8] "The Black religious tradition," concluded Bennett, "continues to speak to the Black Episcopalian in the sermons, prayers and gospel songs of the Black church."[9]

The results of Turner's idea of compiling an African-American hymnal, amid the increased momentum of racial consciousness during the late 1970s, culminated in the publication of *Lift Every Voice and Sing: A Collection of Afro-American Spirituals and Other Songs* (1981). Although the idea for this hymnal might have been Turner's, he was no doubt strongly influenced by the spirit of reformation arising within the camp of black Episcopalians. For instance, in 1974, years before Turner thought about producing such a hymnal, Robert Bennett had written, "Today the 'invisible' Black Church within the Episcopal Church is on the verge of recognizing itself as being part of the 'visible' Black Church phenomenon in America."[10] As an affirmation of black Episcopalian visibility in the whole of Afro-Christianity, *Lift Every Voice and Sing* represented a fulfillment of that prophecy.

Lift Every Voice and Sing was a much-needed supplement to the Episcopal Church's *Hymnal 1940*. This official denominational hymnal clearly attests to the black Episcopalian "invisibility" that had led W.E.B. Du Bois to comment in 1903 that the Episcopal Church had "probably done less for the Black people than any other aggregation of Christians."[11] While the preface to the 1940 hymnal claims that special effort was made to include hymns that "voice the social aspirations of our day," those aspirations evidently included neither the black voice nor the aspiration of black Episcopalians to be liberated from repression within their own denomination. There is no black voice in the *Hymnal 1940* because there is no black hymnody, save a single spiritual, "Were You There" (which is not a song of liberation but a "sorrow song"). Indeed, this one piece is clearly identified as a "Negro spiritual," but the *Hymnal 1940 Companion* (1949) detracts from even that meager "visibility" of the black contribution to American Christianity. Completely neglecting the African people whose experience of enslavement in North America spawned this spiritual, the hymnal companion states that the spiritual is recognized as "one of America's most significant contributions to hymnody." It then cites the research of George Pullen Jackson, a white scholar known for his highly controversial theory that black spirituals are merely modified imitations of white hymns. Citing Jackson's *White and Negro Spirituals* (1943), the authors of the hymnal companion implied, with Jackson, that "Were You There" might have been derived from a white spiritual titled "Have You Heard How They Crucified Our Lord." While the latter never appeared in print, they said, the "Negro version" was first published in William E. Barton's *Old Plantation Hymns* (1899). Their conclusion, while attempting to be fair, subtly denied black Episcopalians any visibility: "Whether originally Negro or white, this deeply moving spiritual passed into folklore between two and three generations ago."[12]

Aside from this spiritual, the only black composer represented in the *Hymnal 1940* is H.T. Burleigh, who set John Oxenham's hymn "In Christ There Is No East or West" to the melody of a black spiritual. The credit for the hymn-tune and harmony read, "Negro Melody adapted by Harry T. Burleigh, 1939." Regarding this setting, the *Hymnal 1940 Companion* comments:

> The first tune, *McKee*, was adapted by Harry T. Burleigh in 1939 from the Negro spiritual "I know the angel's done changed my name." It was named *McKee* in honor of the rector of St. George's Church, New York City, where Mr. Burleigh sang for many years. It was adapted to this text and first published in broadside form. The spiritual dates from the 1884 edition of the Fisk University *Jubilee Songs*, compiled by Theodore F. Seward and George L. White.[13]

While the *Hymnal 1940* contained a mere one black spiritual, itself usurped by the white church as one of "America's most significant contributions to hymnody," on another front too the hymnal rendered black Episcopalians invisible. To black Episcopalians who sang from this hymnal, the mission hymns laden with Social Darwinism were probably repulsive, especially following the black consciousness movement of the late sixties and seventies. Referring to the infamous mission hymn that called Africans "heathens" and "men benighted," Sherodd Albritton (a member of the Standing Committee on Church Music) recognized that "our mission stance in 1979 has certainly got to be expressed in better ways than in the implicit imperialism found in 'From Greenland's Icy Mountains.'"[14] Expressing further understanding of the way in which black Episcopalians must have viewed the *Hymnal 1940*, Albritton said,

> Further, we are alienating whole groups of people sometimes—people who hear themselves excluded by the use of language. When there is genuinely felt hurt, it seems only right to see what can be done about it.

> It is such a small price to pay, changing "white" to "pure". . . or "dumb"
> to "mute". . . in order to avoid further hurt and alienation. In many
> cases very minor adjustments in the text make all the difference, and
> often it actually seems to improve the hymn.[15]

Because of this sort of "alienation," "exclusion," and "invisibility," blacks in the Episcopal Church (like any minority group
dominated by a majority group) admitted to having an "identity
crisis."[16] Because they persisted in remaining members of a
largely white denomination that locked them into this sort of
predicament, scholars of the black church traditionally criticized
black Episcopalians. E. Franklin Frazier was one of the first of
these critics, with his claim that members of the new black
middle class sought to separate themselves from their pasts by
severing relationships with the black Baptist and Methodist
churches and joining the Episcopal, Presbyterian, and Congregational churches, whose cultured worship accorded better
with their new status.[17] Perhaps the most malignant translation
of Frazier's comment was the anonymous remark that "any
Negro who prefers the Book of Common Prayer to the storefront
church is a traitor to his people."[18] Such defamation was not far
removed from Booker T. Washington's claim that, if blacks are
anything but Baptist or Methodist, then white Christians have
been tampering with them.[19]

Naturally, black Episcopalians resented being termed members of the "black bourgeoisie" who were attempting to elude
the black community and the idiosyncrasies of black religion.[20]
They resented the assertion that their worldviews had been tam-
pered with by whites. John Burgess commented thus regarding
the latter accusation in an opening address to the April 1978
Convocation of Black Theologians (sponsored by the Episcopal
Commission for Black Ministries): "It was a stupid remark when
it was made, and it does little credit to those scholars in the field
of the Black Church who seem to hold this view."[21] Furthermore,
said Robert Bennett, "the Black Episcopalian stands in the same
relationship with his white co-religionist that the total Black
community knows in America at large."[22]

In spite of these criticisms, John Burgess (the first black Episcopal diocesan bishop in the United States) identified the self-
affirming, assertive stance that black Episcopalians had to take
regarding their ethnicity. "For conscience sake," said Burgess

first, "we Black Episcopalians must understand that we are legitimate, not only in the eyes of these people, but to White Episcopalians as well."[23] Second, in response to those who sought to discount black Episcopalians as participants in the black experience and who argued that they are not a part of the black church, Burgess implores black Episcopalians confidently to define their own place: "If we believe they are wrong, it is our task so to interpret our place among them that they are no longer uncomfortable with us and will welcome our contribution as an enrichment of the total Black religious experience."[24]

During the seventies, black Episcopalians began to interpret their place within the black church. Robert E. Hood asserted that, "Black Episcopalians are . . . as licit and legitimate heirs to the rich legacy of the black experience in terms of its being shaped by the institution of slavery as black Christians from the more numerous Baptist and Methodist traditions."[25] Bennett claimed that "the Black Episcopalian has demonstrated the authenticity of his religious commitment by his persistent struggle to maintain his racial-ethnic identity within a larger Church body which has not readily acknowledged his presence."[26]

The need to be recognized as "licit and legitimate heirs to the black religious legacy" was evident not only in the black Episcopalians' publication, *Lift Every Voice and Sing*, but more specifically in their belief that they had played a meaningful part in the creation of the black spirituals compiled therein. Bennett stated that black Episcopalians of the antebellum South "described their plantation Holy Communion services in the spiritual, 'Let us break bread together on our knees.'"[27] In an essay titled "Music among Blacks in the Episcopal Church" (located in the back of *Lift Every Voice and Sing*), Episcopal music scholar Irene Jackson-Brown expounds on Bennett's suggestive remark:

> This passing comment of Bennett's suggests that Blacks within the Episcopal Church contributed to the growing body of Afro-American religious folksong to be known later as spirituals. Bennett seems to imply that the spiritual "Let Us Break Bread Together" originated among Black Episcopalians, possibly since the kneeling stance is assumed in communion and probably because the administering of the Holy Sacraments is central to Episcopalian liturgy. Perhaps what is most intriguing about Bennett's hypothesis is that Blacks other than those who were under the influence of the Methodists and Baptists were not to be excluded from certain musical practices that were popular among the masses of Blacks.

These musical practices included the singing of religious folksongs—to be later known as spirituals—and the practice referred to as "lining-out."[28]

Jackson-Brown's essay (which "establishes the historical framework for this hymnal")[29] identifies the renowned arranger of spirituals, Carl R. Diton, as one who served the Episcopal Church as organist at the Saint Thomas Episcopal Church in Philadelphia during the twenties.[30] Perhaps because of their association with the Episcopal Church, and out of a wish for black Episcopalians to be recognized as legitimate heirs to the black religious legacy, Jackson-Brown included "Let Us Break Bread Together" and a representative spiritual arranged by Diton in her compilation of *Lift Every Voice and Sing*.

The most effective means by which Episcopalians have claimed their place in the black church perhaps has not been by conjecturing that they may have been responsible for the creation of "Let Us Break Bread Together" or by pointing out black Episcopalian composers who have made contributions to the preservation of the spirituals, but by publishing *Lift Every Voice and Sing*. Some black Episcopalian preachers may preach in the traditional black mode and others may not, but if black Episcopalians sing the songs of the black church, as proven by their production and use of this collection of black hymns, then their legitimacy and right to authentic partnership in the black church is undeniable. What *Lift Every Voice and Sing* therefore has demonstrated (to those who doubted it) is that "black" and "Episcopalian" are not necessarily contradictory entities. As Van S. Bird said, referring to Du Bois' notion of the divided black soul, "The 'two-ness' of being Black and American is neither overcome nor transcended in the Christian community. We are not Episcopalians; we are Black Episcopalians."[31]

In a sense, one could claim that *Lift Every Voice and Sing* is the embodiment of the divided black soul—the "two-ness" of being black and American—and for this reason is of paramount historical importance. Yet some black hymnologists have overlooked its distinctive contribution to the diverse entity known as "black hymnody," just as some black religion scholars historically have excluded black Episcopalians from membership in the consortium known as "the black church." For instance, in an article on "The Hymnals of the Black Church," musicologist Eileen Southern lists the three black church hymnals published in the early eighties—*Songs of Zion* (1981), *Lift Every Voice and Sing* (1981), and *Yes, Lord!* (1982). She then ignores the Episcopal songbook and proceeds to discuss the significance of the Methodist (United Methodist) and Pentecostal (Church of God in Christ) collections. Of the Episcopal and Methodist hymnals published during the same year, she chooses *Songs of Zion* to join Richard Allen's *Collection of Spiritual Songs and Hymns* (1801) and *Gospel Pearls* (1921) as the most important songbooks in the history of black church hymnody.[32] Although Portia Maultsby does not detail the historical importance of *Lift Every Voice and Sing*, she at least treats it as equal to *Songs of Zion*. First, she notes the overlap in content of the two hymnals—the two share twenty-four hymns, fifteen spirituals, and four gospels.[33] Second, while tacitly recognizing the importance of Allen's 1801 hymnbook, she seems to add *Lift Every Voice and Sing* to Southern's rather limited list of monumental black church hymnals: "*Lift Every Voice and Sing* and *Songs of Zion* are two welcomed additions to the only existing hymnal, *Gospel Pearls*, that acknowledge the broad range of output of Black Americans in their praise to God," says Maultsby. "All three hymnals share a unique feature—they include a representative number of traditional hymns by both Black and White composers."[34]

A unique feature that *Lift Every Voice and Sing* shares with *Gospel Pearls* and Richard Allen's 1801 hymnbook (a feature not shared by *Songs of Zion*) is that its hymns are arranged solely for congregational singing. There has always been a majority voice asserting the importance of congregational singing,[35] and *Lift Every Voice and Sing* echoes it. In her prefatory "Comments on the Selections," Irene Jackson-Brown says, "In the preparation of *Lift Every Voice and Sing*, songs were selected for their effectiveness as congregational songs and for the ease by which they could be learned and sung by the average person in the pew."

The 151 congregational songs in *Lift Every Voice and Sing* include spirituals, standard hymns, gospel hymns (by black and white writers), traditional and contemporary gospel songs, a few Ghanian and Nigerian folk songs, and a Civil Rights song ("We Shall Overcome"). Included are several "standard" hymns by Watts and Wesley and, naturally, John Newton's "Amazing Grace," as well as white gospel hymns by such writers as Fanny

J. Crosby, Elisha A. Hoffman, and Civilla D. Martin, all of whose hymns long have been adopted by the black church.

Although *Lift Every Voice and Sing* probably did not enjoy the extensive distribution of *Songs of Zion*, it is in *some* respects a superior volume. First, while both volumes are supplementary hymnals, it has more of the character of a hymnal, in that its 151 pieces are categorized under theological headings rather than according to musical genre, as the works in *Songs of Zion* are. Second, the thirty-eight spirituals in *Lift Every Voice and Sing* were arranged by a far greater variety of black composers. Almost all of the spirituals in *Songs of Zion* were arranged by the editors, J. Jefferson Cleveland and Verolga Nix (there was a mere one historic arrangement by John W. Work, Jr.). In contrast, the arrangers of spirituals in *Lift Every Voice and Sing* include the renowned Edward Boatner, Harry T. Burleigh, Edward C. Deas, R. Nathaniel Dett, Carl R. Diton, Willa A. Townsend, and Clarence Cameron White, as well as such contemporary black musicians as Horace C. Boyer (of the University of Massachusetts, Amherst), Evelyn D. White (of Howard University), and Richard Smallwood (director of Washington, D.C.'s Richard Smallwood Singers). Third, the historic sources from which many of the older spiritual arrangements in *Lift Every Voice and Sing* were drawn are more diverse. In her prefatory "Comment on the Selections," Irene Jackson-Brown notes that some of the music included was not readily accessible, necessitating her searching through dated collections located in such research repositories as the Schomberg Center for Research in Black Culture and the Library of Congress. For instance, all three of John Wesley Work, Jr.'s arrangements—"Free At Last," "Do Lord Remember Me," and "Standing in the Need of Prayer"—were taken from his historic book, *American Negro Songs and Spirituals* (1940). Two of Dett's four arrangements—"Come Unto Me" and "O Holy Savior"—are credited to *The Dett Collection of Negro Spirituals*, fourth group (1936).

On the other hand, *Lift Every Voice and Sing* and *Songs of Zion* are relatively equivalent in terms of their representation of black gospel music. The Episcopal volume includes pieces by C.A. Tindley (including "We'll Understand It Better By and By"), Thomas A. Dorsey ("Take My Hand, Precious Lord"), Doris M. Akers ("Lead Me, Guide Me" and "Sweet, Sweet Spirit"), Lucie

E. Campbell ("He'll Understand and Say 'Well Done' "), Kenneth Morris ("Yes, God Is Real"), and Andrae Crouch (including "Bless the Lord"). The volume would not have been complete without the piece after which it was named, James Weldon Johnson's "Lift Every Voice and Sing" (set by his brother J. Rosamond Johnson). Illustrating the breadth of *Lift Every Voice and Sing* is Duke Ellington's "Come Sunday," from his jazz suite *Black, Brown and Beige,* and Richard Smallwood's arrangement of "Reach Out and Touch Somebody's Hand," by the husband-and-wife duo Ashford and Simpson (Nick Ashford and Valerie Simpson).

Complementing this traditional (and some not-so-traditional) black hymnody is liturgical music, located in the back of the volume. Included are music for the Episcopal Eucharist, a setting of the "Preces and Responses for Morning or Evening Prayer Rite II," and Anglican chants and canticles. The two Eucharist settings were composed by black musicians William B. Cooper and Timothy Gibson. Cooper, who contributed numerous pieces of service music, was long organist and choirmaster at Saint Martin's Episcopal Church in Harlem. This mix of black spirituals that originated in the "invisible" black church and liturgical music of the institutional church perhaps reflects the ethnic mix among American Episcopalians of African descent. On the one hand are native black American Episcopalians, who Gavin White says have "a liturgical tone which is neither High nor Low but a distinct blending of their own." On the other hand are native West Indian Episcopalians who immigrated en masse to North America during the twenties and thirties, and who, White says, have (save for Jamaicans) a liturgical tone that is "ultra-High."[36]

Perhaps illustrating the removal of all black Episcopalians from the "Low" liturgical tone especially typical in Holiness and Pentecostal worship is the absence in *Lift Every Voice and Sing* of hymns by the prolific and exceptional Holiness hymnist C.P. Jones. That this oversight (as critical as would be overlooking C.A. Tindley) occurred in both *Lift Every Voice and Sing* and *Songs of Zion* divulges more than the lack of breadth of these collections of black church hymnody. What really is revealed here is the greater theological cultural gap between the black constituencies in predominantly white denominations, on the one hand,

and the black Holiness churchgoers and Pentecostals, on the other—a gap greater than that between the black Baptist and Methodist churches and the black Holiness and Pentecostal churches.

While both the Episcopal and United Methodist hymnbooks overlooked C.P. Jones, one aspect of *Lift Every Voice and Sing* that gives it a "higher" liturgical tone than *Songs of Zion* is the list of suggestions provided by the compilers for singing the spirituals in this volume. The prefatory "Keys to Musical Interpretation, Performance, and Meaningful Worship" in the Methodist collection suggest that the words "the," "this," and "that" be pronounced "de," "dis," and "dat." Although the compilers of the Episcopal collection did not alter such vernacular as "Done made my vow to the Lord" or "I ain't goin' study war no more," neither do they request the use of dialect. Since "the," "this," and "that" are also one-syllable words and therefore do not require any modification in the melodic rhythm, there is no reason for proper English-speaking middle-class African Americans to mock an old southern dialect.

R. Nathaniel Dett spoke to this very matter back in 1936, in an essay titled "The Development of the Negro Spiritual," the introduction to the fourth group of *The Dett Collection of Negro Spirituals*. Himself a Presbyterian, Dett identified the presence of dialect in the spirituals as one reason the songs had difficulty being accepted in churches with a characteristically refined style of worship. "It is possible that the publication of the spirituals in broad dialect has been an influence operating to keep the songs from formal religious worship," said Dett, "especially since dialect has been one of the peculiarly American means of obtaining a laugh not only at the Negro's but at almost anybody's expense."[37]

Dett actually had begun to speak about the broader implications of this issue about a decade and a half earlier, in a longer essay written in 1920, "The Development of Negro Religious Music." In this piece he began to formulate his argument for "developing" (arranging) the spirituals to be more suitable to refined worship:

> It is a well-known fact that in practically none of the colored churches of the better class, does the primitive Negro folk song find any place. This is not altogether due to the charge often made that the Negro is trying to

forget or divorce himself from the past. The trouble is that many songs probably full of real or implied significance seem almost meaningless since Emancipation; and when placed alongside of the religious art song and church anthem of the present day appear unspeakably crude, even ludicrous.[38]

While seven years later Dett criticized those same black people "of the better class" for not having "outgrown" shame at these songs,[39] Franklin Turner, in his introduction to *Lift Every Voice and Sing*, articulated the same complaint a half century later:

Unfortunately, Afro-Americans, particularly those in predominantly white churches, have not felt comfortable using their own music in formal services, but instead relegated this music to use at civic and social gatherings. Although Black Episcopalians could not or would not use spirituals in their formal worship, they constantly hummed and sang these songs in private.

Even before the liturgical movement, some priests and congregations experimented with indigenizing the liturgy to the church by incorporating Negro spirituals. This practice was not widespread because it was not encouraged and was thought to be unacceptable, inappropriate, and "not Episcopal." Some said that spirituals could not fit into the Episcopal liturgy.

Although Dett, early on, chided black people "of the better class" for not having "outgrown" this sort of sentiment,[40] his understanding of their viewpoint at that stage of their racial "development" may apply equally to the feelings of some contemporary black Episcopalians: "It is quite natural that in his present state of development the Negro would greatly prize, not only education itself, but also all evidences of educational advancement; so that the laying aside of the hymn and anthem book in order to sing songs which, being merely traditional, require neither thought nor training to perform, would be regarded by many colored people as a backward step in the progress of the race toward so-called 'better things.'"[41]

Time has shown that Dett had a legitimate point, but during his day he came under much criticism for his efforts to "develop" the spiritual in a form usable in refined church worship. For instance, on 21 April 1920 he received a letter from George P. Phenix, the college principal at Hampton Institute, where Dett directed the choir. "As sung by the choir a week ago," chided Phenix, "our spirituals were in a sense de-spiritualized."[42] Similarly, in a letter of 3 February 1945 to Arna Bontemps, W.C. Handy remarked, "Dett did not come up in the deep south as I did, and too, he had much of the education of a man who is trying to keep us in a certain category, as it relates to what we call Negro music."[43] Dett never felt that arrangements of the spirituals would actually "improve" the songs,[44] he only felt that "development" would make them less crude and more congenial for cultured worship. There is no doubt, however, that it has been due to the "development" of the spiritual by Dett and other black composers represented in *Lift Every Voice and Sing* that Bishop John Burgess, in his preface to the volume, is able to claim some victory in changing the attitudes of black Episcopalians: "It has taken a long time for spirituals to gain acceptance in the Episcopal Church. Even with the publishing of this supplement to the Church Hymnal, there will be many who still question its appropriateness. . . . What was once dismissed as hardly worthy of liturgical notice is now evaluated as artistry that compares favorably, musically and emotionally, with the greatest music within the Christian tradition."

While the status of the spiritual in the Episcopal liturgy remains controversial, but is increasingly acceptable, the inclusion in *Lift Every Voice* of Duke Ellington's "Come Sunday" (from his jazz suite *Black, Brown and Beige*) focused attention on an even more delicate issue, one long the subject of theological debate in the black church. On the one hand, there were those religionists, black and white, who felt that jazz had no place in Christian worship, let alone in a hymnbook. They maintained that the character of inherently secular music was not made sacred just by bringing it into a church or including it in a sacred book.[45] Such sentiments must, of course, be considered in light of the fact that Thomas A. Dorsey's gospel songs, now cherished even by fundamentalists, once were rejected by the clergy and laity of the black church as too much imbued with the harmonies and rhythms of blues.

That the inclusion of Ellington's piece in *Lift Every Voice and Sing* apparently was not problematical for the compilers was partly due to two movements that Turner mentions in his introduction to the hymnal: (1) the liturgical renewal movement and (2) the racial consciousness movement. Turner says, "With the civil rights, Black awareness, and liturgical movement of the

1950s and 60s, Black Americans gained courage to boldly pro-
claim and affirm their religious heritage, including their music.
The liturgical movement of the church was intended to more
closely relate worship to the cultural experiences of the people.
Hence the experiment with folk, jazz, and soul masses."

Evidence of the impact of the liturgical movement in the Episcopal Church are the existence of a gospel Mass, *Eucharist of the
Soul*, composed by Lena McLin, and two supplements to the
Hymnal 1940, published in 1979—*Hymns III* and *Songs for Celebration*. *Hymns III*, for instance, contains a rather jazz-like setting
(complete with guitar chords) of "Go Tell It on the Mountain,"
arranged by black composer Hale Smith, a consultant for *Lift
Every Voice and Sing*. Regarding this piece, the prefatory "Performance Notes" states, "for the setting of the Spiritual, 'Go Tell it
on the Mountain,' the compilers chose an indigenous harmo-
nization best suited for performance on the piano." Similarly,
Songs for Celebration contains less formal music for folk masses,
with chords for guitar accompaniment. Third, *Eucharist of the
Soul*, a mass written by black composer Lena McLin, was composed under a commission from black priest William James
Walker, vicar-pastor of the Holy Cross Episcopal Church in Chicago. Intended to be used with the Eucharist Rite II of the Episcopal Church, McLin successfully brought together traditional
black gospel and the Episcopal liturgical setting.

While these were some of the developments within the Episcopal Church that prepared the way for Ellington's piece to be
included in *Lift Every Voice and Sing*, these modernisms did not
compensate for the deficiency of black hymnody in the *Hymnal
1940*. Like the *Hymnal 1940*, *Hymns III* had only one spiritual,
"Go Tell It on the Mountain," which was not even recognized as
being of African-American origin; it was listed as an "anonymous American folk hymn." Similarly, *Songs for Celebration*
contained a scant one spiritual, "Lord, I Want to Be a Christian,"
which also is listed as an "American spiritual," rather than as an
"Afro-American spiritual."

There is no doubt, therefore, that the efforts leading up to the
publication of *Lift Every Voice and Sing* increased the acceptance
of cultural pluralism in the larger church. For instance, the preface of the new denominational hymnal, the *Hymnal 1982*, states
that one of the goals of the hymnal is "to reflect the nature of

today's Church by including . . . works representing many cultures." Hence, included are texts and music from African-American, Asian-American, Hispanic, and Native American cultures. Representing the culture of black Episcopalians are a total of six spirituals (all appropriately identified as "Afro-American spirituals"), two Ghanaian songs (the same ones as in *Lift Every Voice and Sing*), and the Black National Anthem (James Weldon's Johnson's "Lift Every Voice and Sing"). Of the six spirituals, "Let Us Break Bread Together" was arranged by black Episcopalian musician David Hurd, "Go Down, Moses" by Horace C. Boyer, and "Go Tell It on the Mountain" adapted by John W. Work, Jr., and arranged by Boyer. The tune for "In Christ There Is No East or West" (which is the melody to a spiritual) was adapted and harmonized by H.T. Burleigh.

One of the persons who helped to bring to the *Hymnal 1982* this element of greater inclusiveness is seminary professor David Hurd, the only black member of the music committee for the *Hymnal 1982*, a consultant for *Lift Every Voice and Sing*, and a committee member for *Lift Every Voice and Sing II*, presently being compiled by Horace C. Boyer. Hurd's contribution to the *Hymnal 1982* far surpassed mere service on the music committee and arranging a black spiritual. Illustrating his West Indian bent toward a "high" liturgical tone, he also composed or arranged numerous melodies for the Episcopal service and provided original music for nine hymns written over a period ranging from the sixth century to the twentieth century.

This substantive contribution by a black Episcopalian to the larger Episcopal Church is a breakthrough partly traceable to the publication of *Lift Every Voice and Sing*. It is because this African-American song collection had an impact on the racial inclusiveness of the *Hymnal 1982* that Robert E. Hood could praise the initiative and impetus of blacks in forging their own history within the church: "Fortunately, there are various efforts currently at work even amongst black Episcopalians who no longer are convinced of the ability of the Episcopal Church to become a multicultural church willingly and who, therefore, are intent on preserving their rightful black legacy alongside the musical, liturgical, and homiletical traditions of this fundamentally white church."[46]

Historically, it has been only when black people have become convinced of the inability of America to become a multicultural nation that they have become intent on preserving their rightful legacy alongside the historical, cultural, and philosophical traditions of white America. Bennett's claim that black Episcopalians stand in the same relationship to the large Episcopal Church as black citizens do to America as a whole,[47] then, suggests that, were it not for blacks remaining in predominantly white denominations and making a decisive move to preserve their African American legacy, there would be no *Lift Every Voice and Sing*. The fact that the only other modern collections containing such a concentration of black church hymnody are *Songs of Zion* and *Lead Me, Guide Me* (of the Catholic Church) seems to support this theory.

In the end, what *Lift Every Voice and Sing* teaches us is not just that black Episcopalians stand in the same relationship to the larger Episcopal Church as black citizens to the larger nation, but that "black" and "Episcopalian" are not mutually exclusive terms. In the words of Van S. Bird, "Not only can Black and Anglican traditions coexist; they do exist in a potentially creative and constructive tension."[48] In this regard, Gavin White calls the "Negro Episcopalian Church" a "success story"—not only has it survived, ultimately it has been creative in its survival.[49]

CHAPTER 10

The Roman Catholic Church

> Having learned in this Congress the admirable and
> remarkable efforts thus far accomplished for the benefit of
> the African race, either in this country or on the African
> continent, by the various religious orders of the Catholic
> Church, we tender these zealous and noble hearted
> pioneers of the Gospel the expression of our admiration
> and gratitude, and trust they will continue the work of
> devotion done for the regeneration of our people.
> —*The First Negro Catholic Congress, 1889*[1]

> The Catholic church will remain religiously ineffective in
> the black community unless it can effectively syncretize
> African culture with Catholic worship, just as the black
> Protestant church two centuries ago syncretized African
> culture and Biblical religion.
> —*Pope Paul VI*[2]

While W. E. B. Du Bois criticized the Episcopal Church in 1903 for
having done less for black people than any other denomination,[3]
four years earlier he had commented that the Catholic Church in
the prior decade had made noteworthy progress in its work
among blacks and was determined to do more in the future.[4] In
the years prior to the turn of the century, there were numerous
developments among black Catholics to which Du Bois may
have been referring. Two orders of black nuns were founded—
the Oblates of Providence in 1829 and the Sisters of the Holy
Family in 1842. In 1884, a national newspaper was founded by
Daniel A. Rudd, a black Catholic layman of Cincinnati. Rudd
also engineered five Negro Catholic congresses between 1889
and 1894, which addressed the basic question of the relationship
between black Catholics and their church.[5] As Du Bois percep-
tively foresaw, during the ensuing decades, black Catholics did

accomplish more within their church. In 1909, a fraternal order for black Catholic laypersons was founded in Mobile, Alabama, called the Knights of Saint Peter Claver. In 1917, another black sisterhood was founded, the Franciscan Handmaids of the Most Pure Heart of Mary.

The next surge of developments occurred in the years following the Civil Rights movement—the founding of the Black Catholic Clergy Caucus and the National Black Sisters' Conference in 1968, and the creation of the Black Lay Catholic Caucus and the National Office for Black Catholics (NOBC) in 1970. Of major importance, too, was the 1987 publication of the first collection of black hymnody under the auspices of the Black Catholic Clergy Caucus, *Lead Me, Guide Me: The African American Catholic Hymnal.* The publication of this hymnal is not only symbolic of the progress black Catholics have made in their church over the last century, it is also one of their most important achievements.

The little that can be said of a black hymnic tradition in the Catholic Church is fairly recent in origin. The call by the Second Vatican Council in 1963 for liturgical renewal and musical acculturation no doubt was in good part responsible for the present use of black hymnody in the Catholic liturgy and for the publication of *Lead Me, Guide Me.* But there are some additional factors to consider, one of which is the work of a black priest born in Selma, Alabama, Father Clarence Joseph Rivers. Rivers is known in Catholic circles for having launched the renewal in American Catholic music with the publication of his first musical composition, *American Mass Program* (1963), a collection of songs for cantor and congregation. It is significant that this composition, which brought together black spirituals and Gregorian chant, was published prior to the celebration of the first English Mass in Kiel Auditorium, Saint Louis, in August 1964. Rivers' efforts initially led to a folk liturgical revival among white Catholics; only in the late sixties did that revival reach the black Catholic community.[6]

In spite of these rapid developments during the sixties, Rivers' work toward liturgical renewal actually commenced about five years before Vatican II and the publication of his *American Mass Program,* both in 1963. His first efforts, he recalled, date back to around 1956:

Before the pioneering work that we, somewhat unwittingly, began to develop at St. Joseph's Church in Cincinnati between the years 1956 and 1964, it can scarcely be said that the Roman Catholic Church in the Black community was on the road at all. . . . Our liturgical pilgrimage had not even begun. In fact the only effort that I know of, that attempted, before that period, to bring together Black culture and Catholic worship within the United States were the efforts of a particular religious sister from somewhere, I believe, in Oklahoma. She attempted to cover the language of the Latin Mass with unadapted melodies from Negro Spirituals. I remember the Kyrie was sung to the exact tune of "Nobody Knows The Trouble I See." The melody was an ill fitting garment for the words, however noble the idea behind the effort; the effort itself was less than successful. But I do remember someone saying around the time that Sister might well have been more successful had she tried to adapt the basic style and the various elements of Black music to the needs of our liturgical texts without forcing . . . a shotgun wedding of existing melodies with incompatible texts.[7]

There was at least one other effort earlier than the one cited by Rivers, but it occurred in the Episcopal Church, the closest doctrinal and liturgical relative to the Roman Catholic Church. It involved a priest who, presiding over a "Negro mission" near Cincinnati, brought black spirituals into the Episcopal liturgy. The successful venture was documented in 1934 by a religious sister named Esther Mary, N.C.T. In her article, "Spirituals in the Church," Sister Mary advocated the use of this indigenous music in the Episcopal liturgy as a means of meeting the religious needs of black worshipers. In setting up her argument in favor of acculturation, Sister Mary painted the scene of what certainly was one of the earliest efforts at liturgical indigenization among blacks in American Episcopal worship:

It is solemn Evensong at the mission of St. Simon of Cyrene, near Cincinnati, Ohio. Fr. Wilson the priest in charge, has just announced: "The service of Holy Baptism will be found on page 273 of the Prayer Book." With the acolytes he goes to the center of the sanctuary. As he turns to the font, the words ring out: "It's me, It's me, O Lord." Like an answering wave comes from the congregation of colored people— "Standing in the need of prayer." Fifteen minutes later as the closing prayer in the service of Holy Baptism is finished and the procession of priest and acolytes starts toward the sanctuary, again the priest's voice resounds with— "Swing low, sweet chariot." Fervently the congregation continues: "Coming for to carry me home."[8]

Sister Mary proceeded to say that, at the mission, they sang two settings of the service of Holy Communion based on spirituals, one titled "The Communion Office," published in 1925 by Rev. A. Myron Cochran, and the other composed specifically for the mission by Father Wilson and Harold Frederic (formerly of Cincinnati). Both settings, she said, were very popular among the black worshipers.[9]

In the several years following the founding of Saint Simon's Mission, Sister Mary had found that the spirituals had come to play an important role in worship and in the life of the church. For three reasons, she said, they were helpful in ministering to black Christians: (1) the spirituals were a natural form of religious expression for these worshipers, (2) they possessed a beauty not dependent upon vocal training, and (3) they comprised a body of truly exquisite religious song.[10] Regarding her second point, Sister Mary said, "It is interesting to see how natural the singing of even unfamiliar spirituals is to people of St. Simon's. For that reason, while other forms of Church music must be diligently rehearsed, little time has to be spent upon practising the spirituals." With sensitivity and insight, she concluded, "They do not need to be practised, they have been lived."[11]

Prior to (and even after) the Second Vatican Council, the idea of a "black liturgy" was an uncomfortable one for many white leaders in the Catholic Church (and for white leaders in the Episcopal Church, too). Rivers recalled that a former Archbishop of Cincinnati forbade his use of spirituals in the Catholic liturgy, on the grounds that they were secular music.[12] Sister Francesca Thompson similarly recalled that a certain Reverend Mother once remarked to her that the spirituals were "all right" but were not for use in the church.[13] On the other hand, judging from a comment by Sister Mary regarding the Episcopal Church, there were probably a few persons concerned not so much that the spirituals would profane the sacred liturgy, but more that the liturgy would rob the spirituals of a certain authenticity. She said, "While the singing of spirituals in a dignified service may rob them of a certain mode of expression, again when rightly used the religious fervor produced will be as genuine and deep as that aroused in a more primitive atmosphere. Songs having as universal an appeal as spirituals do not need their original setting to give power to their message. Else why the Psalms?"[14] Finally, Sister Mary drew quite a prophetic conclusion from her experiences: "We read and talk much of the value and even necessity of using native Chinese music in the Church of China, of doing the same in Japan. Are we in this country using to the full the priceless heritage of Negro spirituals in our churches ministering to colored people?"[15]

Rivers' response to this question, as applied to his own religious group, was that the Catholic Church in North America had not made adequate advances in employing the musical heritage of blacks until the early 1970s, when the National Office for Black Catholics (NOBC) developed a Department of Culture and Worship to further this end.[16] Moreover, it was only after Rivers had begun successfully to promote the use of black sacred music in predominantly black parishes, through workshops sponsored by the Department of Culture and Worship, that he realized that the music could only be authentic if it were accompanied by a fully Africanized liturgy, including black preaching, praying, and reading. He said, "It was this dichotomy between relatively excellent performance in music and absolutely lousy performance in spoken prayer and reading and preaching that led some specialists in Black culture to wonder if it were really possible to combine Black culture and Catholic worship."[17] In response to this problem, Rivers began advocating a fully "integrated" black liturgy.[18]

Given Rivers' lifetime work of forming an integrated black liturgy for black parishes, it is not surprising that *The African-American Catholic Hymnal* was dedicated to him: "Renowned Liturgist and Musician Father Clarence Jos. Rivers, Ph.D., who paved the way for liturgical inculturation and inspired Black Catholics to bring their artistic genius to Catholic worship." In one of the hymnal's two introductory essays, "The Gift of African American Sacred Song," by the late Sister Thea Bowman, Rivers was further acknowledged:

> In the sixties, Father Clarence Joseph Rivers revitalized Catholic worship, inaugurated a revolution in liturgical music, stirred international interest in the indigenization of Catholic Liturgy, and brought new hope, joy, and spirit to millions of Black Americans when he introduced the melodies, rhythms, harmonies, symbols and rituals of African American Sacred Song into Roman Catholic worship. His *American Mass Program* and subsequent compositions and recordings popularized Black music for Catholic worship. His *Soulfull Worship* and *The Spirit in Worship* analyzed the history, theology, theory and practice of Black sacred song

and its appropriateness and effectiveness in Catholic liturgy and worship.

Although Rivers was a leading figure in liturgical renewal in the American Catholic Church, it was during the black cultural revolution of the seventies that the burgeoning racial and cultural price of black Americans led to momentous developments. Father J.-Glenn Murray, in his introductory essay to the *Lead Me, Guide Me* hymnal, "The Liturgy of the Roman Rite and African American Worship," lauds Vatican II for its call for liturgical renewal in the church. In contrast, Presbyterian hymnologist Melva Costen, in her review of the hymnal, credits the movement led by the Reverend Martin Luther King, Jr. She says that, while the Second Vatican Council is usually recognized as the cause of numerous hymnal revisions and publications, the black community identifies the Civil Rights movement as the source of these changes.[19] Hymnologist William Farley Smith agrees with Costen, stating that the "ethnic nationalism" found in *The African American Catholic Hymnal* is a positive response to the Civil Rights movement. He concludes that black Catholics deserve acclaim for daring to liberate themselves from imposed traditions in order to reclaim some of their rightful heritage.[20] Sensing that there may be those within the white Christian community who fear this "new wave of ethnic nationalism," Smith says that, "much like Christ, *Lead Me, Guide Me* . . . is come neither to hurt nor destroy, but to bring a light to all who would deny the richness and usefulness of musical expression created by a vibrant culture of God-loving people."[21]

It was during this period of "ethnic nationalism" that the question of whether black Catholics could be both black and Catholic became a major issue—so major, in fact, that many blacks began leaving the Catholic Church because they could not reconcile the two.[22] Rivers responded that "from a theoretical point of view the very name of Catholic means Universal, a Church that is open to all . . . cultures; and if a *black* Catholic is not possible then there is no such thing as a *catholic* Church."[23] Convinced that there could develop a fully integrated black liturgy, Rivers argued further that, if black slaves could be true to their Afrocentricity while simultaneously becoming Christians, then so could blacks today be true to their African characters as Catholics.[24] Put plainly by Catholic theologian Diana Hayes,

"Black Catholics can no longer be required to 'sing the Lord's song in a foreign land.' Black Catholics have decided to take down their harps from the willows where they have hung for so long and to make that foreign land their own."[25]

When the 1970 National Convention of Black Lay Catholics resolved that black Catholics are first black and then Catholic,[26] what was really being called for was a liturgy that was first and foremost reflective of their ethnic heritage—what Father William Norvel defined as a "Black Liturgy":

> A Black Liturgy is the corporate worship of God by a Black people who constitute that priestly society which is the Church. It is essential that this liturgy spring out of the Afro-Americans' culture and experiences. For it is out of these experiences that a viable atmosphere of worship and a meaningful mode of expression is created whereby the whole man with his fears, aspirations, joys, and uncertainties is expressed through spirituals, a sermon, brotherhood, and the Eucharist.[27]

Diana Hayes is equally enthusiastic about the notion of a black liturgy, which she identifies as the consequence of "black Catholic revivalism" (black ethnicity): "The result is the emergence of a worship form which recognizes and proclaims that the unique contributions of the African past, the ongoing black life experience and Catholic ritual and sacramentality are compatible and belong together. Out of this rich synthesis has come a form of worship which celebrates being black and Catholic in a way which is not only self-affirming but also community-building and nurturing."[28]

Bishop James Lyke (now an archbishop), who coordinated the African-American Catholic hymnal project, has also commented on the viability of a black liturgy, but more specifically as it relates to the theology of liberation. Through his view of black liturgy as a means of black liberation, he resolves an issue raised implicitly by such Catholic theologians as Edward K. Braxton: whether or not there even exists a black Catholic theology.[29] Lyke says:

> In the Sacred Liturgy, we discover and renew our identity and we bring our unique Black expression to divine worship. If we are a people traveling the liberation road, then we must leave behind the accretions of the past to which we had been enslaved, and celebrate our liturgies in the soulful spontaneity of our culture. This is what Pope Paul VI had in mind when in July of 1969, he told African Catholics, "you will be capable of bringing to the Catholic Church the precious and original

contribution of 'negritude,' which she needs particularly in this historic hour."[30]

Clarence Williams agrees that embracing the task of indigenization and bringing black expression into Catholic worship is evidence of the process of black liberation within the rather confining structure of the Catholic Church.[31]

On the other hand, Rivers had been equally concerned that traditional forms of black sacred music be authentically performed by black Catholics who often are unaccustomed to the tradition. While Sister Mary found in the thirties that the black Episcopalians at Saint Simon's Mission had to spend little time practicing the spirituals, in that they had "lived" them, this is not the case with most contemporary black Catholics, who have never had to really "live" the spirituals. In order to learn to perform authentically and not caricature traditional black music, said Rivers, contemporary black Catholics must turn to their Protestant counterparts who have long "lived" the music and who maintain its traditional performance practices.[32]

Hence, when Rivers became director of the Department of Culture and Worship, National Office for Black Catholics, and sponsored the first Afro-American liturgy workshop in July 1971, among the Protestants he contracted for the event were Pentecostal (Church of God in Christ) recording artist Edwin Hawkins and the Hawkins Family Singers.[33] From the concert culminating this week-long workshop was edited and published a two-record album titled *Freeing the Spirit.*

The following year, the workshop was held in New Orleans at Xavier University, and Edwin Hawkins again participated. During the ensuing years, the annual event was held in various locations throughout the country and involved musicians such as Robert Ray and Avon Gillespie. Gillespie, who has a number of pieces in *Lead Me, Guide Me,* instructed worship participants to be less inhibited about using their bodies in worship. He told them that, while many people freely dance on Saturday night, the very same people are overly restrained on Sunday morning. In order for Sunday worship to be an authentically worshipful community expression, concluded Gillespie, it must reflect the ritual values of that community.[34]

While Rivers long had been concerned that the liturgies in black Catholic parishes become Africanized by means such as those suggested by Gillespie, he was equally insistent that these parishes not abandon their Catholic traditions and become inauthentically Catholic in their haste to become authentically black.[35] Said Rivers, "Who knows . . . what original, unique richness might be created by black Catholics if they could overcome the temptation to discard traditional Catholic music 'because it is the music of our enslavers.'"[36] Repeatedly Rivers stressed the importance of black Catholics not abandoning the musical traditions of their church: "Among blacks themselves, it must be realized, there will be varying cultural preferences, all of which may be valid so long as black people themselves choose them because they find them to be of human value. And so when we are talking about adapting Afro-American culture to Roman Catholicism we must be careful to allow black people to choose freely among the things they find to be of human value."[37] What this means, according to Murray, writing in his introductory essay to *Lead Me, Guide Me* concerning both traditions, is

> If our celebration of the Eucharistic Liturgy (and by extension, all the other liturgical rites) is to be both Catholic and Black, then those whose responsibility it is to plan and execute worship must continue to *study* the Roman Liturgy in order to understand its inner dynamics, come to *appreciate* the significance and integrity of each of its parts, *learn* those places where improvisation may legitimately occur, *keep the assembly central, read* voraciously about inculturation, and *remain open* to the Spirit. It can and must be done!

In order for black Catholics to express the unique mix of their ethnic heritage and their church, Murray specifies, they need to be attentive not only to their Euro-American legacy of Latin chants, motets, and hymns, but also to their Afro-American legacy of spirituals, gospels, adopted and adapted hymns, and contemporary works by black Catholic composers.

The composed liturgies of Rivers are emblematic of this fusion and of what is required of one who plans and executes an indigenized Catholic liturgy. In his book *Soulfull Worship* are nine liturgical "celebrations" involving more than forty songs representing both the Roman Catholic and the African-American traditions—Gregorian chant, standard hymns, black spirituals, and pieces composed by Rivers himself.[38] The synthesis has proven to be very successful for those who have attended Rivers' workshops and employed his liturgies in their parishes. Even Sister Mary, back in 1934, recognized the appropriateness of interweaving the spirituals and traditional Episcopal music: "Because of their very simplicity," she said, "they seem appropriate in the service of Solemn Evensong as the Plainsong Magnificat which follows them, and the use of two such different types of music in one service, rather than seeming incongruous, tends to enhance the beauty of each kind."[39]

Regarding this interweaving of spirituals and Catholic service music, Murray, in his introductory essay in *Lead Me, Guide Me*, outlines the structure of the Eucharistic liturgy and suggests that selections from the repertory of black hymnody may be used as a prelude to the liturgy or the sermon. An even more detailed suggestion has been given by Glenn R. Hufnagel, who employed black hymnody in his music ministry at the Our Lady of Lourdes Church in Buffalo:

> What I propose here is the use of the spiritual with the responsorial psalm of the Mass, as follows: The antiphon of the psalm is replaced with the refrain of a spiritual expressing the same idea and mood. The antiphon is simply a line from the psalm pulled out and highlighted. By replacing it with a refrain, none of the psalm is lost; but both the spiritual and the psalm are "unlocked" by juxtaposition with a different form of expression. Both "blossom" with new meaning and power. The psalm verses may then be read by the lector (with soft transitional music underneath); or, if the verses are fairly regular in structure, they may be set to a melody, or improvised on a psalm tone or blues chant. The spiritual, with its own verses, can then be used elsewhere to lend unity to the service, perhaps as an entrance, communion or closing hymn. . . . The rapprochement of psalm and spiritual is, after all, not so radical. The Psalms are the songs of Scripture; the spirituals are the Psalms of slavery.[40]

Hufnagel's comment that the psalms and the spirituals are kindred genres is absolutely correct. Indeed, *psalm*, a term essentially synonymous with *song*, denotes a lyric poem that was intended to be set to music. Psalm titles such as "To the Chief Musician," "A Song or Psalm of David," and "A Song of Degrees" imply this. Even though the psalms were created between the first and seventh centuries B.C. and the spirituals were created during the eighteenth and nineteenth centuries A.D., there always has been an intimate connection between them: (1) The 150 psalms and the entire corpus of spirituals express the same ideas and moods. (2) The composers of the psalms and spirituals created their music specifically for religious worship, which explains why both genres are often exhortative and edifying. (3) Both psalms and spirituals do more than document biblical history as told in many of the Old Testament narratives; they also capture the worldview of those who created the music, including how they perceived such things as life and death. (4) The symbolism in both the psalms and spirituals is sufficiently broad to make their messages in today's liturgy about as meaningful to the contemporary worshiper as to the original creators. (5) In terms of literary form, the psalms, like the spirituals, employ parallel syntax, refrain, recapitulation, repetition, and strophic and responsorial form. (6) Perhaps the most striking similarity exists specifically between the psalm "lament" and the spiritual "sorrow song": both commence with an individual or community cry for help to overcome sorrow, oppression, or transgression, and conclude faithfully and joyfully on a high pitch of praise.

Hufnagel, pursuant to his suggestion, classes the psalms and the spirituals in corresponding categories. He categorizes the psalms under the themes of joy, creation, help, praise, and thanksgiving, and then gives a corresponding list of spirituals that he uses as substitutes. His list of spirituals is supplemented with other favorite hymns of the black tradition, including pieces by Rivers. Under his category of "Help (Prayer) Psalms," for instance, are listed Psalms 23, 25, 27, 30, 32, 34, 40, 54, 71, 72, 77, 90, 91, 95, 112, and 121, and such possible substitutes as "Balm in Gilead," "Do Lord," "Hush! Hush!," "I Got a Home in that Rock," "I've Been 'Buked," "I Want Jesus to Walk with Me," "Keep Me from Sinkin' Down," "The Battle Hymn of the Republic" (the refrain), and "Rock of Ages" (the first line).[41]

The synthesis of two differing traditions, which Hufnagel accomplished in his music ministry, is superbly captured in *The African American Catholic Hymnal*. Bishop James P. Lyke, coordinator of the hymnal project, and the Reverend William Norvel, president of the National Black Catholic Clergy Caucus, make this comment in their preface:[42]

> *Lead Me, Guide Me* is born of the needs and aspirations of Black Catholics for music that reflects both our African American heritage and our

Catholic faith. For a long time, but particularly within the last two decades, Black Catholics and the pastoral staffs who minister to our people have increasingly seen the need for liturgical and devotional settings and hymnody that lend themselves to the unique and varied styles of song and expression that are characteristic of our people.

Among the black Catholics who early recognized the need for liturgical settings and devotional hymnody was Avon Gillespie, who, according to the hymnal's preface, developed a proposal for such a hymnal in 1978. Another was Father James T. Menkhus, who in 1981 reiterated Gillespie's call for a hymnal. While an associate pastor of Saint Martin's in Baltimore, Menkhus discovered a real need for a special hymnal that could be used in that church's Gospel Mass. Initially he thought that the church could simply purchase a hymnal existing on the market, and he was surprised to find that there was no such hymnal available that expressed the black Catholic "charism."[43] Menkhus said, "So where is the book or hymnal that has compiled the modern efforts of a gifted people? Where, within the Catholic Church, have we gathered the produce of gifted black artists?"[44] Assuming that the delay in producing such a volume was due to financial difficulties, Menkhus concluded, "We encourage the Catholic bishops to consider underwriting such a project."[45]

Whether the problem in producing a black Catholic hymnal was financial, cultural, or political, the official authorization for such a volume finally came in April 1983, according to the preface, from Father Donald Clark, then president of the National Black Catholic Clergy Caucus. Perhaps Clark's impetus was not just the need expressed by such black Catholics as Gillespie and Menkhus, but also the 1982 resolution of the Bishops' Committee on the Liturgy: "There are a diversity of ways of living the Catholic faith, according to the gifts, opportunities and vocations of diverse Catholics. Liturgical celebration should reflect this diversity, and all expressions of faith should be cherished and nurtured. Concern for community should not become oppressive by the insistence that one *kind* of community style is normative for all Catholics."[46] Four years after its authorization in 1983, the hymnal was published by the Catholic press, GIA Publications, in Chicago.

The fusion of the black and Catholic traditions in *Lead Me, Guide Me* is evident in the appearance of the volume. "The very appearance of *Lead Me, Guide Me* is striking and makes a distinct statement regarding the strong African-American heritage of black Catholics," says Wendelin Watson:

> It is a hardbound laminated cover in the colors of the Black American liberation flag—red, black, and green—which symbolize black heritage and solidarity with black African peoples. The flags of many African nations are made up of these colors which symbolize the shed blood, the race/color, and the land of its peoples. The title, *Lead Me, Guide Me,* appears at the bottom of the front cover in bright green letters against a black and red design characteristic of African kinte cloths. On the spine of the hymnal in small letters are the initials of the Catholic publishing company, the Gregorian Institute of America.[47]

The Catholic heritage, says Watson, is also symbolically represented in the outer design of the hymnal:

> Spanning nearly the length of the lefthand side of the front cover is a large capital *P* (black and trimmed in red) which is the ancient Greek symbol, a *kyro*, used by the early Christian community to represent Christ. Usually a part of the cross which stands on the lectern in Catholic churches, the vertical line of the *P* extends downward forming a Cross or *X*. On the back cover is a large capital *M* (also black and trimmed in red) which refers to the blessed Mary to whom high veneration is given by Catholic believers. Perhaps these symbols at the beginning and ending of the hymnal are representative of the Catholic faith expressed in the 565 pieces of music there between.[48]

In terms of its black hymnic content, *Lead Me, Guide Me* includes approximately fifty-five black spirituals arranged by such historic figures as John Wesley Work, Jr., and Willa A. Townsend, and by such contemporary musicians as David Hurd, Richard Smallwood, Evelyn D. White, Verolga Nix, and the late J. Jefferson Cleveland.[49] From the black gospel hymn era (1900–1930) are two pieces by C.A. Tindley. Although there are no hymns of C.P. Jones representing the black Holiness gospel hymn tradition, there are two praise songs by Jones' longtime friend of the Pentecostal tradition, C.H. Mason—"My Soul Loves Jesus" and "Yes, Lord." From the golden age of gospel (1930–69) are pieces by Doris Akers, Lucie E. Campbell, Thomas A. Dorsey, Roberta Martin, Kenneth Morris, and Clara Ward. From the modern era (1969–present) are pieces by such performing artists as James Cleveland, Andrae Crouch, and Elbernita Clark (of the Clark Sisters). In addition to these songs, which fall under the rubric of black gospel, are the various hymns of the white Christian tradition that have long been adopted and adapted by black worshipers—a few favorites of Watts and Wesley; the gospel hymns of Fanny J. Crosby, Elisha A. Hoffman, and their contemporaries; and the modern gospel songs of the William and Gloria Gaither duo. Among the contemporary hymnody by black composers not written in a gospel vein is Roland M. Carter's "Let the Heav'n Light Shine on Me," from his *Five Choral Responses* (1978), and a number of pieces in English translation taken from Howard S. Olson's collection of African hymns, titled *Lead Us Lord* (1977).

The pieces that fall under the hymnal's heading of "Social Concern" not only reflect a post-seventies Afro-Christian worldview, they also illustrate the range of hymns black Christians have composed, adopted, and adapted over the course of their history in North America. Of the nine pieces in this section, almost half are spirituals—"Glory, Glory, Hallelujah," "Free At Last," "O Freedom," and "Go Down, Moses." Also included is the anthem of the Civil Rights movement ("We Shall Overcome"), the Black National Anthem ("Lift Every Voice and Sing"), and two pieces thematizing Martin Luther King's "dream," Robert Manuel's "Keep the Dream Alive" and Ruth Manier's "He Had a Dream."

The two pieces about King further exemplify the diversity of musical styles found in the hymnal and among black musical compositions. Manier's piece, with its repetition, simple dotted melody, and guitar chords, has the air of a folksong. Even its words are folk-like in their repetitiveness. Manuel's piece, on the other hand, is set to a standard four-part harmony and is more conservatively hymnic in nature. Also, in contrast to the former piece, the poetry is more refined.

Also included in *Lead Me, Guide Me* is a variety of Catholic hymnody, ranging from Thomas Aquinas' "O Salutaris" ("O Saving Victim") and "Tantum Ergo" ("Come Adore") to Edward V. Bonnemere's jazz-styled "Christ Is Coming: Prepare the Way" (complete with guitar chords). Similarly, the Marian hymns range from the thirteenth century "Ave Maria" (in Latin) to an African folk hymn, "Salamu Maria." The Masses range from the Latin *Missa de Angelis* to Rivers' *Mass Dedicated to the Brotherhood of Man* (1970). Musical settings for various parts of the Mass—for instance, the Agnus Dei ("Lamb of God")—range from the "standard" setting by black Episcopalian David Hurd to the gospel setting by black African Methodist Episcopalian Robert Ray (from his celebrated *Gospel Mass* of 1981).

In addition to Father Rivers, the other black Catholic composers represented in *Lead Me, Guide Me* are Edmund Broussard, who served on the Hymnal Committee; Marjorie Gabriel-Burrow of the National Association of Black Catholic Administrators; Avon Gillespie, a university music professor; Rawn Harbor and Leon C. Roberts, both of the National Association of Black Catholic Musicians; Grayson Warren Brown; and Edward V. Bonnemere, New York jazz musician. In the hymnal's preface, special recognition is given to Gabriel-Burrow, Harbor, and Roberts, who comprised the subcommittee that studied and selected the hymns and composed and arranged many of them. "To state it pointedly," reads the preface, "without this gifted and dedicated trio, there would be no African American Catholic Hymnal." In many respects, it can also be said that, without the pioneering work of Rivers, there would be no hymnal; it was because of him, says the late Sister Bowman in her introductory essay, that Harbor, Brown, Bonnemere, and Roberts began to compose music for the Catholic liturgy.

All of Bonnemere's pieces initially were composed for Saint Thomas the Apostle Church in Harlem, where he serves as musical director.[50] Two of his several pieces in *Lead Me, Guide Me* have been extracted from his extended liturgical compositions *Advent Jazz Vespers II* and *Mary, Cause of Our Joy*. Roberts' contribution to *Lead Me, Guide Me* includes a substantial part of the service music and psalm refrains at the back of the hymnal and his *Mass of Saint Augustine* (1981). Brown's contribution includes service music, psalm refrains, and his Mass *Cast Your Bread Upon the Water* (1985).

Roberts' Mass is especially appropriately titled for inclusion in this *African American Catholic Hymnal,* for the great African theologian Saint Augustine, said Peter Sarpong, Bishop of Kumasi, Ghana, made so much use of the culture of North Africa during his lifetime that the Roman Catholic Church was known there as the "African Church."[51] Not only is Roberts' Mass appropriately titled, it is also an excellent piece of music composition, which

William Farley Smith recognizes as having black musical characteristics:

> The music of Leon C. Roberts, in his "Mass of Saint Augustine" . . . is all at once aesthetically beautiful, spiritually provocative, innovatively daring and, at the same time, definitely bears musical seeds and devices born of the African-American experience. Here, spiritual and gospel music elements have been successfully wedded to the ancient hymns of the Catholic Mass. . . . Roberts handles the music genre with much knowledge and passes on to the reader coded language indicative of authentic African-American performance practice.[52]

Indeed, *Mass of Saint Augustine* is black music, even though it is cast in the European genre of the Mass. Rivers had long repeated his argument that blackness should not be stereotyped or limited to any particular form or definition.[53] This point was rightly stressed by him, for he probably knows all too well the definitions limiting black music to specific and identifiable musical characteristics. Rivers sides with such contemporary black composers as Olly Wilson, who said:

> We're just going to have to say that Black music is simply music written by Black people. We can talk about certain idioms, about jazz, gospel, soul, African music, early Afro-American music, but it is difficult to pinpoint the music of the contemporary composer in the same way. Implicit behind this is the inference that there is a way for Black composers to compose . . . and if you do not compose this way, you are not Black.
>
> I would prefer to believe that you are in fact a result of all your experiences so that a Black man cannot exist outside of his Blackness. That's why I say when I write a piece, if I'm honest with myself . . . it obviously reveals my Blackness, whether it is demonstrated or not, whether you hear it or not.[54]

In addition to bringing together traditional black hymnody and contemporary sacred music by black Catholics and thus reconciling the apparent discrepancy between being black and Catholic, *Lead Me, Guide Me* is important for another reason: it communicates to the larger black community the self-determination of black Catholics. Effectively communicating with the black community, and assuring them that black Catholic pronouncements and black Catholic theology are not merely the resolutions and theology of the white Catholic hierarchy, is an important concern of black Catholic leaders.[55] By proving that they are no longer "musically enslaved" by the liturgical restrictions previously placed on them by the Catholic authorities,[56] black Catholics make a statement to the wider black community that they are about the task of self-determination.

It is likely that part of the need black Catholics have to illustrate their self-determination to the larger black community through such means as the publication of *Lead Me, Guide Me,* is their longtime quest to procure black converts from the Protestant denominations. For whatever reasons (educational, political, economic, social, or personal) black Christians convert to Roman Catholicism, without liturgical acculturation the church's liturgical practices will remain too foreign to potential converts. As Father Joseph M. Davis commented a decade and a half ago—and this remains true today—the rather static condition of Catholicism among blacks is due to the fact it has not yet become an institution that truly belongs to black people.[57] "The acculturation of black Catholics to white Catholic religious expression as the right Catholic way has been a rude awakening for new black Catholic converts. . . . Once inside the Church, they were introduced to services which utilized an 'alien' music (and until recently, a foreign language.)"[58] Concluded Davis:

> The fundamental concept of the Church's mission in this country distinguished between *ordinary* and *extraordinary.* The ordinary work was in the white community; the extraordinary was in the black community. Church personnel functioning from this viewpoint conceived of their task as converting, in the full sense of the word, black people not only to the one, *true* Church, but also to a "better" way of life. The subtle implication was that black people were also being converted *away from* something, and that was from a culture, tradition and heritage which was not in itself significant, valid or civilizing. The music, dance, diction, patterns of speech and manner of behaving were thought of as some kind of "aberration" from the normal or white man's style of life.[59]

The need to show potential converts of the larger black community that conversion to Roman Catholicism does not necessitate conversion away from their cultural heritage, was no doubt a factor giving *Lead Me, Guide: The African American Catholic Hymnal* a strong ecumenical bent.[60] Regarding this aspect of ecumenism, the preface to the hymnal states: "Black Catholics, who embody various religious and cultural traditions, wish to share our gifts with the wider ecclesial community and draw from the great musical corpus of our Roman Catholic tradition and that of our Sister Churches. Thus *Lead Me, Guide Me* is both universal and particular as well as ecumenical in composition." That *The African American Catholic Hymnal* has in fact been received ecumenically is certain proof that black Catholics themselves have begun to be received by the larger black church community.

Postscript

The leading African-American cultural critics of today—C. Eric Lincoln, Molefi Asante, James H. Cone, Maulana Karenga, Manning Marable, Cornel West, and many other prophetic pragmatists pointing our way toward the twenty-first century—agree that two major concerns facing African Americans are *self-identity* and *self-determination*. Because the hymns sung in the black church are an essential aspect of the religious worldview of black Christians, a study of these hymns, as deposited in the hymnbooks of ten denominations, has been my approach to tracing the status and progress of their theological and doctrinal beliefs and social perspectives over the last two centuries. By peering through the hymnological lens and studying the content of denominational hymnals, I have sometimes stated directly and other times only implied that the black church registers a distinct need for renewed self-identity and self-determination.

The intent of this assessment and this entire critical summary is not to denigrate the black church, which historically has been the most important institution owned and operated by African Americans. But the reality is implicit in the foregoing hymnological history: the black church still tends to be held captive by a kind of theological, doctrinal, and social backwardness that works to stifle impetus toward black self-identity and self-determination in the larger social milieu. Religion itself is not necessarily responsible; religion need not be limited to being a mere stage in the process of human maturation, and does not necessarily quell human aspiration and achievement. African-American self-identify and self-determination should be achievable in and through theological, doctrinal, and social progressiveness.

By what means, then, can Afro-Christians more rapidly alleviate these problems that are reflected in black church hymnody and progress, via the vehicle of their religion, toward racial liberation? First of all, it must be recognized that the problem is not simply *reflected* in the hymnody; to a considerable degree the problem *is* the hymnody. Replacing extant hymnody with a radically aggressive song that realistically remembers past obstacles African Americans have overcome and points to future hurdles they must overcome certainly would help launch the race toward the achievement of corporate personhood. Such a new corpus of church music could build upon the base of the spirituals and Civil Rights songs to include modern expressions of faith and worship that cross the moods and meanings of antislavery and Social Gospel hymnody.

Of course, this radical step is at present an impracticality, if not an impossibility. The black Christian populace seems too entrenched in tradition, too attached to the old "songs of Zion," suddenly to accept more compelling Afrocentric expressions of self-identity and self-determination. A far less extreme, then, would be to omit or modify hymns containing negative racist and sexist language and imagery, as the more modern black hymnals have done, slowly but surely, since the Civil Rights movement began. Just as sexist language contributes to the perpetuation of a tradition of female subjugation, so is language that portrays "black" as evil and inferior, and "white" as sacred and supreme, unhealthy to the minds and spirits of black people. Malcolm X once commented in a speech: "My mother was a Christian and my father was a Christian, and I used to hear them when I was a little child sing songs, 'Washing me white as snow.' My father was a black man and my mother was a black woman, and yet the songs that they sang in their church were designed to fill their hearts with the desire to be white."[1] For this very reason, Henry McNeal Turner, the nineteenth-century AME bishop, prevented his congregations from singing "Wash me and I shall be *whiter* than snow." Washing, he explained, is meant to make one clean, not "white." The problem, to repeat, is not simply *reflected* in the hymnody; to a considerable degree the problem *is* the hymnody.

Something else can be done to press black Christians forward, against the prevailing odds, toward human fulfillment through the medium of their religion. The images in black churches can be modified as a way of giving new meaning to some of the old hymns. Unfortunately, some black churches still display the image of the "lily-white" Jesus, which was a master-to-slave hand-me-down from the white church during slavery (as much of our hymnody was). This image, accompanied by dated hymns containing archaic and oppressive language, is preventing masses of black Christians from breaking free of the psychic and spiritual bondage that impedes self-identity and self-determination.[2]

As a product of the black church who has joined its ordained ministry and embraced the ongoing scholarly tradition of prophetic pragmatism,[3] I hope that this hymnological history will help the black church recognize some of its inner strengths and its weaknesses and thereby attain greater self-identity and self-determination as we move into the twenty-first century.

Notes

Chapter 1

1. Richard Allen, *The Life Experience and Gospel Labors of the Rt. Rev. Richard Allen* (Nashville, Tenn.: Abingdon, 1960), 25.
2. See Eileen Southern, ed., *Readings in Black American Music* (New York: Norton, 1971), 52–61, containing an introduction to and partial reprint of Richard Allen's *A Collection of Hymns and Spiritual Songs* (1801); Eileen Southern, *The Music of Black Americans* (New York: Norton, 1971), 85–93; and Eileen Southern, "Hymnals of the Black Church," *Journal of the Interdenominational Theological Seminary* 14, nos. 1 and 2 (Fall 1986-Spring 1987): 127–140.
3. Southern, "Hymnals of the Black Church," 127.
4. Ibid., 130, 132.
5. Ibid., 127.
6. Southern, *Music of Black Americans*, 86.
7. Allen, *Life Experience*, 76. The hymn in Allen's autobiography is titled "Ye Ministers That Called to Preaching." At least one stanza was moved around, as were several lines.
8. *The Doctrines and Discipline of the African Methodist Episcopal Church* (Philadelphia: John H. Cunningham, 1817; rptd. Nashville, Tenn.: AME Publishing House, 1985). The preface is signed by Richard Allen, Daniel Coker, and James Champion.
9. Southern, "Hymnals of the Black Church," 132; Southern, *Music of Black Americans*, 92–93.
10. Southern, "Hymnals of the Black Church," 32–33.
11. Respectively, R.R. Wright, Jr., *The Encyclopedia of the African Methodist Episcopal Church* (Philadelphia: Book Concern of the AME Chuch, 1947), 352; and Daniel A. Payne, *Recollections of Seventy Years* (1888; rptd. New York: Arno and the *New York Times*, 1968), 233.
12. Wright, *Encyclopedia of the AMEC*, 352.
13. Payne, *Recollections*, 233.
14. Ibid., 234–35.
15. Ibid., 235, 237.
16. "Methodist Hymnody," in *AMEC Hymnal* (Nashville, Tenn.: AMEC Publishing House, 1954), 544.

17. "Proceedings of the General Conference of 1876," AME Church, 155.
18. Signed by Bishop Daniel A. Payne, A.W. Wayman, Jabez P. Vampbell, James A. Shorter, T.M.D. Ward, John M. Brown.
19. R.R. Wright, Jr., *The Bishops of the African Methodist Episcopal Church* (Nashville, Tenn.: AME Publishing House, 1963), 332.
20. See Edwin S. Redkey, ed., *Respect Black: The Writings and Speeches of Henry McNeal Turner* (New York: Arno, 1971), 176.
21. Henry McNeal Turner, "Compiler's Remarks," in *The Hymn Book of the African Methodist Episcopal Church*, comp. H.M. Turner (1876). The remarks were signed by H.M. Turner in Savannah, Ga., on 2 June 1873.
22. Payne, *Recollections*, 254, 255.
23. Ibid., 253–54.
24. Ibid., 252.
25. Wright, *Bishops of the AMEC*, 337.
26. Signed on behalf of the Episcopal Council by Bishops T.M.D. Ward and B.T. Tanner.
27. Signed by Bishops Henry McNeal Turner, Wesley John Gaines, Benjamin William Arnett, Benjamin Tucker Tanner, Abraham Grant, Benjamin Franklin Lee, Moses Buckingham Salter, James Anderson Handy, William Benjamin Derrick, and Josiah Haynes Armstrong.
28. Wright, *Encyclopedia of the AMEC*, 264.
29. Charles E. Stewart, "Our Church Music," *AME Review* 36, no. 2 (Oct. 1919):339–40.
30. Ibid., 340.
31. See Wright, *Encyclopedia of the AMEC*, 92.
32. "Methodist Hymnody," 547.
33. James Lynch, "Our Proper Attitude," in Daniel A. Payne, *The Semi-Centenary and the Retrospection of the African Methodist Episcopal Church* (Baltimore, Md.: Sherwood, 1866; rptd. Freeport, N.Y.: Books for Libraries, 1972), 166.

Chapter 2

1. Cited in Milton C. Sernett, ed., *Afro-American Religious History: A Documentary Witness* (Durham, N.C.: Duke Univ. Press, 1985), 151–52. Original source: Christopher Rush, *A Short Account of the Rise and Progress of the African Methodist Episcopal Church in America* (New York: Christopher Rush, 1843).
2. Let me clear up any possible confusion caused by references to AMEZ hymnbooks dated otherwise, for instance, those dates given in the bibliography of William J. Walls, *The African Methodist Episcopal Zion Church: Reality of the Black Church* (Charlotte, N.C.: AME Zion Publishing House, 1974). The 1869 hymnbook was a reprinting of the 1858 volume (I discuss this below). Any cited dates 1878 and 1937 are simply copyright dates found in the 1909 AMEZ hymnal. Recopyrighted by the AMEZ Church in

1937, the 1909 AMEZ hymnal was a duplicate of the Methodist Episcopal hymnal copyrighted in 1878.

3. The preface was signed by Jas. Simmons, general superintendent, and Solomon T. Scott, assistant superintendent.

4. Walls, *AMEZ Church*, 336.

5. James W. Hood, *One Hundred Years of the African Methodist Episcopal Zion Church* (New York: AME Zion Book Concern, 1895), 103.

6. *A Collections of Hymns, for the Use of the Methodist Episcopal Church* (New York: J. Emory and B. Waugh, for the Methodist Episcopal Church, 1831).

7. *Miriam's Timbrel: Sacred Songs Suited to Revival Occasions: and also for Anti-Slavery, Peace, Temperance, and Reform Meetings*, 2d ed., comp. John P. Betker (Mansfield, Ohio: [Wesleyan Methodist Church], 1853).

8. Walls, *AMEZ Church*, 335.

9. *Hymns for the Use of the Methodist Episcopal Church* (New York: Carlton & Lanahan; Cincinnati, Ohio: Hitchcock & Walden, 1849).

10. Signed by Bishops Joseph J. Clinton, Samson D. Talbot, J.W. Loguen, S.T. Jones, John J. Moore, and J.W. Hood. See also Walls, *AMEZ Church*, 117–18.

11. Cited in Walls, *AMEZ Church*, 464–65.

12. *New Hymn and Tune Book: An Offering of Praise for the Use of the African M.E. Zion Church of America* (New York: AME Zion Book Concern, 1892). The copy I examined at the Library of Congress was actually a word hymnal.

13. Robert G. McCutchan, *Our Hymnody: A Manual of the Methodist Hymnal* (New York: Methodist Book Concern, 1937), 507–8. See also Philip Phillips, *Song Pilgrimage Around the World* (Chicago: Fairbanks, Palmer & Co., 1880).

14. This is cited in David Henry Bradley, Sr., *A History of the AME Zion Church*, pt. 2, *1872–1968* (Nashville, Tenn.: Parthenon Press, 1970), 480. The copy of the 1892 *New Hymn and Tune Book* that I examined at the Library of Congress had no prefatory statement.

15. Two of the 32 added pieces were duplicates of pieces already in the original AMEZ hymnbook of 1872 (the ME hymnbook of 1849).

16. The numbers indicate that there were only 65 hymns (1152–1216), but an added hymn was numbered 1168-1/2.

17. Beneath this heading appeared, in parentheses, "For Music, see 'Harp of Zion'."

18. See John Wesley Smith, "Thou Uncreated Source of Love"; J.A.D. Bloice, "Oh How Often Have I Grieved Thee"; Singleton T. Jones, "O What Amazing Bliss"; John J. Moore, "The Aged Sire Has Gone to Rest." Respectively, compare with Philip Doddridge, "Ye Servants of the Lord"; Isaac Watts, "Come Holy Spirit, Heavenly Dove" and "Come Ye that Love the Lord"; and Thomas Kelly, "The Lord is Risen Indeed." In *New Hymn and Tune Book* (1892).

19. See *AME Zion Quarterly Review* (Oct. 1891):23–31; as cited in Walls, *AMEZ Church*, 577.

20. Singleton T. Jones, "O What Amazing Bliss," "Mid Scenes of Sorrow Here," "Far From the Lord, We Long Have Strayed."

21. John Wesley Smith, "As One Who Sits at Ev'ning."
22. Walls, *AMEZ Church*, 555.
23. Benjamin Franklin Wheeler, *Cullings from Zion's Poets* (1907), 122; as cited in Walls, *AMEZ Church*, 559.
24. Walls, *AMEZ Church*, 118. The Book Concern, founded in New York in 1840, moved to Charlotte, N.C., in 1898.
25. *Hymnal of the Methodist Episcopal Church* (New York: Phillips & Hunt; Cincinnati, Ohio: Walden & Stowe, 1882).
26. Ibid.
27. Signed by Bishops J.S. Caldwell, L.W. Kyles, J.W. Wood, P.A. Wallace, B.G. Shaw, E.D.W. Jones, W.J. Walls, J.W. Martin, C.C. Alleyne, W.W. Matthews.
28. Signed by Bishops W.J. Walls, Chairman; W.H. Davenport; James W. Eichelberger, Jr.; H.J. Callis; Buford F. Gordon; James Claire Taylor; S.G. Spottswood; R.W. Sherrill; J.L. Black.
29. *Soul Echoes: A Collection of Songs for Religious Meetings*, 1st ed. (Philadelphia: Soul Echoes Publishing Co., 1909). The address of the publisher was given: 420 S. 11th St., Philadelphia.
30. *Soul Echoes: A Collection of Songs for Religious Meetings*, 2d. (rev.) ed. (1909). This information appeared on the inside cover of Bishop W.J. Wall's enlarged facsimile reprint edition, *Soul Echoes: A Collection of Songs for Religious Meetings*, 3d. ed. (1964); it was not on the inside cover of the copy of the second edition that I examined at the AMEZ's Hood Theological Seminary, Salisbury, N.C. Stylistic considerations suggest that it is the statement added to the second songbook and subsequently carried over to the 1964 reprint of *Soul Echoes*. For instance, the capitalization of "First Book" was more characteristic of writing in 1909 than in 1964.
31. Walls, *AMEZ Church*, 118–19.
32. David Henry Bradley, *History*, 481.
33. "Commission's Statement," *AME Zion Hymnal* (1957).
34. David Henry Bradley, *History*, 481–82.
35. Walls, *AMEZ Church*, 473.
36. *Minutes, Twenty-Seventh Quadrennial Session*, 1924, 115–16, as cited in Walls, *AMEZ Church*, 474.
37. McCutchan, *Our Hymnody*, 11, 12.
38. *Official Journal of the 34th Quadrennial Session*, 1952, 76–77, as cited in David Henry Bradley, *History*, 482.
39. *AMEC Hymnal* (Nashville, Tenn.: AMEC Publishing House, 1954).
40. *Official Journal of the 35th Quadrennial Session*, 1956, 127, as cited in David Henry Bradley, *History*, 127.
41. Walls, *AMEZ Church*, 119.
42. *Official Journal of the 36th Quadrennial Session*, 1960, 322, as cited in David Henry Bradley, *History*, 483.
43. Signed by Bishops W.J. Walls, J.W. Martin, C.C. Alleyne, W.C. Brown, W.W. Slade, J.C. Taylor, R.L. Jones, H.T. Bedford, H.B. Shaw, S.G. Spottswood, W.A. Stewart, D.C. Pope.

44. Included were 90 hymns by Charles Wesley, 7 by John Wesley (4 translations, 2 alterations, and 1 original), and 3 by Samuel Wesley.
45. Walls, *AMEZ Church*, 120.
46. Excluded are the 2 by Rev. J.A.D. Bloice; the 1 hymn each by Richard Haywood Stitt, John E. Price, and William T. Biddle; and 1 of Rev. Benjamin F. Wheeler's 4.

Chapter 3

1. Cited in Milton C. Sernett, ed., *Afro-American Religious History* (Durham, N.C.: Duke Univ. Press, 1985), 236. Original source: Lucius H. Holsey, *Autobiography, Sermons, and Addresses and Essays of Bishop L.H. Holsey, D.D.* (Atlanta, Ga.: Franklin Publishing Co., 1898).
2. The preface defines "improvised hymns" as "the traditional hymns of Christianity . . . 'worked-over' emotionally and given emphasis and interpretations that suited the social, cultural, and psychological needs of Black Christians."
3. *The Hymnal of the Christian Methodist Episcopal Church* (Memphis, Tenn.: CME Publishing House, 1987).
4. Othal H. Lakey, *The History of the CME Church* (Memphis, Tenn.: CME Publishing House, 1985), 586.
5. Ibid., 341.
6. C.H. Phillips, *The History of the Colored Methodist Episcopal Church in America* (Jackson, Tenn.: Publishing House of the CME Church, 1925), 527.
7. Lawrence L. Reddick III, "The Newly Published C.M.E. Hymnal," *Christian Index* 120, no. 20 (15 Oct. 1987):2.
8. In *The Hymnal of the Christian Methodist Episcopal Church* (1987), following the "Hymn of Christian Methodism" is "An Order of Worship" and then the opening hymn. The backmatter includes responsive readings, biblical references for the responsive readings, aids to worship (calls to worship, prayers of confession, invocations), the CME rituals for the sacraments of the Lord's Supper and Baptism, and a ritual for the confirmation and reception of persons into the church.
9. Reddick, "Newly Published," 2.
10. Lakey, *History of the CMEC*, 221.
11. Ibid., 300.
12. *The Hymnal of the Christian Methodist Episcopal Church* (Memphis, Tenn.: CME Publishing House, 1987), preface.
13. Phillips, *History of the CME Church*, 117.
14. *Hymn Book of the Methodist Episcopal Church, South* (Nashville, Tenn.: Publishing House of the ME Church, South, 1889). This postulate was derived after a careful comparison of the CME hymnal and the ME Church, South, hymnals of 1869, 1875, 1881, 1884, and 1889.
15. The only distinctions are that Holsey apparently singularized the words "Perfection" (section I) and "Office" (section III), and deleted the listing of the index from the table of contents.

16. *Hymn Book of the Colored M.E. Church in America* (Jackson, Tenn.: CME Book Concern, 1891). This statement is based on a careful examination of the 1891 hymnal in the Library of Congress.

17. Holsey deleted the indexes of subjects and first lines of stanzas, and "The Ritual, the General Rules and Articles of Religion of the Methodist Episcopal Church, South." He maintained the "Index of First Lines of Hymns" but did not list it in the table of contents, as had the model hymnal.

18. Philip P. Bliss and Ira D. Sankey, *Gospel Hymns and Sacred Songs* (1875); No. 2, again by Bliss and Sankey; and Nos. 3 (1878), 4, 5, and 6 by Ira D. Sankey, James McGranahan, and George C. Stebbins. The six volumes were compiled into *Gospel Hymns: Nos. 1 to 6 Complete* in 1894. All of the 25 pieces added from the latter source were listed under the section "Supplement-Miscellaneous," and neglected to credit the hymnwriters as in the original source.

19. Phillips, *History of the CME Church*, 236.

20. Ibid., 525.

21. F. M. Hamilton, comp., *Songs of Love and Mercy: Adapted to the Use of Sunday Schools, Epworth Leagues, Revivals, Prayer Meetings and Special Occasions* (Jackson, Tenn.: CME Publishing House, 1904). The volume in fact could have been used for a wide range of needs, for only six of the songs were clearly oriented toward youths; one of these was Hamilton's hymn, "Epworth Leaguers."

22. Phillips, *History of the CME Church*, 424.

23. One of the anthems was Hamilton's setting of G.A. Payne's text, "God Is Our Refuge," for choir, duets, and solo (four pages). The other was his setting of Psalm 30:1–5 for solo voices and quartet (six pages). Incidentally, all but 3 of Hamilton's hymns had choruses.

24. Five other persons who might have been members of the CME Church are Charles A. Dryscoll, who set 11 of the hymns (4 of which are by Hamilton and 1 by Cobb); S.G. Brown, author of 4 hymns (3 set by Dryscoll and 1 by F.M. Hamilton); Rev. J.W. West, author of 3 (2 set by Hamilton and 1 by Dryscoll); and G.A. Payne, author of 2 (1 each set by Dryscoll and Hamilton). This conjecture is based on the fact that the pieces of the persons named (Dryscoll, Brown, West, and Payne), along with the pieces of known CMEs (F.M. Hamilton, Hattie Hamilton, and Cobb) were the only hymns in the songbook specifically copyrighted by the CME Church.

25. "The Old Ship of Zion" and "Is This Not the Land of Beulah?"

26. Phillips, *History of the CME Church*, 423.

27. Had the church not decided at its 1890 General Conference to divide Hamilton's elected position of editor/book agent (with him continuing as editor and Rev. I.H. Anderson being elected the new book agent), it would have been Hamilton's name on the 1891 CME hymnal as book agent, rather than Anderson's. Nonetheless, Hamilton did serve on the 1906 Commission on Federation, among whose concerns was the consideration of a "common hymnbook" for the three black Methodist denominations. Phillips, *History of the CME Church*, 348.

28. F.M. Hamilton was author of "The Cause of the Origin and Growth of the CME Church" (1905), "Hand Book on Church Government," "Practical Thoughts," "A Conversation on the CME Church," and "A Plain Account of the CME Church." Prior to Bishop Phillips' denominational history of 1925, the church, wrote Phillips in his book's preface, "has been indebted to Rev. F.M. Hamilton for his 'Plain Account of the C.M.E. Church,' a pamphlet of 136 pages. This has been our only published record and has met a long-felt want." Phillips, *History of the CME Church*, 5.

29. Lakey, *History of the CMEC*, 341.

30. See "Doing God's Will," "We Shall Meet There By and By," "To the Harvest Fields Make Haste," "The Master Calls! Go Work To-Day," "We Are Working for the Lord."

31. "A Mighty Army," "Do You See Them Coming," "The Church Is Marching Onward," "We Are Working for the Lord," "Think On These Things."

32. "We Are Working for the Lord," "Will You Be There?," "The Path the Master Trod," "Let Us Look to Jesus," "March On, Fight On," "Over On the Other Shore."

33. F.M. Hamilton, "Blessed Are the Pure in Heart," in *Songs of Love and Mercy.*

34. Phillips, *History of the CME Church*, 343–44.

35. Ibid., 379.

36. Ibid., 366.

37. "Fourteen Points against the Organic Union of the African Methodist Episcopal, African Methodist Episcopal Zion, and the Colored Methodist Episcopal Churches under the Proposed Birmingham Plan as a Basis of Union." The speech was first delivered on 16 March 1920, and subsequently in St. Louis, Mo.; Petersberg, Va.; Charlotte, N.C.; Springfield, Ohio; and other cities. Phillips, *History of the CME Church*, 615.

38. A "common hymnbook" was one of six items he listed. Cited in Phillips, *History of the CME Church*, 542.

39. *Hymnal of the CME Church* (1987), preface.

40. Ibid.

41. Phillips, *History of the CME Church*, 332.

42. John Wesley, *A Collection of Psalms and Hymns* (Charles-Town, S.C.: Lewis Timothy, 1737). Of the 70 selections, almost half were composed by Isaac Watts. Aside from a few pieces by obscure writers, the remaining were by Samuel Wesley, Sr. (1), Samuel Wesley, Jr. (5), John Austin (7), George Herbert (6), and Joseph Addison (2). In addition were 8 translations by John Wesley from Spanish (1), French (1), and German (5) sources. John L. Nuelsen, *John Wesley and the German Hymn*, trans. Theo Parry et al. (Yorkshire, England: A.S. Holbrook, 1972), 28.

   While some scholars consider the *Bay Psalm Book* (1640) to be the first hymnbook published in America, it actually contained metricized psalms rather than hymns. I agree with Harry Eskew and Hugh T. McElrath that John Wesley's *A Collection of Psalms and Hymns* was the first. See Eskew and McElrath, *Sing with Understanding: An Introduction to Christian Hymnody* (Nashville, Tenn.: Broadman, 1980), 121.

43. For instance, rather than including some of the 54 hymns, arrangements, and settings of Rev. F.M. Hamilton, as found in *Love and Mercy,* there are three hymns by Juanita Griffey Hines, the Baptist composer who served on the committee that compiled the National Baptist hymnal. The point is that it is doubtful that CMEs are familiar with either Mrs. Hines or her hymns.

44. Lakey, *History of the CMEC,* 126, 125.

45. Reddick, "Newly Published," 3.

Chapter 4

1. Cited in Gayraud S. Wilmore and James H. Cone, *Black Theology: A Documentary History, 1966–1979* (Maryknoll, N.Y.: Orbis, 1979), 268.

2. William B. McClain, *Black People in the Methodist Church: Whither Thou Goest?* (Cambridge, Mass.: Shenckman, 1984), 98, 83.

3. *Doctrines and Discipline of the Methodist Church* (New York: Methodist Publishing House, 1939), 27–28.

4. Harry V. Richardson, *Dark Salvation: The Story of Methodism as It Developed Among Blacks in America* (Garden City, N.Y.: Anchor/Doubleday, 1976), 273–74.

5. *Doctrines and Discipline of the Methodist Church* (1939), 696.

6. *The Book of Discipline of the United Methodist Church* (Nashville, Tenn.: United Methodist Publishing House, 1972), 87.

7. Grant S. Shockley, Earl D.C. Brewer, and Marie Townsend, *Black Pastors and Churches in United Methodism* (Atlanta, Ga.: Center for Research in Social Change, Emory University, 1976), 1.

8. Ibid.

9. *Book of Discipline of the UM Church* (1972), 336–37.

10. *Supplement to the Book of Hymns* (Nashville, Tenn.: United Methodist Publishing House, 1982), *Hymns from the Four Winds: A Collection of Asian American Hymns* (Nashville, Tenn.: Abingdon, 1983). For the Hispanic community, the UM Church produced in Spanish translation an abridged edition of *The Book of Hymns,* titled *Himnario Metodista* (Nashville, Tenn.: United Methodist Publishing House, 1973).

11. With the help of minority members of the Hymnal Revision Committee and special consultants, *The Book of Hymns* (Nashville, Tenn.: United Methodist Publishing House, 1989)—the first hymnbook to be published following the elimination of the Central Jurisdiction—includes a carefully selected group of 84 hymns representing the 4 major ethnic groups of the church.

12. Over 325,000 copies of *Songs of Zion* (Nashville, Tenn.: Abingdon, 1981) were sold or distributed.

13. McClain, *Black People,* 86.

14. Richardson, *Dark Salvation,* 275.

15. Harry V. Richardson, "The Role of Blacks in the United Methodist Church," in *Black Methodism Basic Beliefs,* ed. G. Lovelace Champion (N.p.: 1980), 108.

Chapter 5

1. Cited in Milton C. Sernett, ed., *Afro-American Religious History* (Durham, N.C.: Duke Univ. Press, 1985), 280. Original source: Elias C. Morris, *Sermons, Addresses and Reminiscences and Important Correspondence* (Nashville, Tenn.: National Baptist Publishing Board, 1901).
2. See Miles Mark Fisher's discussion of hymns by early English and American Baptists and of *The Baptist Hymnal* in Fisher, *A Short History of the Baptist Denomination* (Nashville, Tenn.: Sunday School Publishing Board, 1933), 146–49.
3. Some of the original headings in the model hymnal were made into subheadings in the new hymnal, and some of the subheadings of the original hymnal were omitted altogether in the new one.
4. R.H. Boyd, *A Story of the National Baptist Publishing Board* (Nashville, Tenn.: National Baptist Publishing Board, [ca. 1915]), 130.
5. *Journal of the 20th Annual Session of the National Baptist Convention*, Richmond, Va., 12–17 Sept. 1900 (Nashville, Tenn.: National Baptist Publishing Board, 1900), 81.
6. *Journal of the 22nd Annual Session of the National Baptist Convention*, Birmingham, Ala., 17–22 Sept. 1902 (Nashville, Tenn.: National Baptist Publishing Board, 1902), 64.
7. Boyd, *Story of the National*, 13.
8. Ibid., 14.
9. "Publisher's Note," *The National Baptist Hymnal* (Nashville, Tenn.: National Baptist Publishing Board, 1903).
10. *Journal of the 20th Annual Session of the National Baptist Convention*, 1900, 82–83. Boyd, *Story of the National*, also lists, with brief descriptions, theological and historical books, sermons, sermon outlines, catechisms, pastor's guides, and so forth. He tells us that *Choice Songs No. 1* contained 64 select pieces with music.
11. *Journal of the 21st Annual Session of the National Baptist Convention*, Cincinnati, Ohio, 11–16 Sept. 1901 (Nashville, Tenn.: National Baptist Publishing Board, 1901), 72. *The National Baptist Hymnal* was listed as well, but without description, probably because it was not actually available until 1903. In an advertisement closing the published minutes of 1903 (and subsequent minutes), it was noted that all of the songbooks contained music and employed either round or shaped notes (and often both) for notation.
12. *Journal of the 21st Annual Session of the National Baptist Convention*, 1901, 68.
13. *Minutes of the Twenty-Fourth Annual Session of the National Baptist Convention*, Austin, Tex. 14–19 Sept. 1904 (Nashville, Tenn.: National Baptist Publishing Board, 1904), 109–110.
14. Ibid., 110.
15. "Publisher's Note," *The National Baptist Hymnal* (1903).
16. "Preface," *The National Baptist Hymnal* (1903). The hymns' texts were located above and below the tunes, which were at the center of each page.

17. *Minutes,* 1904, 110.
18. As early as 1901, Boyd was also advertising in the closing pages of the minutes various types of organs and pianos. With all of the songbooks being produced, Boyd, a shrewd businessman, must have known that it was expedient to sell instruments with which people could accompany their singing from these many volumes. In 1901, the "National Baptist Organ" was advertised (said name was etched above the stops). The notice read: "We can furnish you with both Parlor and Chapel Organs at moderate prices. Our instruments are of the highest grade and one in a community will convince you of their merit and quality. We carry also an excellent grade of pianos." The backmatter of the 1903 minutes contained advertisements for three different organ models and one piano.
19. Edward A. Freeman, *The Epoch of Negro Baptists and the Foreign Mission Board* (Kansas City, Ks.: Central Seminary Press, 1953), 96.
20. For information on Charles H. Pace, see Mary Ann L. Tyler, "The Music of Charles Henry Pace and Its Relationship to the Afro-American Church Experience," Ph.D. diss., Univ. of Pittsburgh, 1980.
21. James E. Gayle headed the black-owned James E. Gayle & Sons Publishers of New Orleans. He was a member of the convention's Original Goodwill Singers.
22. *National Jubilee Melodies,* 2d. ed. (Nashville, Tenn.: National Baptist Publishing Board, 1916), contained 75 more songs than the previous one.
23. Owen D. Pelt and Ralph Lee Smith, *The Story of the National Baptists* (New York: Vantage, 1960), 112.
24. Eileen Southern, "Hymnals of the Black Church," *Journal of the Interdenominational Theological Center* 14, nos. 1–2 (Fall 1986-Spring 1987):136.
25. Ibid.
26. Willa A. Townsend compiled two other volumes: *Selected Gems: For Use on Children's Day, Mother's Day and Other Occasions* (N.p.:N.d.); and *Holiday Entertainer* (N.p.:N.d.).
27. Lucie E. Campbell, who had a number of songs in *Gospel Pearls,* was an important figure in the National Baptist Convention, USA, Inc. In addition to serving as music director at Tabernacle Baptist Church in Memphis, she was music director of the National Baptist Sunday School and Baptist Young People's Union (BYPU) Congress from 1916 to the year of her death, 1963. She also served as vice president-at-large of the National Baptist Music Convention and president of the National Baptist Choral Society, both auxiliaries of the larger incorporated convention. Although Campbell's choirs performed choral music, her philosophy of church music was supportive of congregational singing. "Music convokes the congregation and gives them a means of united worship, praise and exhortation," she wrote. "The spiritual life of the church has largely developed through congregational singing. Let *all* the people praise him, not just the choir." Lucie E. Campbell, "Music," in *Miss Lucie Speaks,* ed. William M. Washington (Nashville, Tenn.: Sunday School Publishing Board, 1971), 46.
28. *Thirteenth Annual Report of the Sunday School Publishing Board of the National Baptist Convention, U.S.A.,* Detroit, Mich., 7–12 Sept. 1927 (Nashville, Tenn.: Sunday School Publishing Board, 1927), 7.

29. Ibid., 8.
30. The new edition of *Inspirational Melodies* (it was the new edition of either issue one or two) was also published by the National BYPU Board. The Music Committee included E.W.D. Isaac, Sr.; his son E.W.D. Isaac, Jr.; Lucie Campbell; P. James Bryant; Viola T. Hill; Wittie A. Biggins; Isaac C. Reddie; R.M. Rideout; H.E. Harris; H. Louise Holland; Josie E. Isaac, Isaac, Sr.'s wife, W.A. McKinney; Helen Walker; and B.J. Barnes.
31. Luvenia A. George, "Lucie E. Campbell: Baptist Composer and Educator," *Black Perspective in Music* 15, no. 1 (Spring 1987):34. The song was dedicated to Connie M. Rosemond, "the blind gospel singer," whom Campbell discovered and had perform her song before the 1919 Baptist convention in Atlantic City.
32. Pelt and R. L. Smith, *Story of the National Baptists*, 113.
33. Ibid., 113–17.
34. Ibid., 117.
35. *Journal of the Forty-fourth Annual Session of the National Baptist Convention*, Nashville, Tenn.: 10–15 Sept. 1924 (Nashville, Tenn.: Sunday School Publishing Board, 1924), 162–63.
36. *Thirteenth Annual Report of the Sunday School Publishing Board of the National Baptist Convention, U.S.A.* (Nashville, Tenn.: Sunday School Publishing Board, 1927), 7.
37. Pelt and R. L. Smith, *Story of the National Baptists*, 118.
38. One contemporary hymnist of the Townsend Convention whose works are being neglected is Elizabeth Maddox Huntley, the St. Louis resident whose collection of 15 original hymns (text and music) is *Songs of Faith and Power* (St. Louis, Mo.: Privately published, 1975).
39. Known as "The National Baptist Singing Ambassador" because of his worldwide concertizing, bass baritone J. Robert Bradley is currently music director of the National Baptist Congress of Christian Education and director of music promotions for the Sunday School Publishing Board. Lucie E. Campbell, who discovered Bradley, dedicated to him her song "Signed and Sealed with His Blood." Bradley also was a member of the convention's Original Goodwill Singers, along with James E. Gayle, Cleavon Derrick, Thomas H. Shelby, W.S. Ellington, Jr., and E.W.D. Isaac, Jr. Bradley. Personal communication to Jon Michael Spencer.
40. J. Robert Bradley, cited in Brenda J. Holland, "Standards in the Worship Music of Our People," *Informer* 41, no. 3 (Sept.–Nov. 1988):8.
41. Ibid.
42. Ibid., 9.
43. Southern, "Hymnals of the Black Church," 137.
44. Chairperson Davis is music director of the National Baptist Sunday School and Baptist Training Union Congress, and is director of music at New Bethel Baptist Church in Indianapolis, where her husband is pastor.
45. See the newspaper piece on Margaret P. Douroux by P.L. Yates, "Famed Composer Margaret Pleasant Douroux to Build Gospel Music House," *National Baptist Union Review* 93, no. 4 (Feb. 1989):3, 8.
46. Joseph H. Jackson, *Unholy Shadows and Freedom's Holy Light* (Nashville, Tenn.: Townsend Press, 1967), 120.

47. Of special interest in *The New National Baptist Hymnal* (1977) are the pieces by the late Gordon Blaine Hancock, a Baptist minister, black Social Gospeler, and noted sociologist who long taught at Virginia Union University. His hymns, however, are not of a social nature.

48. The last hymn in *The Progressive Baptist Hymnal* is also numbered 503. However, in the replacement process, 6 hymn numbers were omitted, leaving a total of 497 hymns.

Chapter 6

1. Charles Price Jones, "Autobiographical Sketch of Charles Price Jones," in *History of Church of Christ (Holiness), U.S.A., 1895–1965*, ed. Otho B. Cobbins (Chicago: National Publishing Board, Church of Christ (Holiness), USA, 1966), 21–32. Rptd. in *Journal of Black Sacred Music* 2, no. 2 (Fall 1988):54.

2. Ibid., 54.

3. Ibid., 58.

4. Charles Price Jones, "The Battle Royal," annual address to the 34th Annual Holiness Convention, Los Angeles, Calif., 24–31 Aug. 1930, 8. Indeed, the official founding date of the Church of Christ (Holiness), USA, in 1897 was not a part of the "come-out" stampede of 1870–90, during which Holiness churches grew rapidly.

5. Jones included in *Jesus Only Nos. 1 and 2* (1901) three hymns by William Rosborough. None of Rosborough's three hymns in *Jesus Only Nos. 1 and 2* appears in later Baptists hymnals along with his many other hymns.

6. Charles Price Jones, "Autobiographical Sketch," 55.

7. Charles Price Jones, *Jesus Only Nos. 1 and 2* back cover.

8. Ibid.

9. Charles Price Jones, "The History of My Songs," in Ortho B. Cobbins, *History of the Church of Christ (Holiness), U.S.A. 1895–1965* (Chicago: National Publishing Board, Church of Christ (Holiness), U.S.A. 1966), 422; rpted. in *Journal of Black Sacred Music* 2, no. 2 (Fall 1988):73ff.

10. Charles Price Jones, *His Fullness* (enlarged), cover page.

11. Charles Price Jones, "Battle Royal," 18.

12. Charles Price Jones, "History of My Songs," in Cobbins, *History of the Church*, 416.

13. The title *Jesus Only* is not at all related to the anti-Trinitarian or unitarian "Jesus Only" movement of the "Oneness Pentecostals," which commenced in 1913. These "Jesus Only Pentecostals" or "Jesus Onlies" rejected the Trinity and baptized "in the name of Jesus."

14. Charles Price Jones, "History of My Songs," in Cobbins, *History of the Church*, 422.

15. Ibid., 416.

16. Although the Baptists rejected Jones early in the history of their denomination, he wrote in 1935, "This would not occur now for they have advanced in spirituality and tolerance. All discord comes from misunder-

standing. We have learned to love one another and some of the most highly and strictly spiritual men I know are Baptist. God bless them. Amen." Charles Price Jones, "Autobiographical Sketch," 55.

17. Cobbins, *History of the Church*, 27, 53.
18. Ibid., 432.
19. Ibid., 55.
20. In fact, about a third of the popular hymns in Charles Price Jones, *Jesus Only Nos. 1 and 2* are also in the 6-volume gospel hymn series which commenced publication in 1875 and culminated in 1894 with a cumulative volume: Ira Sankey, Philip P. Bliss, James McGranahan, and George C. Stebbins, eds., *Gospel Hymns: Nos. 1 to 6 Complete*.
21. Vinson Synan, *The Holiness-Pentecostal Movement in the United States* (Grand Rapids, Mich.: Eerdmans, 1971), 58.
22. Charles Price Jones, annual message to the National Convention of the Churches of Christ—Holiness, Jackson, Miss., 23–30 Aug. 1931, 13.
23. Charles Price Jones, "History of My Songs," in Cobbins, *History of the Church*, 418.
24. Ibid., 405.
25. Ibid.
26. Ibid., 407.
27. Ibid., 401.
28. Ibid., 409.
29. Ibid., 404.
30. Ibid.
31. Ibid., 413–15.

Chapter 7

1. Responsive reading from "Church Decree," in "Program of the Seventy-Eighth Annual General Assembly," 1981.
2. Cited in Bishop J.W. Jenkins, "Preface," in "Program of the Seventy-Eighth Annual General Assembly," 1981: "Thanks to the God of the Universe from whom all blessings flow, and to all of our loyal, obedient, self-sacrificing and wonderful workers of The House of God Church, Keith Dominion, as found in Timothy 3:15–16."
3. Frank S. Mead, *Handbook of Denominations in the United States*, rev. ed. (Nashville, Tenn.: Abingdon, 1961), 71.
4. Joseph R. Washington, Jr., *Black Sects and Cults* (Garden City, N.Y.: Anchor/Doubleday, 1973), 77.
5. Ibid., 71.
6. The volume being examined, *Spiritual Songs and Hymns*, is, according to the foreword by M.F.L. Keith, the second release—"The 1944 Edition, the second publication of Spiritual Songs and Hymns, which were compiled by Bishop M.L. Tate."
7. Hugh J. Roberts, *"Spiritual Songs and Hymns: A Review," Journal of Black Sacred Music* 2, no. 2 (Fall 1988):90–93.

8. Cheryl Townsend Gilkes, "The Role of Women in the Sanctified Church," *Journal of Religious Thought* 43, no. 1 (Spring-Summer, 1986):40.
9. Washington, *Black Sects*, 65.
10. Roberts, *"Spiritual Songs,"* 95.
11. Responsive reading from the "Church Decree," in "Program of the Seventy-Eighth Annual General Assembly," 1981.
12. Bishop J. W. Jenkins, "Preface," in "Program of the Seventy-Eighth Annual General Assembly," 1981.
13. Program of the Eighty-First Annual General Assembly, 1984, includes this segment form the "Church Decree" as a part of the opening responsive reading for the assembly.
14. Roberts, *"Spiritual Songs,"* 93.
15. "The Rev. Rubin Lacy," interview by David Evans, *Blues Unlimited* 43 (May 1967):13.
16. "Living Blues Interview: Lowell Fulson," *Living Blues* 2, no. 5 (Summer 1971):22.
17. Flora Molton, unpublished interview by Eleanor Ellis, *Living Blues* files, Center for the Study of Southern Culture, Univ. of Mississippi, University, Miss.
18. Washington, *Black Sects*, 108–109.
19. Gilkes, "Role of Women," 33, 41.
20. Hans A. Baer wrote about a Spiritualist leader, Mother Hurley, to whose honor Mother's Day was dedicated. One of her followers called her the "greatest mother who ever lived." Hans A. Baer, *The Black Spiritual Movement: A Religious Response to Racism* (Knoxville: Univ. of Tennessee Press, 1984), 107.

Chapter 8

1. Elsie W. Mason, *The Man, Charles Harrison Mason* (N.p.: N.d.), 18–19. See the story in Milton C. Sernett, ed., *Afro-American Religious History: A Documentary Witness* (Durham, N.C.: Duke Univ. Press, 1985), 285–95.
2. Elsie W. Mason, *The Man, Charles Harrison Mason*, 14.
3. "Testimonies," *Apostolic Faith* 1, no. 12 (Jan. 1908):4.
4. Walter J. Hollenweger, "Foreword," in Iain MacRobert, *The Black Roots and White Racism of Early Pentecostalism in the USA* (New York: St. Martin's, 1988), xiii.
5. This list is assembled from testimonies published in *Apostolic Faith* (1906–1908). Christmas carols were also among the repertoire. Said one testimony: "At an all-day meeting on Christmas, we had a Christmas carol in tongues. . . . It was interpreted by one who knew the language: 'Glory to God in the highest and on earth peace, good will to men.'" In "The Heavenly Anthem," *Apostolic Faith* 1, no. 5 (Jan. 1907):3.
6. Walter J. Hollenweger, *The Pentecostals* (Minneapolis, Minn.: Augsburg, 1972), 464.

7. See Jon Michael Spencer, "The Heavenly Anthem: Holy Ghost Singing in the Primal Pentecostal Revival (1906–1909)," *Journal of Black Sacred Music* 1, no. 1 (Spring 1987):1–33.

8. Jennie Moore, "Music from Heaven," *Apostolic Faith* 1, no. 8 (May 1907):3. Jennie Moore was a young woman who later married William J. Seymour, pastor of the Azusa Mission.

9. *Apostolic Faith* 1, no. 4 (Dec. 1906):2.

10. Rachel Harper Sizelove, "The Temple: How the Shekinah of God's Glory Fell on the People in the Early Days at the Azusa Street Mission in Los Angeles, California," *Word and Work* 58, no. 5 (May 1936):2, 12.

11. Garry Seabron, "*The Jackson Bible Universal Selected Gospel Songs:* A Review," *Journal of Black Sacred Music* 2, no. 2 (Fall 1988):96.

12. Ibid., 101. That *The Jackson Bible Universal Selected Gospel Songs* is a source documenting hymns favored by early black Pentecostals of the Deep South is suggested by the fact that only 6 of the 35 songs reappear in the official COGIC hymnal published almost 40 years later: *Yes, Lord!: The Church of God in Christ Hymnal* (Memphis, Tenn.: COGIC Publishing Board, in association with the Benson Co., Nashville, Tenn., 1981).

13. Seabron, "*Jackson Bible*," 96.

14. Ibid., 98. See *Official Manual with the Doctrines and Discipline of the Church of God in Christ* (Memphis, Tenn.: Church of God in Christ Publishing House, 1973), 73.

15. Seabron, "*Jackson Bible*," 96.

16. *Official Manual with the Doctrines and Discipline of COGIC*, 51.

17. This black Pentecostal denomination was for ten years associated with the predominantly white Fire Baptized Holiness Association of America, founded in 1898, before founding a separate black denomination in 1908.

18. *Hymnal of the F.B.H. Church* (Atlanta, Ga.: Board of Publication of the FBH Church of God of the Americas/Fuller Press, 1966), 100–162. The table of contents, however, is in the front of the book, following the contents of the discipline.

19. *Yes, Lord!* (1982).

20. Eileen Southern, "Hymnals of the Black Church," *Journal of the Inter-denominational Theological Center* 14, nos. 1–2 (Fall 1986-Spring 1987):138.

21. Donna McNeil Cox, "Contemporary Trends in the Music Ministry of the Church of God in Christ," *Journal of Black Sacred Music* 2, no. 2 (Fall 1988):24.

22. Following the hymns are "Responsive Scripture Readings" and "Aids to Worship." The latter includes "The Statement of Faith," "Calls to Worship," "Invocations," "Thanksgiving Prayer," "The Lord's Prayer," "The Ten Commandments," "The Beatitudes," "The Nicene Creed," "The Apostles Creed," and "Benedictions." Topical and scriptural indices for the scripture readings follow, along with an alphabetical index of hymn titles and first lines, and a topical index of hymns. Indexes of authors/composers, tunes, and meters are not included.

23. That this hymn was sung daily (sometimes in tongues) is documented in "Bible Pentecost," *Apostolic Faith* 1, no. 3 (Nov. 1906):1; and in Frank Bar-

tleman, *Azusa Street* (Plainfield, N.J.: Logos International, 1980), 57. *Azusa Street* is a reprint of Frank Bartleman, *How Pentecost Came to Los Angeles* (1925).

24. Southern, "Hymnals of the Black Church," 139.
25. *Official Manual with the Doctrines and Discipline of COGIC*, 127–28. See also 130.
26. Southern, "Hymnals of the Black Church," 139.
27. *Official Manual with the Doctrines and Discipline of COGIC*, 56–58.
28. Bartleman, *Azusa Street*, 57.
29. Cox, "Contemporary Trends," 24.
30. Ibid., 26.
31. Ibid., 26–27.
32. Ibid., 26.
33. William C. Turner, Jr., "Singing in the Holy Convocation of the United Holy Church of America," *Journal of Black Sacred Music* 2, no. 2 (Fall 1988):21.
34. Dovie Marie Simmons and Olivia L. Martin, *Down Behind the Sun: The Story of Arenia Cornelia Mallory* (Memphis, Tenn.: Riverside Press, 1983), 39–41.
35. Ibid., 41.
36. C.G. Brown, "Observations of Elder C.H. Mason, Chief Apostle," in *The History and Life Work of Elder C.H. Mason*, ed. Mary Mason (N.p.: N.d.), 88–89.
37. Ibid., 91 (emphasis added).
38. Ibid., 92 (emphasis added).
39. Ibid., 91.
40. Elsie W. Mason, *The Man, Charles Harrison Mason*, 16 (emphasis added).
41. Ibid (emphasis added).
42. "Testimonies," 4.

Chapter 9

1. Cited in George F. Bragg, *History of the Afro-American Group of the Episcopal Church* (Baltimore, Md.: Church Advocate Press, 1922), 60.
2. William Douglass, *Annals of the First African Church in the USA, Now Styled the African Episcopal Church of St. Thomas, Philadelphia* (Philadelphia: King & Baird, 1862), 104, as cited in Ann C. Lammers, "The Rev. Absalom Jones and the Episcopal Church: Christian Theology and Black Consciousness in a New Alliance," *Historical Magazine of the Protestant Episcopal Church* 51, no. 2 (June 1982):179.
3. Richard Allen, *The Life Experience and Gospel Labors of the Rt. Rev. Richard Allen* (Nashville, Tenn.: Abingdon, 1960), 25.
4. Lammers, "Rev. Absalom Jones," 166–67.
5. Ibid., 183.
6. Irene V. Jackson, "Music Among Blacks in the Episcopal Church: Some Preliminary Considerations," *Historical Magazine of the Protestant Episcopal Church* 49 (1980):21–36; rptd. in *More Than Dancing: Essays on Afro-American Music and Musicians*, ed. Irene V. Jackson (Westport, Conn.: Greenwood,

1985), 116, 117, 119. Also reprinted in *Lift Every Voice and Sing: A Collection of Afro-American Spirituals and Other Songs* (New York: Church Hymnal Corp. 1981).

7. Robert A. Bennett, "Black Episcopalians: A History from the Colonial Period to the Present," *Historical Magazine of the Protestant Episcopal Church* 43, no. 3 (Sept. 1974):244–45.

8. Robert A. Bennett, "Scripture and Tradition Speak to the Black Episcopalian," *Saint Luke's Journal of Theology* 22, no. 4 (Sept. 1979):317.

9. Ibid., 320.

10. Bennett, "Black Episcopalians," 242.

11. W.E.B. Du Bois, *The Negro Church* (Atlanta, Ga.: Atlanta Univ. Press, 1903), 139, cited in Bennett, "Black Episcopalians," 239.

12. *The Hymnal 1940 Companion,* 3d ed. (New York: Church Pension Fund, 1940), 61.

13. Ibid., 174.

14. Sherodd Albritton, "What's Going On with the Hymnal," *Historical Magazine of the Protestant Episcopal Church* 48, no. 2 (June 1979):142.

15. Ibid., 143.

16. Bennett, "Scripture and Tradition," 314.

17. E. Franklin Frazier, *The Negro Church in America* (New York: Schocken, 1974), 83.

18. Anonymous speaker cited in Gavin White, "Patriarch McGuire and the Episcopal Church," *Historical Magazine of the Protestant Episcopal Church* 38, no. 2 (June 1969):140.

19. Booker T. Washington, cited in John M. Burgess, "Opening Presentation," Convocation of Black Theologians, April 1978, *Saint Luke's Journal of Theology* 22, no. 4 (Sept. 1979):245.

20. Bennett, "Black Episcopalians," 232.

21. Burgess, "Opening Presentation," 245.

22. Bennett, "Black Episcopalians," 232.

23. Burgess, "Opening Presentation," 245.

24. Ibid., 246.

25. R.E. Hood, "Christian Witness and Social Transformation," pt. 2, *Saint Luke's Journal of Theology* 22, no. 4 (Sept. 1979):305.

26. Bennett, "Black Episcopalians," 232.

27. Ibid., 239, cited in Irene V. Jackson, "Music among Blacks," in Jackson, *More Than Dancing,* 110.

28. Irene V. Jackson, "Music among Blacks," 111.

29. Irene Jackson-Brown, "Comments on the Selections," in *Lift Every Voice and Sing* (New York: Church Hymnal Corporation), 1981.

30. Irene V. Jackson, "Music among Blacks," 120.

31. Van S. Bird, "Christian Witness and Social Transformation," pt. 1, *Saint Luke's Journal of Theology* 22, no. 4 (Sept. 1979):294.

32. Eileen Southern, "The Hymnals of the Black Church," *Journal of the Interdenominational Theological Center* 14, nos. 1–2 (Fall 1986-Spring 1987):137.

33. Portia K. Maultsby, review of *Lift Every Voice and Sing* and *Songs of Zion,* in *The Hymn* 33, no. 3 (July 1982):195.

34. Ibid., 196.
35. For the debate, as carried in the Episcopal Church on during the nineteenth century, see Jane Rasmussen, *Musical Taste: As a Religious Question in Nineteenth-Century America* (Lewiston, N.Y.: Edwin Mellen, 1986), esp. 37–91.
36. White, "Patriarch McGuire," 122–23.
37. R. Nathaniel Dett, "The Development of the Negro Spiritual," in *The Dett Collection of Negro Spirituals*, 4th group (Minneapolis, Minn.: Schmitt, Hall & McCreary, 1936), 3.
38. R. Nathaniel Dett, "The Development of Negro Religious Music," *Journal of Black Sacred Music* 2, no. 1 (Spring 1988):65. This article is one part of a four-part essay, "Negro Music," which won the Bowdoin Literary Prize at Harvard University in 1920. Available at Main Library, Harvard University, Cambridge, Mass.
39. R. Nathaniel Dett, review of Howard W. Odum and Guy B. Johnson, *Negro Workday Songs*, in *Southern Workman* 56 (1927):46.
40. Ibid.
41. Dett, "Development of Negro Religious Music," 66.
42. Cited in Jon Michael Spencer, *As the Black School Sings: Black Music Collections at Black Universities and Colleges, with a Union List of Book Holdings* (Westport, Conn.: Greenwood, 1987), 38.
43. Ibid., 30.
44. R. Nathaniel Dett, "Negro Idioms in Motets and Anthems," program notes, concert by the Hampton Institute Choir, Symphony Hall, Boston, 10 Mar. 1929.
45. William L. Banks, *The Black Church in the U.S.: Its Origin, Growth, Contributions, and Outlook* (Shelbyville, Tenn.: Bible and Literature Missionary Foundation, 1972), 113.
46. R.E. Hood, "From a Headstart to a Deadstart: The Historical Basis for Black Indifference Toward the Episcopal Church, 1800–1860," *Historical Magazine of the Protestant Episcopal Church* 51, no. 3 (Sept. 1982):296.
47. Bennett, "Black Episcopalians," 232.
48. Bird, "Christian Witness," 295.
49. White, "Patriarch McGuire," 140.

Chapter 10

1. Cited in Milton C. Sernett, ed., *Afro-American Religious History: A Documentary Witness* (Durham, N.C.: Duke Univ. Press, 1985), 270.
2. Pope Paul VI, St. Peter's, Rome, 29 Oct. 1967, cited in Diana L. Hayes, "Black Catholic Revivalism: The Emergence of a New Form of Worship," *Journal of the Interdenominational Theological Center* 14, nos. 1–2 (Fall 1986–Spring 1987): 104.
3. W.E.B. Du Bois, *The Negro Church* (Atlanta, Ga.: Atlanta Univ., 1903), 139.
4. W.E.B. Du Bois, *The Philadelphia Negro* (1899; rptd. New York: Schocken, 1967), 219.

5. See David Spaulding, "The Negro Catholic Congresses, 1889–1894," *Freeing the Spirit* 1, no. 3 (Summer 1972):7.
6. Clarence Joseph Rivers, "Thank God We Ain't What We Was: The State of the Liturgy in the Black Catholic Community," *Freeing the Spirit* 6, no. 2 (Spring 1979):30.
7. Ibid., 29.
8. Sister Esther Mary, "Spirituals in the Church," *Southern Workman* 63 (1934):308–309.
9. Ibid., 312.
10. Ibid., 309–10.
11. Ibid., 310.
12. Rivers, "Thank God We Ain't What We Was," 29.
13. Francesca Thompson, "Black, Catholic, and Stayin' that Way," *U.S. Catholic*, Oct. 1988, 33–34.
14. Mary, "Spirituals in the Church," 313.
15. Ibid.
16. Rivers, "Thank God We Ain't What We Was," 31.
17. Ibid., 30.
18. See Clarence Joseph Rivers, "The Homily in Integrated Worship," *Freeing the Spirit* 1, no. 4 (Fall-Winter 1972):37–43, and Clarence Joseph Rivers, "To Train a Preacher . . . Train a Performer," 2, no. 1 (Spring 1973):49–51.
19. Melva Wilson Costen, "Published Hymnals in the Afro-American Tradition," *The Hymn* 40, no. 1 (Jan. 1989):17.
20. William Farley Smith, review of *Lead Me, Guide Me: The African American Catholic Hymnal,* in *The Hymn* 40, no. 1 (Jan. 1989):13–14.
21. Ibid., 14.
22. "The Resolutions of the National Convention of Black Lay Catholics," *Freeing the Spirit* 1, no. 3 (Summer 1972):42.
23. Clarence Joseph Rivers, *Soulfull Worship* (Washington, D.C.: National Office for Black Catholics, 1974), 17.
24. Clarence Joseph Rivers, "From that Day On," *Freeing the Spirit* 3, no. 4 (1975):19.
25. Hayes, "Black Catholic Revivalism," 105.
26. "Resolutions of the National Convention of Black Lay Catholics," 42.
27. William Norvel, "The Meaning of Black Liturgy," *Freeing the Spirit* 1, no. 1 (Aug. 1971):5.
28. Hayes, "Black Catholic Revivalism," 87–88.
29. Edward K. Braxton, "Toward a Black Catholic Theology," *Freeing the Spirit* 5, no. 2 (1977):3.
30. See James Lyke, "Black Liturgy/Black Liberation," *Freeing the Spirit* 1, no. 1 (Aug. 1971):17.
31. Clarence Williams, "The Future of the Black Catholic Church," *Freeing the Spirit* 5, no. 4 (1976):36.
32. Clarence Joseph Rivers, "Music and the Liberation of Black Catholics," *Freeing the Spirit* 1, no. 1 (Aug. 1971):27.
33. See the National Office of Black Catholics' interview with Hawkins in *Freeing the Spirit* 1, no. 2 (Spring 1972):7–9.

34. J. Michael McMahon, "Afro-American Workshop," *Freeing the Spirit* 4, no. 3 (1976):22–24.
35. Rivers, "Thank God We Ain't What We Was," 32.
36. Clarence Joseph Rivers, "So You Want to Start a Choir,"*Freeing the Spirit* 1, no. 2 (Spring 1972):35.
37. Rivers, *Soulfull Worship,* 20–21.
38. Ibid., 159.
39. Mary, 310.
40. Glenn R. Hufnagel, "Spirituals and Poetry in Catholic Worship," *Freeing the Spirit* 7, no. 1 (Spring 1981):23.
41. Ibid., 27.
42. The preface was symbolically signed on 4 Apr. 1987, the anniversary of the deaths of both St. Benedict the Black and Martin Luther King, Jr.
43. James T. Menkhus, "Gifted People Need Gifts, Too," *Freeing the Spirit* 7, no. 1 (Spring 1981):34.
44. Ibid.
45. Ibid.
46. Virgil C. Funk, ed., *Music in Catholic Worship: The NPM Commentary* (Washington, D.C.: National Association of Pastoral Musicians, 1972), 46–47.
47. Wendelin J. Watson, Review of *Lead Me, Guide Me: The African American Catholic Hymnal,* in *Journal of Black Sacred Music* 3, no. 1 (Spring 1989):69.
48. Ibid.
49. The co-arrangements by Jefferson and Nix, who were editor and assistant editor, respectively, of *Songs of Zion,* are credited to the latter hymnbook.
50. Rivers, "So You Want to Start a Choir," 33.
51. Peter Sarpong, "African Religion and Catholic Worship," *Freeing the Spirit* 4, no. 4 (1977):19.
52. William Farley Smith, review of *Lead Me, Guide Me,* 15.
53. Rivers, "So You Want to Start a Choir," 35.
54. Olly Wilson, "Black Composers and the Avant Garde," in *Black Music in Our Culture,* ed. Dominique Rene de Lerma (Kent, Ohio: Kent State Univ. Press, 1970), 71–73.
55. Clarence Joseph Rivers, "Toward Unanimity," *Freeing the Spirit* 1, no. 3 (Summer 1972):3.
56. Rivers, "Music and the Liberation of Black Catholics," 26.
57. Joseph M. Davis, "The Position of the Catholic Church in the Black Community," *Freeing the Spirit* 1, no. 3 (Spring 1972):19.
58. Joseph M. Davis, "Reflections on a Central Office for Black Catholicism," *Freeing the Spirit* 3, no. 1 (Summer 1972):34.
59. Ibid., 35.
60. According to hymnologist Melva Costen, the hymnal has succeeded in reaching the wider religious community. She says that, because of the inclusion of traditional hymns, gospel songs, and music composed by black Catholics, the hymnal will certainly find a place among black Protestants. Costen, "Published Hymnals," 13.

Postscript

1. Malcolm X, "The Black Man's History" (recorded speech; tape in collection of Jon Michael Spencer).
2. See Na'im Akbar, *Chains and Images of Psychological Slavery* (Jersey City, N.J.: New Mind Productions, 1984), 45–58.
3. Cornel West, *The American Evasion of Philosophy: A Genealogy of Pragmatism* (Madison: Univ. of Wisconsin Press, 1989), 212, 230, 239.

Bibliography

Select Works

Cone, James H. *For My People: Black Theology and the Black Church.* Maryknoll, N.Y.: Orbis Books, 1984.

DuBois, W.E.B. *The Negro Church.* Atlanta, Ga.: Atlanta University Press, 1903.

Frazier, E. Franklin. *The Negro Church in America.* New York: Schocken, 1974.

Jackson, Irene V., ed. *More Than Dancing: Essays on Afro-American Music and Musicians.* Westport, Conn.: Greenwood, 1985.

Keck, George R., and Sherrill V. Martin, eds. *Feel the Spirit: Studies in Nineteenth-Century Afro-American Music* (Westport, Conn.: Greenwood, 1988).

Lincoln, C. Eric, ed. *The Black Experience in Religion.* Garden City, N.Y.: Anchor/Doubleday, 1974.

Lincoln, C. Eric, and Lawrence H. Mamiya. *The Black Church and the African American Experience.* Durham, N.C.: Duke University Press, 1990.

Mapson, J. Wendell, Jr. *The Ministry of Music in the Black Church.* Valley Forge, Pa.: Judson Press, 1984.

Mays, Benjamin E., and Joseph W. Nicholson. *The Negro Church.* New York: Russell and Russell, 1969.

McClain, William B. *Come Sunday: The Liturgy of Zion.* Nashville, Tenn.: Abingdon, 1990.

Rivers, Clarence Joseph. *Soulfull Worship.* Washington, D.C.: National Office of Black Catholics, 1974.

Sernett, Milton C., ed. *Afro-American Religious History: A Documentary Witness.* Durham, N.C.: Duke University Press, 1985.

Southern, Eileen. *The Music of Black Americans: A History.* New York: Norton, 1971.

———, ed. *Readings in Black American Music.* New York: Norton, 1971.

Spencer, Jon Michael. *Protest and Praise: Sacred Music of Black Religion.* Minneapolis, Minn.: Fortress Press, 1990.

———. *Sacred Symphony: The Chanted Sermon of the Black Preacher.* Westport, Conn.: Greenwood, 1987.

———, ed. *Unsung Hymns by Black and Unknown Bards.* Special issue of *Black Sacred Music: A Journal of Theomusicology* 4, no. 1 (Spring 1990).

Walker, Wyatt Tee. *"Somebody's Calling My Name": Black Sacred Music and Social Change.* Valley Forge, Pa.: Judson Press, 1979.

Whalum, Wendel P. "Black Hymnody." *Review and Expositor* 70, no. 3 (Summer 1973):341–55.
Wilmore, Gayraud C., ed. *African American Religious Studies.* Durham, N.C.: Duke University Press, 1989.
Woodson, Carter G. *The History of the Negro Church.* Washington, D.C.: Associated Publishers, 1921.

Denominational Hymnbooks Cited

Chapter 1
The African Methodist Episcopal Church

A Collection of Spiritual Songs and Hymns, Selected from Various Authors. Compiled by Richard Allen. Philadelphia: Printed by John Ormrod, 1801.
A Collection of Hymns and Spiritual Songs, from Various Authors. Compiled by Richard Allen. Philadelphia: Printed by T.L. Plowman, 1801.
The African Methodist Pocket Hymn Book. Philadelphia: AME Book Concern, 1816.
The African Methodist Episcopal Church Hymn Book. New York: AME Book Concern, 1837.
The Hymn Book of the African Methodist Episcopal Church. Philadelphia: AME Book Concern, 1876.
The African Methodist Episcopal Hymn and Tune Book. Philadelphia: AME Book Concern, 1898.
The Richard Allen AME Hymnal. Philadelphia: AME Book Concern, 1941 [or 1946].
AMEC Hymnal. Nashville, Tenn.: AME Publishing House, 1954.
AMEC Bicentennial Hymnal. Nashville, Tenn.: AME Publishing House, 1984.

Chapter 2
The African Methodist Episcopal Zion Church

[*Hymns for the Use of the African Methodist Episcopal Zion Church*]. New York: AME Zion Book Concern, 1839.
Hymns for the Use of the African Methodist Episcopal Zion Church. New York: AME Zion Book Concern, 1858.
A Collection of Hymns for the Use of the African Methodist Episcopal Zion Church in America. New York: Methodist Book Concern, 1872.
New Hymn and Tune Book: An Offering of Praise for the Use of the African M.E. Zion Church of America. New York: AME Zion Book Concern, 1892.
New Hymn and Tune Book for the Use of the African M.E. Zion Church. Charlotte, N.C.: AME Zion Publishing House, 1909.
The AME Zion Hymnal. Charlotte, N.C.: AME Zion Publishing House, 1957.

Chapter 3
The Christian Methodist Episcopal Church

Hymn Book of the Colored M.E. Church in America. Jackson, Tenn.: CME Book
    Concern, 1891.
The Hymnal of the Christian Methodist Episcopal Church. Memphis, Tenn.: CME
    Publishing House, 1987.

Chapter 4
The United Methodist Church

Songs of Zion. Nashville, Tenn.: Abingdon Press, 1981.

Chapter 5
The National Baptists

The National Baptist Hymnal. Nashville, Tenn.: National Baptist Publishing
    Board, 1903. [National Baptist Convention, USA.]
The National Baptist Hymn Book. Nashville, Tenn.: National Baptist Publishing
    Board, 1905. [National Baptist Convention, USA.]
The Baptist Standard Hymnal. Nashville, Tenn.: Sunday School Publishing
    Board, 1924. [National Baptist Convention, USA.]
The New National Baptist Hymnal. Nashville, Tenn.: National Baptist Publishing
    Board, 1977. [National Baptist Convention.]
The Progressive Baptist Hymnal. Washington, D.C.: Progressive National Baptist
    Convention, 1976. [Progressive National Baptist Convention.]
The New Progressive Baptist Hymnal. Washington, D.C.: Progressive National
    Baptist Convention, 1982. [Progressive National Baptist Convention.]

Chapter 6
The Church of Christ (Holiness), USA

Jesus Only. Compiled by Charles Price Jones. [Jackson, Miss.: Truth Publishing
    Co.?], 1899.
Jesus Only Nos. 1 and 2. Compiled by Charles Price Jones. Jackson, Miss.: Truth
    Publishing Co., 1901. [Printed by the National Baptist Publishing Board.]
His Fullness. Compiled by Charles Price Jones. [Nashville, Tenn.: Printed by
    National Baptist Publishing Board?], 1906.
His Fullness. Enlarged ed. Compiled by Charles Price Jones. Nashville, Tenn.:
    Printed by National Baptist Publishing Board, 1928.
Jesus Only Songs and Hymns Standard Hymnal. Los Angeles: Jones Benefit Foun-
    dation, 1940. [Ninth edition published in 1966.]
His Fullness Songs. Jackson, Miss.: National Publishing Board of the Church of
    Christ (Holiness), USA, 1977.

Chapter 7
The House of God Church

Spiritual Songs and Hymns. Ed. Mary F.L. Keith. Chattanooga, Tenn.: [The
House of God Church, c. 1944].
Spiritual Songs and Hymns. [Nashville, Tenn.: House of God Church, after
1962].

Chapter 8
The Church of God in Christ

Yes, Lord!: The Church of God in Christ Hymnal. Memphis, Tenn.: Church of God
in Christ Publishing Board, 1982.

Chapter 9
The Episcopal Church

Lift Every Voice and Sing: A Collection of Afro-American Spirituals and Other Songs.
New York: Church Hymnal Corporation, 1981.

Chapter 10
The Roman Catholic Church

Lead Me, Guide Me: The African American Catholic Hymnal. Chicago: G.I.A. Publications, 1987.

General Index

Abbey, M. E., 66
Absalom Jones Theological Institute, 167
Abyssinian Baptist Church, 92
Adams, Sarah F., 122, 148
Adams, Wellington A., 89, 90
Addison, Joseph, 90
African hymns, 195
African Methodist Episcopal Church, x, xi, 3–24, 26, 37, 53, 56, 75; combined hymnal with AME Zion Church, 19, 37–39, 40, 94; first book of discipline, 6–7
African Methodist Episcopal Zion Church, x, 19, 25–43, 53, 56, 75; combined hymnal with AME Church, 19, 37–39, 40, 94; sesquicentennial celebration, 42
African National Congress, 67
Akers, Doris, x, 21, 56, 57, 71, 93, 96, 151, 154, 174, 194
Alabama State University, 18
Albritton, Sherodd, 169–70
Allen, Richard, 3, 7, 19, 21, 25, 27, 96, 166, 173; hymnbooks of, 4–6, 20, 85; ordination as bishop, 6
Allyne, Betty Lee Roberts, 42
Allyne, Cameron C., 42
Alwyn, Austin, 86
AME Book Concern. *See* AME Publishing House
AME hymnbooks: of 1801, 4–6, 8, 13, 20, 22, 85; of 1818, 4, 7–8, 22; of 1837, 4, 8, 11, 13, 22; of 1876, 4, 9–15, 16, 18, 22, 23; of 1892, 4, 15–

17, 22, 23, 38, 42; of 1898, 16, 17, 18, 19; of 1941, 4, 17, 18, 19, 20, 22, 23, 38; of 1954, 4, 14, 20, 21, 22, 23, 41; of 1984, 4, 14, 20–23
AME Publishing House, 7, 8, 10, 15, 16, 17, 19, 20, 38
AME Review, 17
AME Zion Book Concern. *See* AME Zion Publishing House
AME Zion hymnbooks: of 1839, 26, 29; of 1858, 26–28, 29; of 1872, 26, 28–29; of 1892, 26, 29–33; of 1909, 26, 34–35, 39; of 1957, 25–26, 37, 38, 40–43
AME Zion Publishing House, 25, 26, 29, 34, 36, 39
American Baptist Publication Society, 76, 77, 78
American National Baptist Convention, 75
Anderson, Amelia Gaynor, 107
Anderson, Vivienne L., 21
antislavery hymnody, 12–13, 27, 33, 201
Apostolic Faith, The, 142, 143
Aquinas, Thomas, 195
Asante, Molefi Kete, 200
Ashford and Simpson, 175
Austin, R. Alwyn, 89
Azusa Street Revival, 140–43, 151, 156, 161

Ballantine, William G., 22
Ballinger, Bruce, 157

Seward, Theodore F., 169
sexist language, 21, 201
Seymour, William J., 140, 141
Shade, Will, 132
Shakers, 142
Sherwood, W. H., 84, 85, 87
Shockley, Grant, 60
Short Talks on Music or Rudiments of Vocal Music, 81
Shuford, Dovie, 139
Simpson, Albert B., 110, 155
Simpson, K. Eloise, 37
Sisters of the Holy Family, 182
Skipwith, J. H., 89, 92
Smallwood, Richard, 174, 175, 194
Smiley, John H., 86, 89
Smith, C. S., 17
Smith, H. W., 30
Smith, Hale, 179
Smith, John Wesley, 30, 31
Smith, Ralph, 88, 91
Smith, William D., 36
Smith, William Farley, 64, 71, 187, 197
Social Christianity, 22
Social Darwinism in hymns, xii, 21–22, 91, 152, 169
Social Gospel movement, 12, 22, 23, 24, 41, 112, 138; hymns of, 22, 93, 111, 112, 153, 201
Sontonga, Enoch, 67
Soulfull Worship, 186, 190
Southern, Eileen, 4, 7, 85–86, 87, 92, 96, 148, 152, 155, 172–73
Southern Baptist Convention, 87, 95
Southern University, 18
Spafford, Horatio G., 67, 106
Spearman, Daniel G., 107
Spirit in Worship, The, 186
spirituals, 167, 183; arranging of, 88, 176; created by Episcopalians, 171–72; created during preaching, 84; in Catholic liturgy, 183, 191–92, 197; in Episcopal liturgy, 184–86, 191; in hymnals, 20, 21, 36, 42, 45, 50, 62, 64, 68–69, 71, 86, 88, 91, 93, 94, 95, 107, 110, 111, 122,

123, 137, 153, 167, 168, 173, 174, 176, 180, 190, 194, 195, 201; relation to blues, 132–33; relation to psalms, 191–92; in songbook collections, 87, 174
Spottswood, Stephen Gill, 39, 42
Stebbins, George C., 154
Steele, Anne, 26, 76, 90
Stennett, Samuel, 76, 126, 138
Stevenson, Iris, xi, 149–50, 156
Stewart, Charles E., 17–18
Stitt, Richard Haywood, 30, 31
Stone, Samuel J., 126
Story of the National Baptist Publishing Board, 81
Stowe, Harriet Beecher, 138
Sunday School Publishing Board, 85–92, 94
Sweney, John R., 154

Talbot, Frederick H., 21
Tanner, Benjamin Tucker, 11, 15, 17, 20, 21
Tate, Mary L., 119–22, 125, 126, 128, 133, 134, 135, 136, 137
Taylor, James C., 42
Taylor, Jerome, 155
Taylor, Mamie E., 93
theomusicology, xi
Thomas, H. P., 30
Thompson, Francesca, 185
Thompson, Joseph P., 26, 27
Thompson, Will L., 110
Tillman, Charles D., 66, 90, 106, 107, 151, 154
Tindley, Charles Albert, x, 19, 20, 21, 35, 36, 51, 52, 53, 62, 64, 65, 70, 71, 86, 90, 91, 93, 96, 110, 111, 122, 125, 144, 154, 174, 175, 194; hymns analyzed, 65–66
Tindley Temple United Methodist Church, 64, 65
Tobias, J. W., 82
Tobias, T. W. J., 89, 90
tongues: singing in, 142–43, 151; speaking in, 140, 151
Toplady, Augustus M., 138

Music Index